Gary W Friendshuh

A man's story is all that
he will truly ever own.

A PATH LESS TAKEN

The True Life Adventures of

One Man

and His Faith Awakening

Gary W Friendshuh

First U.S. Print Edition

Softcover BW ISBN-13: 978-1-945333-18-7

Available from Amazon.com and other bookstores

For bulk sales and author inquiries: gwfriendshuh@gmail.com

Printed in the U.S.

Acknowledgements

I would like to acknowledge my wife Jeanne whose encouragement, guidance and help were invaluable in completing this work, and Barb Evenson, who started out as my editor and finished up as my friend, and along the way taught me how to be a better writer.

Dedication

I would like to dedicate this book to my children, grandchildren, great grand-children, all of my offspring down through the ages and to those who may be inspired to pass on the story of their journey through life.

Contents

Foreword

A Son's Perspective

by Luke Friendshuh

When Dad said he was hoping to start a family tradition by sharing stories of his life, I wasn't sure he could do it. Years later, when he had most of it done, I was honored when he asked me to write a foreword to what turned out to be his autobiography.

I have so many memories of growing up with Dad, it is hard to know where to start. I remember many life lessons and perspectives that thankfully became a part of who I am.

The most important lesson is that life is an adventure and something to love and be grateful for. He took us on many adventures and proved this to us. Secondly, he taught us the importance of toughness, perseverance and hard work. He made us do tough work that from a child's perspective sometimes seemed overwhelming, but with a combination of high expectations, lots of praise and a firm hand that wouldn't let us skate by or quit, he got us to do things way beyond what we thought was possible and much more than our peers. We were always proud of that.

He also taught us the importance of telling the truth and showed us how honesty builds trust, which is possibly the most important value a human being can have. Lastly, he taught us a love for the wilderness and showed us how to survive and be comfortable in nature without any of the comforts of the modern world. It gave us a primal connection to something that always seemed more real than anything man could create. It gave me an inner strength and power to see peer pressure, fashion, money, wealth, popularity, comfort—all the things I saw other kids worried about—as being ephemeral as the wind. They had no power over me. How can any of those things matter when your very survival is at stake?

Memories are like threads that lead to an infinite set of moments that make up your life. They are also like an onion in that no matter how many layers you peel off, there always seems to be more. So, in the interest of brevity, I will limit myself to a single story for each broad memory. Understand though, that they are mere samples; just a small representation of the myriad of moments that made up my childhood and reinforced the values, lessons and perspective that came from my father.

Loving life and life as an adventure

In addition to almost constantly saying that he loved life, and that life was an adventure, Dad actually lived it out.

We rented a boat to sail in the Bahamas to learn about sailing. We had a great adventure, but we had no experience and many things went wrong. I remember always thinking we would figure it out somehow through Dad's leadership because in every adventure we had, we always came through and then had great stories to tell about it afterward. One never seems to remember the things that go as planned. It is the mishaps and hurdles and adventures one always remembers about trips.

We moved around and built houses in the middle of nowhere. Something I remember being ingrained in me from all the moving we did was that one moved to follow dreams—not because of some career thing. You choose to live where you lived because it would be fun and interesting. We were always really excited about our moves. We were excited to go to Colorado for mountains; we were excited to live in an athletic club in the cool town of Cannon Falls; we were excited to move next to the Cannon River in the underground house we helped build. It seemed like we were always involved in the decisions and Dad made us feel like we were helping decide. I really believed it then, but now that I look back, we couldn't have had much impact on the decision. I think Dad just got us to buy into his dreams. Anyway, I learned from it that life is about chasing your dreams and having adventures! It was a wonderful way to grow up. I have loved change ever since.

Toughness/perseverance/hard work

Hard work and toughness were always important to Dad. I didn't always appreciate those lessons growing up, but I have found them to be some of my most precious lessons as an adult. Again, our lives were full of moments that taught hard work and toughness, but I'll pick just a few memories to describe here.

When we were in grade school, we had to get up early to do chores before school. We had to feed our cows hay and make sure they had water in their water trough. That often meant getting up in the dark, going outside in the bitter cold, breaking ice off the water trough, dragging 50 lb-80 lb bales we could barely lift and walking through foot deep manure that almost went over our rubber boots. In fact, I remember a few times where our boots got stuck in the manure and came off briefly. I remember using twine to hook up to the bales of hay so we could drag them more easily. I remember one morning relishing the ice formations from freezing rain on the barbed wire fence. I also remember actually enjoying the time with my brothers doing the work and sometimes we got yelled at for taking too long because we played King of the Hill on the stacks of hay. I also remember that breakfast always tasted REALLY good after doing that work first thing in the morning. I do NOT remember hating the work or thinking it was too much or ever thinking we could not do it. It was just sort of a fact of life. Getting up early when you don't feel like it, doing work before breakfast and doing unpleasant work since then has always felt easy.

I also remember helping on every single one of the three houses my Dad built while I was growing up. The first one was built when I was four. We didn't do much, but I distinctly remember putting little wooden shims in between the logs and feeling like I contributed. In Colorado, I remember digging the trench for bringing spring water to the house when we first moved in and then mixing and hauling cement in wheelbarrows when I was 12. Finally, for the Cannon Falls house, we often worked 12-hour days for 6 days a week in the summer while we were in high school. Since it was an underground house, it involved jack hammering rocks, digging dirt for retaining walls, building rock retaining walls, framing the house, building the deck, and backfilling behind the walls. It was hard sweaty work during which we worked on our tans. Once again, even though it was hard, we were proud for having contributed and we learned a lot about construction.

Truth and stories

One of my favorite memories was when Dad would come up and tell us bedtime stories. He wouldn't read anything, but he would make the stories up. He was a very good story teller and all of us hung on every word. He often used stories to teach lessons. I remember one lesson standing out in particular. He reinforced over and over how important it was to tell the truth. He even modified the Adam and Eve story from the Bible. He said that he thought perhaps the reason God threw them out of the Garden of Eden wasn't because they ate the apple—it could be because they lied about it afterwards and tried to deceive God.

I also remember an Indian story where four Indians went on a grand adventure. (Dad's stories often involved Indians and they were always the heroes.) One Indian personified Truth, the other Love, another Strength and another Courage. They started arguing about who was the most important. So, each of them left for a short time during the journey to test who would be the most important. Making a long story short, the group always succeeded with one of them missing except when Truth was missing. They couldn't do anything or succeed without Truth because they couldn't trust each other and that was more destructive to their teamwork than living without Love, Courage or Strength. Truth was the only one they couldn't live without. I also remember that Dad reinforced this in real life. We always were in more trouble if we got caught in a lie than if we just admitted the wrong that we committed.

Connection with wilderness

Lastly, I remember Dad's love of the wilderness. We lived it in our adventures in Colorado; we lived it in our trips to the boundary waters and we lived it in our deer hunting trips. We always went to places that had few or no people and were very isolated.

In particular, I remember Dad helping us put together survival kits for deer hunting. He taught us what to do if we got lost or hurt in the woods. He taught us how to use a compass and how to start fires with only the wood and kindling found in the woods. He taught us how to use a mirror to gain attention and how important it was to stay dry. When we went deer hunting in northern Minnesota, we drove miles through logging roads that no one else dared go on. We camped near a lake in a tent with a wood stove. For nine days, we didn't shower or see any form of civilization, and I loved it. If you wanted to get clean, you had to do it in the ice-cold lake (often with a thin layer of ice on it). We went to the bathroom outside and got dirty and grubby.

And when we did shoot a deer, Dad taught us how to clean it. I can remember getting ready for deer hunting on a Friday afternoon at St. Thomas Academy, where I went to high school. I changed out of my clean uniform with a tie and put on my hunting clothes with my survival kit and buck knife on my belt. I had told all my teachers that I would miss a week of school for deer hunting. Sometimes they would look at me funny, but I knew I was going back to the wilderness for a week to learn from the best classroom in the world, to reconnect with what was REAL in life—not school, not grades, not military formations or promotions, not cliques or popularity contests, not even girls or dances—but pure wilderness and isolation.

I feel like I could go on and on—maybe even write my own book—but here is where I will end. I will always cherish the memories, lessons and adventures I shared with my dad while growing up. I have three boys of my own now who have all moved out. I hope that in my own way, I gave them some cherished memories of their own. I shared and taught them different things, and I wasn't ever quite as adventurous with my own kids as Dad was with us. I do regret not doing more of that with my own boys, but each of us has our own strengths and weaknesses and my boys are now living their own adventures. I think they still gained a bit of Grandpa in their life, and I am very grateful for that.

Introduction

Important to Know

I am telling my own story, my adventures through life, primarily for my grandchildren and my great grandchildren, but perhaps it may have something to offer for those who have an interest in a life lived differently from most, or for those searching for their own faith awakening.

All of us travel through life on our own path, but most of us choose, are guided to, or are forced onto one wherein we live our lives like most of those around us. I chose a path less taken.

At age sixteen I spent thirty days in the wilderness halfway between the north shore of Lake Superior and Hudson Bay, and I never saw another human being for twenty-eight days, other than the thirteen-year-old boy with me.

In 1965, at age twenty-two, I moved my pregnant wife and our one-year-old son to Alaska to homestead. The following year I started a plumbing business and have been my own boss ever since. The same year I started my first business, I bought twenty acres of timber on the side of a mountain just outside of Anchorage.

Over the next fifty-plus years I bought and sold over a hundred parcels of land, became a real-estate broker and owned commercial real-estate. I have worked as a plumbing contractor, a guide and outfitter, an athletic club owner, a cow-calf rancher and I have designed and built four homes.

Along the way I had five sons, wrote a book on raising children and a book of children's stories. I built two private handball courts and won a state handball tournament. I went up against a grizzly bear with a knife and a rock and had an awakening in my lifelong search for faith.

I will share my unusual journey through life by telling stories about it, and what a wonderful journey it has been!

I would love to take it over again, but know I cannot. Perhaps the next best thing is to relive it in my mind and in the telling of these adventures. It is one of the joys of old men to do so.

In the past, the saga of a person's life was often passed down from generation to generation. A person was able to learn from this and even lived on for generations through the stories told about him or her. The history of our ancestors and their voyage through life nourished and maintained a sense of family, of who we were and where we came from.

With the advent of electricity, radio, television, and now the computer, these stories seem to have left us. Sharing them is no longer part of our families, and they are no longer a necessary form of entertainment.

I heard very little about my family. I wasn't able to pick up a book and read about my grandparents or aunts or uncles, and was saddened because of it.

I hope you tell your grandchildren about your life's journey, and you pass on your values and carry on a family tradition that perhaps my stories have started.

It does not matter that you are not a writer—I certainly am not. It will be difficult, as this has been difficult for me, but your children and your children's children will, as I hope you will, overlook the presentation and be grateful for the content.

So let the stories, and hopefully the tradition, begin.

Grandfather's quote

Why we tell our story is most important of all.
Our story is what keeps us and all
those in it belonging always.

My original book, *A Path Less Taken: The True Life Adventures of Gary Friendshuh and His Faith Awakening*, contains a lot more about my sons, more pictures, more personal details and poems. It is available on Amazon.

My Grandfather Friendshuh's parents, Louisa and Wilhelm Pfreundschuh

My Grandmother Friendshuh's parents, Sophia and Adam Doerfler

Prologue

Those Who Came Before Me

THE FRIENDSHUH FAMILY

So where does a person's story begin? At birth? I think not. It begins with those who came before him and is influenced by the paths they have taken. And all Americans have a path less taken in their genes. Either they themselves or their relatives took such a path by leaving most others behind while they ventured to a new land.

My father's grandparents, Wilhelm and Louisa Pfreundschuh, came from Uissigheim, Germany, and never became citizens of this country. Mr. Franklin Steel purchased land near Fort Snelling and he sold eighty acres of it in Richfield to a Mr. Altaman, who immediately sold forty acres of the eighty to Wilhelm and Louisa. Perhaps Steel would not sell to a non-citizen.

Wilhelm and Louisa had three children, Annie, Adolf and Joseph Andrew (my father's father). Joseph was born at Fort Snelling on October 17, 1874.

Wilhelm died when Joseph was four years old and Louisa sent to Germany for a woman to come and help her with the children and on the farm.

My grandparents Elizabeth and Joseph Friendshuh (1902)

When Joseph became an adult, following his own path, he changed the spelling of his name to Friendshuh. No one knows why. His brother Adolf dropped the P, so he spelled his name Freundschuh.

When Joseph was twenty-eight he married Elizabeth Doerfler, who was nineteen.

Elizabeth's parents, Sophia Knaeble and Adam Doerfler, came to this country from Bamberg, Bavaria, in Germany and were the first recorded marriage at St. Boniface in Richfield, Minnesota. Soon after their marriage they bought 160 acres in Richfield, just north of what is now 78th Street and Nicollet Ave.

Elizabeth was the last of twelve children. Her mother died when she was three days old, so a married sister raised her until she was five or six and able to take care of herself. Then she moved back to the farm her father, who never remarried, still operated.

Elizabeth had two brothers who were priests. Abbot Bruno and Father Hilary. Both taught at St. John's University, and Abbot Bruno became the head priest and master of the school. In 1902, he rode a horse from St. Cloud, Minnesota, to Saskatchewan, Canada, in search of a place to build a new monastery. The parishioners of his church, probably near the monastery, named the town after him. Years later, some Friendshuhs went to Bruno and were treated like royalty. Assumption Parish in Richfield has an old church book that tells the story.

Elizabeth also had three sisters who were nuns. When Elizabeth started school, she went to the convent to live with her sisters during the school year.

In later life she was called the saint. She was soft spoken and a great cook. She loved farming, and she and her husband, Joseph, bought their own farm just before she had her third child.

Joseph and Elizabeth had sixteen children. Here is a little of what I know of each of their remarkable children.

Cordelia Teresa

Their oldest, Cordelia Teresa, was born July 9, 1903, and married Leo Ostertag in 1925. They lived on a farm in Rosemount, Minnesota, and had twelve children. Some say Cordelia was her mother all over again.

She was a big woman and always had the welcome mat out. I ran into one of her daughters at a Lakeville Mass one Sunday, and she insisted that our entire family come over to her home for breakfast. And it was no small meal! I remember being on their farm when I was little, but all her children were much older than I so I didn't get to know them well. I do remember at the family picnics that all her daughters were as warm and friendly as any person can be.

George

George, their eldest son, was born on January 28, 1905. When he was eleven years old, he saved the life of his younger brother, who had gotten in with a bull. George got his little brother out but while doing so he was gored by the bull. He died three days later on September 16, 1916.

Louis

Next came Louis, who was born on August 6, 1906, and died on December 8, 1906.

Urban

Urban (Urb) was born on January 16, 1908, and like his father he became a dairy farmer. He had three children, George, Gene and Carolyn.

I remember going to his farm in Mora, Minnesota, whenever my father needed to fix a pump or do some plumbing work in the barn. They always expected me to help with the chores, and I remember loving it. The warmth of the barn, the feeling of responsibility and just the comfort of being there made it special. Urb was quiet like Dad, and he loved to play cards. When all of his children moved to Alaska, he and his wife moved there too. They had a home right next to George and Gene, and he hunted and fished with them all the time.

Louise

Louise was born on December 15, 1908, and married Herman Haeg in 1930. They had eight children. One of them, Steve, died in the Korean War. Louise was a super lady who knew all the stories. Perhaps she passed some of them on to her children. Her husband, Herman, was a real character. He worked at the Schmidt Brewery in St. Paul, but they had a farm of sorts in Bloomington. I can remember going there and being able to watch the drive-in movie theater on 78th Street across their field.

Gerald

Gerald (Gary) was born on December 20, 1911, and died of kidney failure at age 23, as a result of scarlet fever.

Anselm

Anselm was born April 20, 1910, and died March 21, 1911.

Arnold

Arnold (AJ) was born on January 26, 1913, and married Margaret on November 11, 1936. They had six children, among them Steve and Big Mark. AJ lived next to my father from the time I was five years old, until the day that he died, when I was probably over fifty.

As a young boy, he was the only one who worked off the farm. He worked for Oxborough Lumber just across Lyndale Avenue, then just a dirt road. Eventually he became manager of the lumber yard and chief of the Bloomington volunteer fire department. He got married during the Minnesota deer hunting season and brought his bride to camp for one night. Every year during hunting camp, he would drive twenty miles to town to call his wife and wish her happy anniversary.

When he bought five hundred acres in northern Wisconsin, he tried to get Dad to buy it with him. I think Mom was the reason Dad

(back) Urb, AJ, Roman, Duke, Al, my father Bill, Claud; (front) Cordelia, Evelyn, Grandma Elizabeth, Grandpa Joseph, Marie, Louise

Grandpa, Al, AJ, Duke, Dad, Claud, Urb and Roman

didn't do just that, but we were welcome there all the time. Spent many a Wisconsin deer hunting season in them there woods. AJ hunted elk on my ranch in Colorado and took a ranch tour here in South Dakota the year before he died.

My only seemingly contact with the spirit world came one morning in Cannon Falls. At a very early hour I was awakened out of a sound sleep by a woman's voice stating, "There is a God." I remember looking at the clock and noting the time. Later that day I got a phone call and learned Aunt Margaret, AJ's bride, had passed away that morning at the exact time I had heard the woman's voice.

Roman

Roman was born on March 7, 1914, and he married Clara in 1936. He was a dairy farmer, and they had ten girls and two boys. Roman was a farmer through and through. He was a bull of a man, and boy did he love his cards. Their farm was in St. Michaels, Minnesota. I can remember squirrel hunting there along with helping all his daughters with the chores.

Paul

Paul (Duke) was born on February 19, 1917, and married Teresa in 1939. They had four children. He moved to California and was a contractor. Paul was called Duke after a mean bull they had by the same name, because he was supposedly so mean.

Willard

Willard was born on October 15, 1915, and died on April 20, 1917.

Alvarez

Alvarez (Al) was born September 10, 1918, and married Winifred in 1941. They had 9 children. He became a dairy farmer on a farm in Albertville, Minnesota. I used to spend a lot of time there, too.

William

My father, William (Bill), was next so I am listing him here, but I will tell his story in a following subtitle. He was born on June 16, 1920, and married Helen Cunningham, my mom, on August 30, 1941.

Claud

Claud, the last of the boys, was born on November 18, 1921, and married Mary Ann Christian in 1943. They had sixteen children. He had a dairy farm in Marystown just south of Shakopee, Minnesota. My mother dated him before she dated Dad. (She probably didn't want sixteen kids and having to help milk cows.)

I spent many a fall on his farm. As a teenager, I used to drive out and hunt squirrels, and I was there each fall with my dad hunting pheasants. When I was still in grade school, I would go spend a weekend or two helping on the farm. Here, too, I was expected to help with all the chores and I remember helping with the haying. In later life, Claude worked for Dad running a backhoe and he was the best I ever saw at it.

Marie

Marie was born on April 20, 1923, and married John Donahue. They had nine children, and one of her sons was killed in Vietnam. She was a very soft-spoken woman and extremely spiritual.

Evelyn

Evelyn was born on April 27, 1926, married Don Swanson and had one child. She moved to California when I was very young, so I didn't get to know her very well.

Two of my favorite Friendshuh family stories kind of illustrate a family on its own path.

My grandfather loved to play cards and towards the end of his wake, the boys started a card game. When one wife complained, they told her their dad was in heaven and if he were here, he would be playing cards too, so they were just remembering and honoring him by doing so.

My grandmother waited for a little over a year before joining her husband in heaven. Both had left wills, but neither stated who was to get their household possessions. The family decided to cut cards to determine who got what. The highest card could choose whatever he or she wanted and so on and so forth. At the time Claud, their youngest son, was the poorest of the lot and he did not own a TV. It just so happens the single most valuable thing Grandma and Grandpa had owned was a large console TV. All the brothers and sisters got together, without Claud, and agreed whoever cut the highest cards would not choose the TV. Well, Claud couldn't believe it when he was sixth or seventh to choose and the TV was still available.

That's the Friendshuhs for ya.

My grandfather's farm on 95th and Lyndale. (In 1940, Lyndale was still a dirt road.)

My mother, Helen, and father, William, on their wedding day

BILL FRIENDSHUH, MY FATHER

Of the sixteen children, my father was the one who most dramatically took his own path. All his brothers and sisters called him Wild Bill.

When their family became so large that my grandfather Joseph had plenty of help in the barn, the two youngest boys, Claude and my father, Bill, stayed inside to help with the housework. Under their mother's guidance, both learned how to clean and do laundry, and also became very good cooks. My father's father was a man no one ever openly challenged or stood up to but Dad wasn't above helping others follow their own path too. When his sister Marie had been forbidden to go out on a date with the man she later married, Dad used a long step-ladder to help her climb out an upstairs window.

In ninth grade Dad was told he couldn't stay after school to play sports, so he quit school. He didn't mind starting each day working in the barn for a couple of hours before school (he had graduated to outside work by the time he was in ninth grade), but if he couldn't play sports, no way was he going to go to school.

Dad wasn't the only one to work off the farm when he got older, but anyone who worked off the farm had to give all of what they earned to their father. Their father in turn gave them a weekly allowance. Anyone who lived at home, regardless of his age, had to continue this practice.

When one of his boys got married and left home, they were given, for the times, a large sum of money. My father only got half of what the others got because when he started dating Mom, he asked for a regular wage. His father's response was if he didn't like the way things were handled on the farm, he could leave. Dad followed his own path and left. He was somewhere between 16 and 18 years old.

My father served with distinction in World War II and received the Silver Star. Dad was a Master Sergeant and was called "the old man" at age twenty-five. After some great battle his outfit was marching through an area that had many dead bloated German soldiers in it. Later that day Dad found out his men were cutting off the fingers of

Dad and me (1945)

the dead soldiers and taking their rings. He called them all over and told them if he caught anyone cutting any part of the dead soldiers, he would shoot them on the spot.

After the war, Dad worked for Earl Blaylock, until he started his own plumbing company. Dad was a great ball player, and he had his own baseball team before he was 19. He was also very strong, but he never would compete with his kids. I could not get him to arm wrestle. Maybe it was because I was too competitive.

He was also a great golfer and could still shoot in the seventies when he was in his late sixties. He was also a very good card player. Once a month, he would play bridge with a friend of mine, my brother Jay, and me, for money. And he loved to hunt pheasants, ducks and mostly deer. But he had a bad back and a bad hip, and in his fifties he had to quit hunting after a hip surgery.

He could also play any musical instrument you put in front of him. And boy, could he sing.

He was a quiet man, yet Mom says before the war he was a ball of fire. She said the war changed him a lot, and he came home different. Dad also showed little or no emotion. He even told me he thought it was inappropriate to kiss my wife in public. I remember when he was helping me build the log house in Lakeville and a police officer brought Mom out crying. She said their home had caught on fire, and the fireman had to break all the windows out. He just took her in his arms and held her. The officer asked him if they would be all right and he said, "Sure." He never showed the slightest bit of emotion—he just did what had to be done.

Dad taught me how to be a man and how to be a hard worker, and he was a man of honor and a man of his word. Like his father before him, he was the undisputed head of his family, yet when I asked him to sign my report card in eleventh grade, he said, "You are a man; sign it yourself." Perhaps it was his requiring me to work and take on responsibility at a very young age that encouraged or allowed me to choose a path less taken. In his later years he mellowed a lot, and although most of his organs were strong, his lungs failed him. He smoked all his life and died of emphysema at age 71.

HEADQUARTERS 79TH INFANTRY DIVISION A.P.O. 79. U.S. ARMY
General Orders 21 August, 1945
Number 188

Award of the Silver Star

Pursuant to authority contained in AR 600-45, the Silver Star is awarded to:

Sergeant William J Friendshuh, 37595837, 313 Infantry, United States Army, for gallantry in action against the enemy on the 27th of March 1945 in Germany. While defending four enemy gun and ammunition pits which had been captured during an attack, the platoon in which Sergeant Friendshuh served as a rifleman came under fire from concentrations of enemy mortar artillery, and small arms fire. Direct hits on the ammunition pits resulted in detonating many explosions which made the pits untenable. With total disregard for his personal safety, Sergeant Friendshuh exposed himself to administer first aid to the wounded and to assist in their evacuation. After carrying one man seventy-five yards in full observation of the enemy and under continuous fire, he remained in the pits until all of the wounded were evacuated. The courage and devotion to duty displayed by Sergeant Friendshuh reflect great credit on himself and the armed forces of the United States. Entered military service from Minnesota.

By Command of Brigadier General Watson

The Hendricksons: (back) Karl Ludvic (Louie), Inga, Paul, Lillian, William; (front) my grandmother Clara, Mrs. Hendrickson, Henry Hendrickson

Grandfather Charles Cunningham about age 10, in front of his father's Illinois farm

THE CUNNINGHAM FAMILY

My personal knowledge of my mother's family begins with her parents, Charles and Clara Cunningham.

My grandmother Clara's family, the Hendricksons, came from Norway. The youngest of six children, she was named Clariece, but following a path less taken she called herself Clara Elizabeth all of her adult life. She even had that name put on her tombstone.

She had two sisters who I never met. Inga was the oldest and lived in Oregon. Lillian served as a nurse overseas during World War I.

I never knew her brother William, but I knew her brothers Paul and Louie. Paul was very intelligent and over 6'6" tall. Perhaps that is where our family gets some of our height. Too bad I didn't get the intellectual part. Louie's actual name was Karl Ludvic. Uncle Louie was a streetcar conductor and lived close to my grandparents. He and his wife, Carrie, used to come out every Christmas and Thanksgiving. He always had a pocket full of change for the kids, and Aunt Carrie baked the best cookies I have ever eaten.

My grandfather Charles's family came from Ireland. Charles was the youngest of the twelve Cunningham children and he grew up on a farm in Deer Grove, Illinois. I never knew any of his brothers or sisters.

When he was four years old, his brother shot his left eye out with a slingshot. At twenty-one, he was hit by a train and the doctors said he could not possibly survive. The pronouncement was wrong, and in 1918 Grandpa married Grandma, who at the time was eighteen.

When she married him, she thought he was thirty. After they had been married for many months, she found out he was actually forty-eight. Grandpa and Grandma had three children, Carolyn, Helen (my mom), and Charles.

Aunt Carolyn, Mom's older sister, was very close to Mom and married later in life. Before marrying Frank Onufrak and moving to the east coast, she was with us for many Christmases and Thanksgivings. Frank was a very tall man with a great work ethic. When I was about fourteen he and I built a rock garden at Dad's home in Bloomington and he taught me a little about defending myself. Frank and Carolyn had one daughter.

My first communion, standing with my grandfather Charles

My grandparents Charles and Clara Cunningham

Uncle Charles also married later in life. Before getting married, he was a big part of my life. He, like his sister, was at our home for most Christmases and Thanksgivings. I remember him not wanting to sit next to the kids at meal time because he didn't want to get hit with food. Mom laughed when he had kids of his own because every father gets spilled on.

I believe he is the one who taught me how to play table tennis. I remember him teaching me how to dribble a basketball and telling me to practice a lot. He and a buddy named Roger took me to several University of Minnesota basketball games.

He worked for West Publishing. He was vice president before he retired and sold his stock for several million dollars. Even before becoming a millionaire, Mom said he would never fly anywhere unless it was first class, so now he could lead his entire life first class. He and his wife Cathy had two children, daughter Dawn and son Greg. Dawn and her family came to visit me on the ranch one summer and seemed to have a good time.

Grandma was thirty years younger than Grandpa, and she jokingly would say, "I can't wait until Charlie kicks the bucket so I can go out and kick up my heels."

Well, she kicked the bucket years before Charlie, but before doing so she was always willing to take care of me and I know she loved me dearly.

In my youth, I did not know what to say to her as she lay on her deathbed. How I wish now I would have just held her hand and told her how much I loved her. She did so much for me, and I did not know how to be there for her. Don't make the same mistake. Those who care for you want nothing more than for you to show or tell them you love them. No matter how awkward it may seem, letting someone know you love them will always, to them, be perfect.

Grandpa was very independent and after Grandma died, he lived alone. He used to walk to Mass and to the grocery store every week, and he loved to play cards. Cribbage was his favorite game. I used to occasionally go in and play with him.

He always lied about his age, as he did when he got married. In later years he always said he was fifteen or twenty years younger than he was. When he started to shake a little at the age of ninety-two or ninety-three and he knew he could no longer keep up the charade, he handled it another way. I was playing cards with him one day, and he said he wanted to tell me something in confidence. He told me he had been lying about his age all these years and he wanted me to know that he was really 106.

When he fell while shoveling snow and broke his hip at the age of ninety-four, the doctors told him he would never walk again. That was not for him, so he just refused to eat and within a month passed on.

HELEN FRIENDSHUH, MY MOTHER

My mother was on a path less taken for a woman of her day. She always taught me to think for myself and she would talk to me about anything. She treated me like a young adult and spent a lot of time giving me pointers about girls. She even told me some off-colored jokes and made sure I had ballroom dancing lessons.

She was very direct and completely comfortable with herself and who I or anyone else was. You always knew how she felt. Once when she came to visit me, I had a ping pong table in my living room. She got a chair, got up on the table and stood there with her arms in the air yelling, "If you don't get this damn table out of your living room I am never coming back!"

When I was eighteen, she could pass for my sister, and at eighty she looked fifty and was still line dancing with her friends. They even put on line dancing shows at senior citizens centers.

When she was a little over eighty years old a lifelong friend lost his wife and invited Mom to travel around the world with him. She said she couldn't afford it. When he told her he would pay for everything, she said in her direct style, "I am not sleeping with you." She did go on the trip and had a good time except she felt her traveling companion was a "party pooper." He was about her age or maybe a little younger but he was ready for bed by 8:00 PM every night.

My mother, Helen, at age 80

She remained very young for her age until my brother took away her car keys when she was about 90. She really went downhill after that and passed away at age 94.

Grandfather's quote

Those who came before us are a large part of who we are, and you will be part of those who follow, so share your story.

For many years I have been accused of seeing the world through rose colored glasses. No wonder! The view is wonderful and it was there from the start. (1943)

1

Early Memories and Starting on My Own Path

I was born in Minneapolis, Minnesota, on July 2, 1943, and arrived butt first (a breech birth). My mother teasingly says I have been backasswward ever since. When I was fifteen months old, I had some serious disease, maybe rheumatic fever, and was not expected to live. Dad was due to be shipped to Italy with his Army outfit. Instead, he was reassigned and allowed to stay. Mom says they agreed to let the doctors try out some medicine or antibiotic on me that had never been used on humans before. It obviously worked.

I had nothing to do with the path that my life's journey was on before I got into third grade, but that is where I either consciously or unconsciously started down a path that was different than most.

When I started third grade, it was at the newly opened Nativity of Mary School in Bloomington. I had a first-year teacher named Miss Smith, who despised me. Perhaps it was partly because I was taking my first steps onto a path less taken. I was one of the very few kids who was always very polite and said, "Yes, Sister" or "No, Sister" and the like. When I was polite to Miss Smith, it angered her. She said she liked the troublemaker in the class much better than me because even though he was always getting into trouble, he was honest about it. She regarded my politeness and respect as being just plain sneaky.

Me on Grandpa's farm. Maybe this is where my love of ranching came from. (1944)

Thankfully Miss Smith's distrust didn't deter me from staying on my own path and continuing to be polite and respectful. My politeness and respect for adults served me well through all of my schooling, and respect for others has served me well throughout my life.

Even at that young age in third grade, it did not matter to me what my peers thought. I felt no peer pressure back then, nor at any other time in my life.

I can remember when a bunch of my grade school buddies showed me how neat they thought it was to bend over and hold their breath and then stand up quick and pass out. They couldn't get me to do it. I just thought it was stupid.

Attending a Catholic school, taught mostly by nuns, also started me down a very different path than most, and not in the way you might think. At this young age I was not entirely comfortable with being on this different path which my mother had guided me to. She always taught me to think for myself, even in matters of faith. Well, it is a lot easier for a young child to just be told what was right or wrong and what he could or could not do. I on the other hand was expected to decide for myself between right or wrong, regardless of what the nuns or anyone else said about it. I struggled with this and thought the other kids were lucky because they didn't have to decide. They just did what the nuns told them to do. Period, The End.

When my aunt got married in a Protestant church, the nuns told me I couldn't go, but I went anyway. At the age of sixteen, when a priest told me I couldn't go into the wilderness for thirty days and miss Mass for four Sundays, I went anyway. But when anyone has to decide on matters of faith, much less a third grader, or even a sixteen-year-old, that individual will always challenge their own decisions as to whether or not they decided correctly in the eyes of their Creator.

As I reflect back over the years, perhaps it has been a good thing to have to search deep within my heart for direction and go through the struggles with faith that this caused. It kept me looking for answers or for the faith I was worried I did not have, and it may even be a small part of the reason for all the blessings that have been bestowed upon me.

A few more random thoughts and stories

When I was eleven years old, I was still learning responsibility and was just beginning to acquire a good work ethic. But as with most eleven-year-olds, even though I seemed to be taking my own path, my self-esteem had a long way to go.

At that age I still loved playing in the sandbox, but somehow I sensed my father did not approve. To this day, I do not know if that really was the case or if I just thought that is how he felt. He was your typical German. He worked hard, said little and was very proud.

That Christmas I remember getting money that I was supposed to use to get myself a special gift. I went to the variety store and bought a really neat Cavalry Fort. It had the fort, cannons, lots of soldiers, lots of cavalry and hundreds of Indians. I was really excited about it; but when I brought it home, once again I sensed my father did not approve. I vaguely remember Mom saying she thought I had spent my money foolishly but this memory, too, may not be correct. I do know I took it back and got something else.

My grandmother turned this into a positive moment. She had been visiting when this all happened, and I think she knew what was going on. She was aware of my inner struggle. The next day, when I was on the floor playing with some toy soldiers, she came up behind me and put her hand on my shoulder and said, "Gary, it's OK to be playing with your toys. You don't have to be ashamed of your wonderful imagination. It is a great gift, and you should be proud of it."

I have always remembered her words. Thank you, Grandma.

My brothers and sister

I can remember taking care of my youngest brother when I was sixteen and seventeen years old. Brent was fifteen years younger than me. When he was four years old, I came home from college and Mom told him that I was his brother; he replied, "No, he is not." When he was seven and eight years old, I sent him about twenty post cards a year from Alaska. He remembers that to this day, and said, "Who at age 21 and 22 does something like that?"

My sister Janet was nine years younger than me and other than babysitting her and remembering her excitement at Christmas time, I have few memories of her childhood.

Now my brother Jay was only four years younger. Because we lived out in the country and for several years I had no friends my age living close by, we did a lot together. When I started playing baseball at age ten, he was right there with me at age six. As I developed and got better, so did he. When I learned to play cards, I taught him. In fact, when I was in eighth grade and he was only in fourth grade we were playing bridge with our parents. When it was just Jay and I, the two of us would bid and play two hands each to practice for the games with our parents. He went on to become a master bridge player and an all-around super card player. We also played lots of games like Monopoly together. He was one of the best game players I ever played with.

Church, cards and staying on my different path

Before Nativity School was built, my family went to Mass in the old Bloomington high school. Once the school was built, we went to Mass in the school gym. Dad saw to it that we never missed Mass. If the weather was bad and we couldn't get there, Dad just had us all say the rosary at home. Dad was a man of faith, but he was your typical German and kept things like that to himself. He was on the parish council and used to go play poker with other members of the council and the parish priest.

My card playing really began because I got kicked out of music class. Bobby Oxborough and I had voices that were too deep, so we were sent to the lunchroom during music class. Perhaps it was because I loved to sing and was not embarrassed about singing loudly. Whatever the reason, I never learned to read a note or carry a tune or stay on key, if these are even things one is taught in a music class. What I did learn is a love for cards, because I always brought a deck, and while the rest of the class was learning music, Bobby and I were playing cards in the lunchroom.

Perhaps it was because I was expected to work at Dad's plumbing shop during the summers and I had to interact with adults more, that I never felt the need to go along with the teenage crowd, and that kept me from doing some of the stupid things kids seem to do. I did try smoking a cigarette or two, but I never could figure out how anyone got by those first few. No one can say they liked it in the beginning. They either did it to impress their friends or because they thought it was cool.

Then there was the time when I was in seventh grade and we were out on Halloween walking by a house with several jack-o-lanterns outside. There were six or seven of us and one of the guys said, "Let's go smash those." The others started to follow, and I hollered, "Stop! Come on guys, some little kid carved those, don't wreck them." They stopped.

Between my sixth and seventh grade year we moved to a new house on Glen Wilding Lane, which was on the Minnesota River bluffs. Dad and his brother AJ built houses just across a ravine from one another, so we had the same main neighbor.

We had a long driveway and in the summertime, with all the leaves on the trees, we couldn't see any neighbors. Dad also built a combination tennis court, shuffleboard court and basketball court, with floodlights on it. As I got a little older, I practically lived on that basketball court.

We also had a ping pong table in the basement. Dad had been the ping pong champion of his outfit, during and after the war. Even after playing for over a year with my friends, I couldn't get three points on Dad. Oftentimes a friend of mine, Pat Mallkee, and I would play for three or four hours at a time, and before I got out of high school, I was finally able to beat Dad.

In my eighth grade year, I took a test to see if I could get into St. Thomas Military Academy, but I was put on a waiting list.

I also took a test to get into De La Salle, where my father had gone to high school for part of one year. I was accepted.

Grandfather's Quote

Walk your own path, not the path of others.

2

Work and Becoming a Man

Before I was ten years old or prior to fifth grade, I do not have any recollection of working. I am sure I had normal household chores, like keeping my room clean, taking out the garbage, clearing the table and raking leaves, but I honestly do not remember many of those things.

At the end of the school year, when I just finished fifth grade, Dad told me I was old enough to start working. He told me I had to come down to the plumbing shop and answer the telephone and put away plumbing fittings. The first summer I was only required to come in for half days. I could get out of going if there was a ball game, or I was busy with some other sporting activity. I was paid 25 cents an hour.

The following summer I was required to be there five days a week, eight hours a day. I was not allowed to sleep in, watch television, or lie around the house. Actually, I don't think we owned a television at this stage in my life. But just like the summer before, I was allowed to miss work for sports or other things my father deemed important. As you can imagine, I made sure I was off doing something as often as I could get away with. I played lots and lots of baseball, did a lot of fishing, and spent a lot of time in the woods hiking or building forts or whatever.

When I did go to work, one of my jobs was answering the telephone. In retrospect, I now realize how valuable a lesson answering the telephone was. I had to answer something like, "Bloomington Plumbing, may I help you?" Then I had to take messages and get them right. I also put away plumbing fittings in the back of the shop. The plumbers would come in the morning and pick out all of fittings they needed for the job each day and load them in buckets. Then at the end of the day they would bring those same buckets back and dump all the fittings on the floor. I learned what all the plumbing fittings were called and where they went, and more importantly I learned to interact with adults. All the guys would come in each morning and sit around and have a cup of coffee and talk about the day's work. Between interacting with the workmen each morning and answering the telephone, I learned to communicate with adults as an adult.

After seventh grade, Dad put a shovel and a set of pipe wrenches in my hand. In the beginning, I do not remember how much actual digging I did. When I worked with the well drillers, I was probably just bringing them wrenches and pipe and things like that. To be honest, I can't really remember a lot about that first summer. I am sure I was probably as much of a bother as I was of help, but I was learning. I also remember my father often telling me what a good worker I was. More importantly, he would tell others, within earshot of me, how good a worker I was. It made me want to live up to all the praise.

It was the summer between my eighth and ninth grade year that I truly became a workman and more importantly became a man. When I was with the well drillers, we were usually driving new wells. Our well rig was run with a rope which would drop a 300-pound weight and drive casing into the sandy ground.

It was hard work. The man who worked the rope and pulleys which lifted and dropped the 300-pound weight had to coordinate with the man bringing him the pipe. More than once if I made a mistake, I got yelled at big time, but I was learning.

Occasionally we would pull a screen to repair an old well. So I learned how to take a pump off and pull out the pipe and the screen from a well and help put it back in. Even though I didn't have a driver's license, Dad would occasionally let me drive the well rig to the job if it was close by. I guess he figured the well rig was more like a tractor than a vehicle.

I was thirteen years old and working with the well drillers when, in my mind, I went from being a child to being a man. I remember the day.

One day we were putting in a new well. We had to put a hole in the concrete on the bottom of the well pit before we started driving the well. Eddie Freundschuh, who I was working with, had to go back to the shop and get some fittings. He left me on the job and told me to break the concrete with a hammer and cold chisel. I can remember striking that cold chisel over and over again, and I was getting nowhere. I started to feel sorry for myself and said to myself that I could not do this. The more I tried, the more frustrated I got and the more I was sure I could not get the job done. I started to cry, and then I caught myself and admonished myself for being a baby.

I sat back, took a deep breath and told myself if Eddie or any other man could break this concrete, so could I. I pulled myself together and did what I had to do. I broke through the concrete, and at the same time broke out of my childhood. I don't know what caused me to have that kind of determination. I just was not going to let Eddie come back and find some snotty-nosed kid with wet eyes who couldn't do the job.

That day I became a man.

I spent more than half the summer with the laborers. I took pride in working hard, having the sweat pour off, and keeping up with the man at my side. Our job was to dig cesspools and septic tanks. By this time I was making a whopping 50 cents an hour. The two of us would have to dig a six-foot diameter hole twelve feet deep and a four-foot diameter hole twenty feet deep.

First, we dug each hole down about four or five feet. Then we laid a concrete ring in the bottom of the hole, either a six-foot diameter ring for the septic tank or a four-foot diameter ring for the cesspools. Next we took curved blocks and set them on this ring all the way around. We laid a second row of blocks on top of the first, then a third and a fourth until the wall was two feet above the ground. Then one of us climbed inside the concrete ring with two buckets. The man in the hole filled one bucket with dirt and put it on a hook at the end of a rope. The other man lifted the bucket out with a gas-powered pulley machine. He dumped that bucket of dirt and lowered the empty bucket back down to the man in the hole, who by this time had filled the other bucket. In this way we got deeper and deeper until, in the case of the cesspool, we were twenty feet in the ground. Two men, usually Nick Friendshuh and I, could put in both the septic tank and cesspool in less than an eight-hour day.

Halfway through a second summer of working with the laborers or well men, I turned fifteen and got my driver's license. By this time it was evident I could keep up with the adult men digging. I went to my father and asked him what Nick and Eddie were making an hour. They were both fathers, and each had at least two children and they were supporting their families. They were making $2.50 an hour. I told Dad I could do every bit as much work as they could, and I thought it was fair that I made the same amount of money. He agreed. So at age fifteen, in 1958, I was taking home $100 a week.

I worked with the well rig and laborers for two summers, but by the time I was into the summer between eleventh and twelfth grade, I began working with the plumbers. At that time, we as plumbers had to cut the cast-iron pipe with a hammer and chisel and pour the joints with hot lead. The lead had to be set with a hammer and caulking irons. All the waste and vent pipe was steel and had to be threaded, and when I started, we threaded it all by hand. We had an electric drill for drilling joists, but we did not have a sawzall. All the joists and rafters had to be cut with a hand saw or a keyhole saw. My arms were as tough as iron. I could whip most anyone at arm wrestling.

When I started my junior year in high school, I began to go to school two nights a week at Dunwoody Institute to become an apprentice plumber. I went on to become a plumber and a master plumber. By age twenty-two, I had started my own plumbing company.

With the exception of about six months helping out a friend, I have never worked for anyone else since. I have been my own boss during all my working years.

Grandfather's Quote

Learn the value of hard work and
work hard at whatever you do.

3

High School

I went to De La Salle High School, which had its main building on the Nicollet Island in downtown Minneapolis. They had a freshman building on 43rd and Blaisdell, very close to where my grandparents lived. There were about four hundred boys in my freshman class.

In retrospect, I believe it was a very big mistake. All the friends I played baseball and basketball with went on to Bloomington High School and started for the varsity basketball and baseball teams. I was as good as any of them.

In a class of four hundred, almost all the good athletes had played for the inner city grade school teams and the coaches knew who they were. I was asked to dribble the basketball down the court for two minutes and then was cut. When I went out for the baseball team, I was one of 150 kids trying out. They hit three hard grounders at me, at shortstop range, and I booted two of them and was cut. I should have just gone to the coach and said, "Put a bat in my hands for a few pitches and see if you want to cut me." But I never did.

I had never played football before and when I tried out I even thought that there were only nine players on a team. I was the last player cut, and I was cut after the first game, which I never got a chance to play in. My father had come to watch and I can still remember how I felt riding home with him and having to tell him I had just been cut.

I started swimming on the swimming team as a freshman. We used to swim laps for a couple of hours, along with doing sprints. We would also swim with a kickboard in front of us, using only our legs. Even as a freshman, my frog kick made me the fastest kicker on the team, but if I tried to flutter kick, I would go backwards.

In my last swimming meet as a freshman, I swam the 100-yard breaststroke in a time of 1:29. I did not practice during the off season; I just grew stronger and more mature. In my first meet as a sophomore, I swam the 100-yard breaststroke in 1:19. I had shaved 10 seconds off my time just by growing older. By the end of the swimming season I had got down to 1:11, and I placed third in the Catholic state tournament.

I made the football team my sophomore year as a defensive lineman. During one of our first practices, some college or pro defensive lineman came and took me under his wing. He taught me many tricks of the trade, and from then on, I was unstoppable. We were allowed to do a lot of things that would be against the rules today. I usually played right over the center and I would cock my forearm way back. As soon as he moved the ball, I would bring it up under his chin and flip him over backwards. He would then get real low and I would bring my forearm down on the back of his head and go over the top of him. During our team scrimmages, I mistreated our starting center so badly that he finally got up off the ground and slugged me in the nose. I was taken by complete surprise, and my nose was broken. The coaches and other players grabbed us before it went any further.

As hard as the coaches made us work at football, I could still go home after practice and do homework. I could even play basketball. But after a grueling swimming workout, I had nothing left.

Swimming is what gave me all my endurance. I could even swim close to 100 yards underwater without coming up for air. When I was at the lake, that made me lots of spending money. I would point to a dock that was over 85 or 90 yards away and bet kids I could swim that far underwater. No one believed I could do it until they bet me and saw it done.

The school spirit at De La Salle was phenomenal. We had great pep rallies, with over 1,500 boys yelling at the top of their lungs. We were even given time off school to go hang a dummy on a competing school's lawn, a time or two.

We also had great school dances. There were many all-girls schools in the area and all the girls came to our dances. At first I was so nervous I almost couldn't get started, but each girl and each dance was a practice session for the next. Soon I was dancing with as many girls as I could and if all went well with one particular girl, I kept coming back to her. I even got a phone number or two.

I disliked it when a girl seemed to be somewhere else rather than with me. I made sure I was attentive to her. If we weren't talking, I looked at her, not at other dancers. My partner was the focus of all my attention. That lesson and the confidence I gained served me well throughout my life.

I also got a lot out of the religion classes at De La Salle. Brother Bernard was my sophomore religion teacher and he was truly great. We had many lively discussions. He had a box where any student could drop a note to ask any question anonymously. I learned a lot through that box. I learned about French kissing, and whether masturbation causes pimples, and many other things.

But the most important thing I took away from that class stayed with me for life. A mortal sin, which might keep you out of heaven, needs three conditions. First, the act has to be a serious matter. Thinking something is serious doesn't make it a mortal sin. Second, you have to absolutely believe the act is a mortal sin. Here you can be on dangerous ground because we all can convince ourselves that what we want is right. The safe way is to accept the church's view in most cases. Third, you have to do it in spite of the fact that it is a serious matter and you know it.

I was only a C student, but I liked English, particularly when it came time to give speeches or talks in front of the class. I also liked algebra, but my favorite classes were the business and accounting classes.

They were thought of as the non-college prep courses for the students the school didn't feel were college material.

Bullshit!

Don't let anyone tell you where you belong or what you are not capable of. If you apply yourself and are interested in something, you can do anything you want to do.

Another sad part of that story is that even the students taking the college prep courses thought of themselves as superior to the other so-called dumb kids.

It was true—I was a poor and slow reader, had a poor vocabulary and I couldn't spell worth a damn, but when I did go to college, it was a breeze. And I'd love to compare the financial earning power and the accomplishments of my life to the so-called "college material" kids.

Take the courses you want to and don't let anyone tell you that you can't do it. Work on your reading though, because I will admit that my poor reading ability (mainly being slow and not being able to sound out words) has been a handicap my entire life.

I don't know why I liked the business courses so much. Maybe it was because my dad was in business, maybe because they seemed so practical and adult, or maybe it was because I had a great teacher. I believe his name was Mr. Graff and he was sharp. He was a little eccentric though. He liked to skip down the halls. He just loved life and it showed, but a lot of kids made fun of him. Little did they know.

A footnote on those business courses that were supposedly below the college-bound kids. When I was in college they offered business courses, but you had to be a junior or senior to take them. I figured that was bullshit and went higher up and said I was paying for college and I should be able to choose my classes. I was told the only way I could take them was to audit them. That meant they wouldn't count for any credits and I didn't have to take any test if I didn't want to.

"Didn't count for any credit"? What the hell is that supposed to mean? What I learn is what should count. Their little ole credit system sucks. I knew a student whose girlfriend took all his tests and did all his homework for him, but guess what—he got his credits. He became a teacher. It didn't matter that he probably learned very little—he had his credits and now he is probably tenured and teaching some college-bound kids.

Well, I took those classes, and they were a breeze. I don't think they covered anything that had not been taught to me in high school. I dominated the class discussions, and I aced their tests, but whoopee ding, I didn't get any credits.

College is great for what you can learn, and there is much to learn other than what you may or may not earn credits for. But it is not necessary to financially succeed in this world and don't let anyone tell you different.

Go if you want to, or go if you don't know what you want, but don't go because you feel you have to in order to get financially ahead in this world.

The main problem I had with high school was that it was full of kids. From the time I turned thirteen years old, I thought of myself as a man. I didn't like being with a bunch of kids. I felt more like an adult than a teenager, and I enjoyed being with adults more because they were not so immature.

Grandfather's Quote

'Adolescent' is a term often used as an excuse for not being all you should be. Don't ever allow yourself this excuse or your kids either for that matter.

4

My First Wilderness Trip

I am not sure where my love for the outdoors, or more particularly the wilderness, came from. When it came to that love, that wanting to be a mountain man, my mother would say, "Where the heck did you come from?" You couldn't get her, or any of her relatives, in a tent to save their lives. And other than for hunting, I don't believe Dad ever camped out or went on wilderness adventures.

Maybe it came from being a Boy Scout, and our campouts or summer camp; or maybe it came from hearing about my Dad's hunting trips. Maybe it was reading Joseph Altsheler and James Fenimore Cooper's novels. I can still remember those stories even today. I loved them, particularly the first in Altsheler's series, *The Young Trailers*. Maybe a person is just born with a love of the outdoors and a love of adventure.

I loved being outdoors, and I loved being self-reliant. The more I think about it, a lot of my outdoor skills did in fact come from my time in the Boy Scouts. If I had realized that earlier, I would have made sure all my boys became scouts.

In Boy Scouts not only did I go on weekend overnights, but I also went to summer camp. That is where I learned to canoe, and I instantly fell in love with canoeing.

Me, ready for the portage

In my interaction with the adults I worked with, I heard about fishing trips on Lake Nipigon or on the Gunflint Trail. A friend of my Dad, Ed Swanson, told me about a trip he took twenty years before to a ranger cabin on Winchell Lake on the Gunflint Trail. He said it was hard to get to, but the fishing was great.

That's all I needed. I could get out of work, take a trip into the wilderness and get in on some super fishing. I sent away for some maps and started planning my trip.

On that first trip, I learned the most important thing you can take into the wilderness, and perhaps on a trip anywhere, is the right companion.

I asked Jim G along. I was fifteen at the time and he was sixteen.

I made a list of the items we would need, called an outfitter on the Gunflint Trail, and lined up a canoe for a week. Because of my scouting, I had all my camping gear, and I ordered a Duluth pack that I still have to this day, forty-nine years later.

In my car, Jim and I headed for Grand Marais on the north shore of Lake Superior and at the head of the Gunflint Trail.

We picked up the canoe and tied it on top of the car, and headed to Poplar Lake where we were to start out. Weight was considered on all that we took along. We had a small light tent, sleeping bags, a light cook kit, matches in a waterproof case, an ax and a bow saw. I had learned in Boy Scouts that you could gather a lot more firewood with a bow saw than with an ax. We also had enough dehydrated food, along with the fish we would catch, to last us the week. We would drink our water right out of the lake.

We loaded the canoe, lashing everything all in along with our fishing rods, and off we went.

We paddled across Poplar Lake and saw a few other canoes before we had to make a portage to Caribou Lake. I had a 50-pound pack on my back and I carried the canoe over my head. Jim carried a slightly larger pack and the rods and reels. If I remember right, the first portage was rather short, but it was up a fairly steep hill.

On the portages you had to make sure you had mosquito lotion on, or else they would carry you away. On the lakes there were no mosquitos, and the scenery was spectacular. Towering pine trees and magnificent rock cliffs all around and the cold blue water was like glass.

Caribou Lake was a much smaller lake than Poplar Lake. It only had a couple of other canoes on it, and it didn't take long until it was time for our next portage. We portaged into Horseshoe Lake and paddled across it without seeing another canoe. After our third portage, we paddled across Gaskin Lake, which took a little longer than Caribou or Horseshoe Lakes. We saw one other canoe.

I was in the stern of the canoe and had far more experience in a canoe than Jim. He was beginning to get tired. He kept asking how much further and asking why we could not just stay right here.

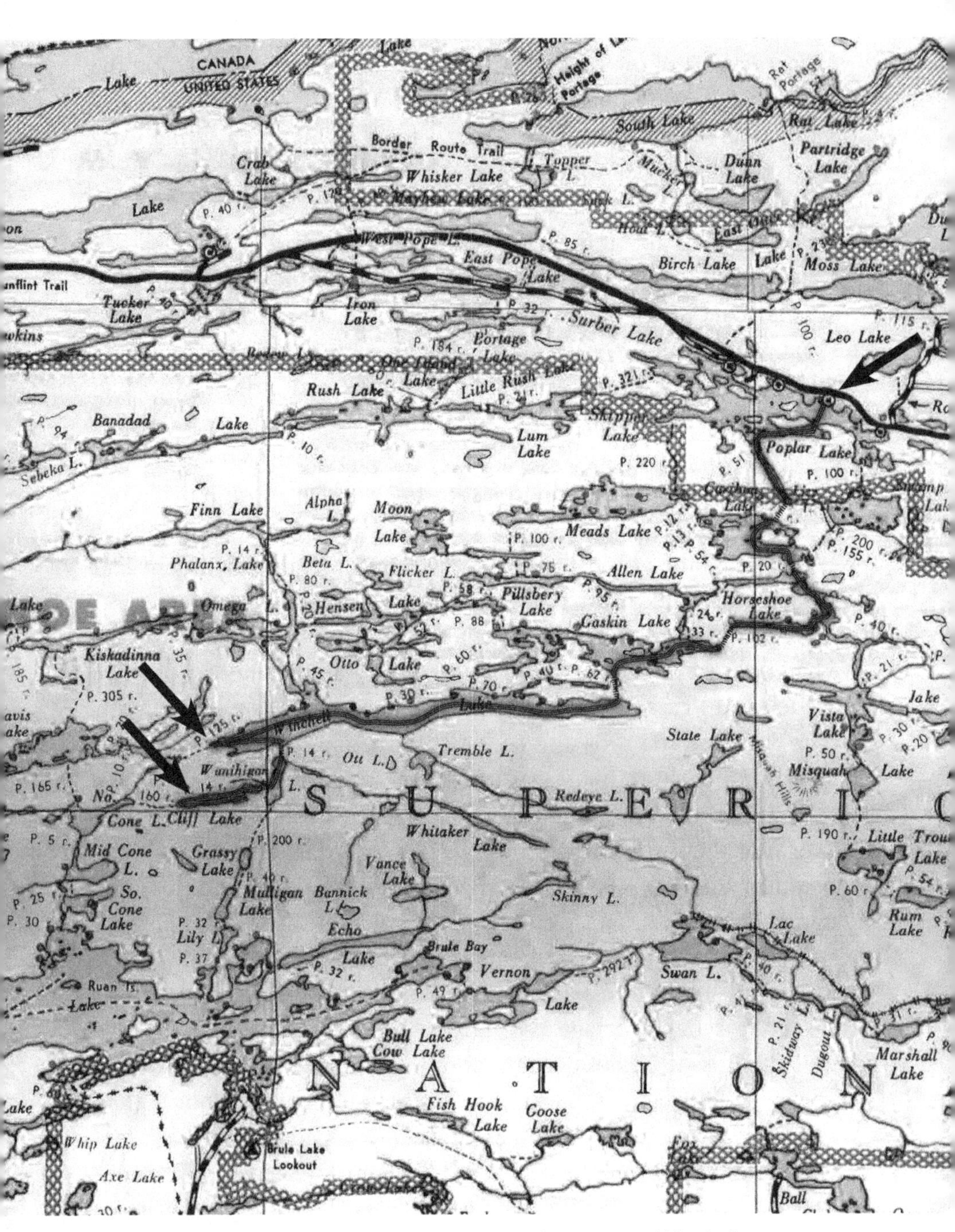

Started at Poplar Lake, made main camp on Winchell Lake and went as far as Cliff Lake

I wanted to get to the ranger cabin. I knew the farther away from the road we got and the harder we were willing to work, the fewer people there would be. And the fishing was sure to be better. Besides, we had talked about the trip and we had planned on going all the way in one full day of paddling.

By the time we had portaged out of Gaskin Lake into Winchell Lake, Jim had had it.

Now Winchell Lake was big and a long paddle across. Jim quit paddling and said this was not fun. He said that it was just hard work.

He was right: it was hard work, but although my arms ached, I loved it.

I made a deal with him. I said if he promised to go on in the morning that we would stop and camp here on Winchell Lake. He agreed.

There were several campsites along the shoreline and we stopped at the next one we came to. We unloaded our gear and then Jim just laid there on shore. I stripped down and jumped into the cold water. Man, it was cold! Yet when we had dipped our cups over the side of the canoe to get a drink, it seemed a little too warm in the drinking of it. Welcome to the bush.

The stars were spectacular, and I was in my element. Jim was miserable. I had to set up the tent, do all the cooking and clean up the few dishes we had. Jim did gather the firewood.

That night we talked and Jim really didn't want to go on. He kept complaining about how his arms hurt and about how much work this was and how this certainly was not his idea of fun.

In the morning I insisted we go on. I told him we had no more portages and that we would soon be there. He reluctantly agreed.

When we got to the end of Winchell Lake, we landed where Ed had said the cabin would be. We pulled the canoe up on the rocks and went ashore. A short ways up the hill was the ruins of a cabin. Three walls were still standing, but the fourth wall was gone and the roof had collapsed.

Jim was pissed. He said this was bullshit, and he wanted to go home. We argued some, and he said again that this was not fun and he was going to go home. Then he headed for the canoe.

I got in his way and told him no way were we leaving and if he tried to go, he would have to fight me first.

This 16-year-old, who was a year older than I and who had bullied me around when we were younger, started to cry. He sat on the ground and balled.

I have never been mean and I certainly have never been a bully, so I figured I had to take this little boy home. I said that I would take him home if he promised to paddle all day and make the trip back to the car with me in one day.

He made the promise, and he kept it. We never said a word to each other, and we made our last portage into Popular Lake in the dark. It was still light enough to see though, and we got back to the car under the stars, having eaten nothing except a few candy bars all day.

I can't remember what I did with the canoe. All I remember is driving the entire way all by myself and getting back about seven hours later. I dropped him off, went home and went to bed.

The next morning I went over to my uncle AJ's home and had a talk with his son Steve, who was twelve years old going on seventeen. I told him what had happened and about how hard the work would be. Despite that, when I asked him if he would like to go, he said sure.

His parents said he could go, so he gathered his gear and we left that same day.

Steve was twelve, but he was over six feet tall and from the pictures probably weighed as much as I did.

He turned out to be the perfect companion. He was big and strong, and could paddle all day and seemed to love it as much as I did.

I was talkative and he was quiet. I loved to sing and he never complained. In later years, when canoeing across a lake together, a small boat with about a 5- or 10-horse motor came along heading in the same direction as us. Steve and I never said a word to each other, but we started paddling harder and harder. It was a long way to shore, and that motor boat never was able to pass us by. We were a great team!

I remember little of that first trip with Steve other than me loving it. I do remember me singing a lot because I loved life and being in the wilderness so much. I also remember going to Cliff Lake, which got its name from the high cliffs along its shore. There were no campsites there. It seemed as though we had gone back in time. We caught a lot of fish there too. We would paddle to one end of the lake, put our fishing lines in, and let the wind blow us back across the lake. We used big red and white Daredevils and caught lots of northern pike. I am sure none were over six or seven pounds though. I have vivid memories of filleting fish on the large rock on the shore. I also remember seeing a steam engine underwater somewhere on one of the lakes.

Oh yeah, then there was the fire. We set up camp and built a cooking fire in the appropriate way. We cleared away all the moss and built a circle of rocks for the fire to go in. But we made a mistake. We hadn't made sure we were down to all dirt. We had the fire going really good and were sitting around finishing up our fish dinner, when smoke started coming out of the ground about twenty feet away. The fire had gotten into the moss and burned underground, then sprang to the surface behind us. We had a hell of a time putting it out because we either had no shovel or a very small camping one. I can remember feeling very panicky. It took a long time. We tore up all the moss within a twenty- or thirty-foot radius and carried untold buckets full of water from the lake, but we finally got it out.

My last memory of the trip was driving home along Lake Superior. The fog was so thick I could not see more than three centerline dashes ahead in the road. Steve was the navigator and had to watch for the "Sharp curves ahead" signs, which told you the maximum safe speed for the corner. I was intently watching the centerline. When he missed one of the sharp curves signs, I never slowed down and almost lost it. I guess the Lord wanted me to be around so I could have my sons, who in turn could have my grandchildren!

Steve, age 12

As I write this almost fifty years later, I realize just how great a friend and perfect companion Steve was. If you can find one like him, you will be truly blessed.

My whole life the Lord has blessed me, and I am not sure why. It seems as though everything I ever did turned to gold. It's been a great journey, this life of mine.

Grandfather's Quote

The most important thing to take with you into the wilderness is the right companion.

Steve working hard in the bow

Me singing, once again, over a fire

5

Thirty Days in the Wilderness

The previous year I had made my first wilderness trip and found the perfect companion to have at my side.

I was now 16 years old and my love of adventure was stronger than ever, so I began planning a month-long canoe trip.

I wanted to be in as pure a wilderness as I could find, so I grabbed a map and looked in Canada for a place with no roads. Halfway between the north shore of Lake Superior and Hudson Bay, there was a small town called Hearst. Just east of there was a one-building town called Mattice, which was on the banks of the Missinaibi River. South of Hearst there were no roads on the map for several hundred miles.

I knew the river flowed north to Hudson Bay, so I figured we could paddle upstream about 100 miles to Brunswick Lake. That way it would be an easy trip back. I did not want to go downstream for 100 miles and have something happen, then have a difficult time getting back.

I sent for the detailed maps and made my list of supplies. I figured we could live off the land, so we didn't have to pack a month's worth of grub.

When we got to Mattice, the people running the store said the river was too swift and dangerous for us to be going upstream by canoe. They told us that just the week before a couple of guys got swamped in the rapids and drowned.

Some of the rapids we shot

We started out anyway. The current was swift, but we were both strong paddlers and we stayed along the shoreline as much as possible. It seemed like we were crawling. It took us three days to get upstream forty miles, but not just because of the current.

This was not the Gunflint Trail. This was true wilderness. No man-made campsites and no trails for the portages we had to make.

One of the portages was over a mile long, and we literally had to chop our way through the brush in order to be able to carry the canoe through. It took us over half a day to make that single portage.

The footgear of choice for canoe travel was tennis shoes. I had tried deer hide moccasins, but when they got wet, they became much too slippery on the rocks. One of the downsides to tennis shoes, or moccasins for that matter, was neither kept out a misdirected hatchet. We used a small hatchet to chop away brush to be able to carry the canoe over the portage. While Steve was clearing brush, he somehow hit his foot. The blood oozed through the top of his tennis shoe. When I got it and his sock off, there was quite a gash in the top of his foot.

Without enough loose skin in the area to consider sewing it together, we cleaned it up as best we could and taped it. We discussed turning back, but Steve assured me he was OK. We agreed to stay there until morning, and if there was no sign of infection, we would go on.

We set up the tent and Steve relaxed inside as I chopped and cleared brush for the rest of the portage. The next morning there was no sign of infection, so I carried the canoe upstream to where we could once again put it in the water. I went back for Steve's pack and carried it for him as he made his way to the canoe.

While I was sitting here writing this, I realized that it has been forty-eight years since that trip. I remember very little of the day-to-day details. I do remember having a very good map of the area. We tried to keep track of our location by counting and noticing each small stream that entered the Missinaibi and keeping track of long straight stretches or sharp curves in the river. When we were approximately forty miles upstream, we came upon a trapper's cabin along the shore.

The cabin was very small and when we opened the door and looked inside, there were a large pair of snowshoes crossed on top of pine boughs on the floor. There was also a small iron stove and a couple of big barrels that had flour and sugar and the like in them. Leaning up against the back of the cabin were large circles made of willow which were used for stretching hides.

We decided to stay for a while.

Rather than using the cabin, we pitched our tent because it had very good mosquito netting. The cabin was built for winter, not for the mosquitos in July.

We drank our water right from the river and used it kind of like a refrigerator. When we wanted some fish to eat, we just went to the refrigerator, threw our line in and in a couple of minutes we had a fish.

The river was also our bathtub. I took a very quick dip each morning in the almost-freezing water.

I was fascinated with the trapper and his way of life, and wanted to take a look around. We took several hikes back into the brush. We learned very quickly that once we got away from the water, mosquito

Me in front of the trapper's cabin

lotion was not enough. With no breeze and thick brush, the mosquitoes came at us in swarms. Every time I took a breath I would suck them up my nose and they got in my eyes constantly. On the water or even along the water's edge they were not bad at all, but in the dense brush they were unbelievable; so every time we went into the brush we had to wear broad-brimmed hats with mosquito netting over them.

The mosquito bites didn't seem to bother Steve much at all, but the no-see-ems really made him swell up. The no-see-ems didn't bother me, but if I got a mosquito bite, it would swell.

On one of our hikes we started noticing blaze marks on the trees, but they were all ten to twelve feet off the ground. That meant when the trapper was here in the winter, the snow had to have been four to seven feet deep on the level.

I remember telling Steve that I wanted to find out who was trapping here and see if he would allow me to come spend a trapping season with him. I did later ask people in the nearby town if they knew who might be trapping up there, but no one knew anything about him.

I can't remember why we decided not to continue upriver to our destination, Brunswick Lake, but I am sure we both agreed to turn back. Perhaps it was because of Steve's foot or because of my poor planning as far as food went. We were not catching rabbits in snares, we were getting tired of fish as our staple, and we had brought very little food.

We decided to make our way back to civilization, stock up on our food supply and take a chain of lakes back into the bush. Without the long portages, we could take more food along and Steve's foot would have a better chance to heal.

Always remember when you are working your body very hard and putting yourself to the test, you are best prepared to handle whatever may arise if you have a belly full of good food.

Take enough food or be prepared to harvest your own variety of it.

We left the cabin early one morning and started downstream. We decided not to make any portages. We had seen all the rapids on the way upstream and thought we were capable of shooting them on the way back.

Steve was over 6'2" tall by now and I remember white water shooting over his head. We had no life jackets. We did have good guardian angels, I guess, because we got turned around once and bounced off a rock or two. But when it was all said and done, we made the entire forty miles before sunset.

Three days in and one day out. That river was moving!

The first thing we both had was pie and ice cream, followed by burgers and fries, followed by pie and ice cream once again. We talked to the locals, found a spot and loaded up with supplies. I do not even remember where we wound up going, but once we left the lake where

Steve, age 13 and already a man

we started, we hit a river. After that, we never saw another human being for the following twenty-three days.

I remember digging a hole in the beach, just back from the lake and allowing the water to fill it in. Once it settled, it was very clear and much colder than lake water, so it was better for drinking. The sand also purified the water.

On this trip I caught a fourteen-pound walleye, but it wasn't much fun. I thought I had a snag and just slowly pulled it to the canoe and then lifted it in.

But most of the time the fishing was loads of fun and the fish put up great fights.

On one occasion the northern were biting so fast and furious that we made a bet. We had to cast our Daredevils into the water at least thirty or forty feet out and then get it back *without* a fish. We reeled the lures in as fast as we could, jerked them out of the water, or tried anything to avoid catching a fish. Usually as soon as the Daredevil hit the water, a fish would take it. Once or twice they took it out of the air just before it hit the water. I do not remember who won the bet, but I do remember it was almost impossible to get the lure back to the canoe without a fish caught on it. They were all over three pounds, but none were over seven or eight pounds. This lasted until we grew too tired of taking fish off the line and quit. I have never experienced any fishing like that ever, before or since. It was a once-in-a-lifetime experience.

For wildlife, we mostly saw moose, ducks, geese and loons. The call of the loon is an awesome sound any time, but it is very special when you are in the wilderness on your own.

We saw moose on the river several times. They were usually standing in the water with their heads submerged. I think they were eating something and also keeping the insects off. If we only paddled towards them when their heads were under water, and froze when they looked up, we could get quite close. We anticipated when they were about to pull their heads out so we could stick our paddles in the water to stop the canoe. If we didn't, the canoe would continue to glide on the water and the movement would scare them off.

Steve was always the bow man, and I was always in the stern. We both stayed on our knees to keep our weight low. Our butts were up against the seats. Steve was a very strong paddler, and he made sure his strokes were always very long. That way I could do a J stroke and keep in time with him. We really could fly over the water.

When not pushing ourselves, I was usually singing. I can even remember spreading my arms over a fire and singing to the sky. Steve never joined in, but he never complained either. One of us cooked, and the other did the dishes. I usually was the first one up, and made breakfast, and he usually cooked the dinners. It was a great life, and he was the best of all companions.

We hunted ducks together too, but after he returned from the service, he gave up hunting and I could never talk him into another canoe trip.

Grandfather's Quote

Pride in the hard way.

Me with the big one

6

Cars and Motorcycles

When I took my driver's test at age fifteen, I failed so badly that the examiner told me that I had better go back and practice for at least a couple of months. I never had any instruction other than from my father, and I scored around 57%.

During the test the examiner told me each time I did something wrong, so I came back the next day and took the test again. I got a 94%.

Dad always said I could spend the money I made any way I wanted, so within a week of getting my driver's license, I bought a 1949 or 1950 Pontiac.

It was a three-speed brown metallic two-door. I put clamps on the front springs to lower the front end and I often took the rear window out so my friends could sit on the ledge behind the back seat and look over the top of the car.

Once I had my own car, I drove to school every day.

Later that year I bought a motorcycle, a Triumph. It was a lot of bike. Dad asked how much I had paid for it and I told him $750. He had just bought a brand-new 1958 Ford for $1,900 but he said, "I will make you a deal. I'll trade you my 1958 Ford for the motorcycle, even up, if you agree to never own a motorcycle again so long as you are living under my roof."

I agreed. I was now a 15-year-old with a brand-new 1958 Ford that I immediately had painted cherry red. Dad was able to sleep well at night because he knew my personality, and he knew a bike could be the end of me.

A footnote: Once I took in a 750 motorcycle in payment for a plumbing job. I had three little kids at home at the time. A little later I was driving it back from giving a plumbing estimate and looked down at the speedometer and saw 105 mph. I decided to sell it. It would be over twenty years later before I bought and kept another bike.

When I got married, I sold my cherry-red Ford and bought a 1962 blue-and-white half-ton Chevy pickup. I have driven mostly pickups or Suburbans ever since.

It was life that was the adventure, not some machine. I bought practical outfits that did a job and helped me get away from the fast lane and back to nature.

Grandfather's Quote

Life should make you high, not some machine.

7

Dealing with Bullies

I hate bullies, and I cannot remember picking a fight in my entire life, yet for some reason, in my youth, I always seemed to be defending myself.

When I was a young boy, there was a bully in our neighborhood named Shelton A. who was very mean. He was three or four years older than I was. He had had polio and walked with a limp. Before a housing development brought new kids to our neighborhood, I mostly played with my younger first cousins, Tom and Steve, and my younger brother Jay. Tom was one year younger, Steve was three years younger and Jay was four years younger.

This bully stopped us when we tried to go to the store. He told us we could not pass unless we paid him or gave him some of the pop bottles we had collected to turn in for pennies.

When I was about eight years old, he caught us in my grandfather's pasture and made us dunk our heads in muddy water at the edge of the pond. I went home crying and went to my father, and he was very upset with me. He asked me why I had dunked my head rather than stand up to him. I was ashamed.

Occasionally another neighbor, Jim G, would be with Shelton and they both would bully us around. Jim was only one year older than I was. One time when I was coming back from the store by myself, he and Shelton tried to get me to pay them for passing. One walked on each side of me and told me I had to pay them for walking on their road.

When I got close to home, I got up the nerve to slug Jim in the stomach and then started running home with Jim chasing me all the way. I was yelling for help and when I got to the front door, Dad was standing in the doorway. Jim ran up to me and slugged me in the stomach, right in front of Dad. Dad asked him why he had done that and Jim said, "Because Gary hit me first." Dad just turned and walked back into the house, and I noticed my uncle Charles was there too.

I went around to the side of the house and sat there in the grass for hours until Uncle Charles left. I was too ashamed to go inside.

I never forgot that feeling.

As I grew older, I got bold enough to wrestle with the bully, and in a short time I found that I was winning. He no longer bothered us after that. Once he quit bothering us, Jim never bothered us either.

As a side note, years later when I was about twenty years old, I had to go to court for a traffic violation. When I got in the courtroom, Shelton, the bully of my youth, was there too. His case came before the judge first. When he was found guilty and given the choice of a $15 fine or three days in jail, he took the three days.

After Shelton stopped his bullying, the next time I had any problem was when I was in seventh grade. During recess I started wrestling with an eighth grader named Dan Gallett. It started out as just fun for both of us, and then perhaps at the urging of other kids, it got a little serious. Then one day Dan got really pissed at this younger kid getting the best of him, and he hauled off and slugged me in the mouth. I backed off. The next day he wanted to fist fight, and I was afraid and would not fight him.

The next couple of days he pushed me around and tried to get me to fight, and each day I was afraid to fight him. It was really getting embarrassing, and I felt like a coward.

After a few days of this, I knew I couldn't take it anymore. I called him and told him to meet me on the corner of Glen Wilding and Bliss

Lane to settle this thing once and for all. I told him to come alone, but he brought his twin brother and some other friends who hid in the bushes.

It is kind of funny, because over forty years later Dan bought some land from me in South Dakota and we became friends. When I asked him if he remembered our meeting on the corner, he said he remembered. I asked him who had won, and he said that he remembered it as being a draw. I remember it quite differently, but we both remembered he never bothered me again after that.

When I went to high school, I went to an inner-city school, and it seemed as though I had to fight my way through it.

Within the first week of starting school, I was playing football with other students on the playground and when our team scored, I would cheer. One of the opposing players told me to knock off the cheering. When I didn't, he gave me a shove and said he was going to meet me after school.

Everyone told me all day long how tough he was and how he was going to kick my ass. I am very ashamed to say that I snuck out the back door and avoided him.

The following day, he caught up with me and gave me a couple of shoves and tried to get me to fight him. I did not fight back, but he did not hit me and just walked away calling me a chicken.

Perhaps the word got out that I was a chicken. Perhaps it was because I was tall and skinny. Whatever the reason, some bully was always pushing me around to prove how tough he was.

I had a couple of fights that didn't amount to much. It usually started by a kid giving me a shove in the hallway at school and me just paying no attention to him. Then he would shove me again and again and finally, he would tell me he was going to meet me after school. Such seemed to be the way of an inner-city school, and I hated it.

Then one day a kid named Beerbom said he was going to kick my ass after school. I don't even remember why, but I was told he was the toughest kid in school and he was a boxer and a super mean kid.

No way was I going to look or act like a chicken again, so I met him in the alley and we started swinging away at each other. I swung my arms wildly and hit him in the face several times. Blood soon began flowing out of his nose, but he threw me to the ground anyway. When I was down, he started kicking me in the head with his engineer boots. All of a sudden we heard sirens as the cops were coming and we started to break up. He said, "We will finish this tomorrow." I took off with my head really hurting. I didn't want to face him again because I felt I had lost. But because of all of his blood, the kids who saw the fight thought I had won. More importantly, Beerbom avoided me and we never fought again.

Shortly thereafter, I was with my youth group at church. I had just bought a blue silk shirt and a pair of white suede shoes. A kid from my freshman class was there and picked a fight with me. I beat him so badly that I closed both of his eyes. His face was all swollen for a couple of weeks, and his blood ruined my new shirt and shoes.

He was a good friend of the Hoffman kid that I had refused to fight my first week of school and the Hoffman kid was afraid of him. Hoffman even came up to me and asked me if I had done that to him. When I said yes, he said that I didn't have to worry, he would never tell anyone what had happened between us.

As you can imagine, I didn't like high school very much, and when I got to the main high school downtown, it was even worse.

I hated fighting, but I hated bullies even more. I never would bully another, and in retrospect, I do not believe any of my five sons did either. Brothers excepted, that is. All brothers have their disagreements, and I suppose you could consider how they sometimes treat or tease each other as bullying.

I was very proud of all of my sons because none of them seemed to have to get into fights in high school. I don't know how they did it, or if it was just the inner-city school I went to. Perhaps in the case of my four older sons, if you picked on one, you would probably have had three others to contend with.

In any case, they can be very proud of themselves for being able to just walk away.

Between my sophomore and junior year I started boxing in Golden Gloves. I fought middleweight and got to the finals of the upper Midwest championships. I was sixteen and I remember seeing my 24-year-old opponent at the weigh-in. His name was Jeff Arnold, and he won the award for the best boxer in the tournament. I lost to him in the championship fight, but I was written up in the Minneapolis paper. I do not believe anyone at my high school ever picked a fight with me again.

When I turned twenty, I told my wife I wanted to go back as a man and fight Golden Gloves. She begged me not to, so I never fought in the ring again. She also begged me not to teach my sons to fight, and I honored her wishes.

I say I never picked a fight, but I do remember one incident as a junior or senior in high school when perhaps I could be accused of trying to do so.

It was after a basketball game with our arch rival, Cretin High School.

I was driving and there were three other De La Salle students in the car with me. We were following a car with four Cretin students in it. They were making gestures at us, and we were making gestures at them. Finally they pulled over, and I pulled over behind them. At the same time, a station wagon with six more Cretin students pulled in right in front of the first Cretin car. When I jumped out of my car to face the four Cretin students, their number had increased to ten.

Unknown to me, my three buddies had jumped back into my car when they saw the other car pull up and I was alone. I rushed right at the ten students, sounding as mean as I could, and gave the first one a hard shove in the chest. All ten of them turned around and started to walk away.

End of story, but not an end to the great lesson that had been learned, and even used in later life against a grizzly bear, but that's another story.

I will tell you about one incident in later life which I feel is important. I was playing poker with my best friend Gene Clinton and several others as a guest in a man's house. I don't even remember the man's name. I'll just call him Bob. Bob got very drunk that night and towards the end of the evening, he started reaching across the table and pulling on my beard. Bob was a very big man, perhaps 260 pounds, and he looked very strong and athletic.

I was so proud of myself for not even being tempted to fight this man that I knew I would have no trouble defeating. We were in his home for God's sake, and he was drunk and didn't really know what he was doing.

I was, however, very shocked when on the way home my best friend said to me that he didn't know how he was going to help defend me. I asked him if he thought I was afraid. He said that he did.

Wow! That really hurt. I told him that I was an accomplished Golden Gloves boxer and was in no way afraid of this man. I am still proud of my restraint, and it taught me that even in front of my best friend, I didn't need to prove anything to anyone.

Grandfather's Quote

A real man doesn't have to prove that he's a man.

Irene

8

Irene and College

I went to River Falls College in Wisconsin. I went to play football and to see if I wanted to continue my education.

When I first got there, I knew it was different from high school and I loved it. I had a room in the boys' dorm and Jim Peterson, my best friend from high school, was my roommate. But soon after, he didn't like the smell of my acne medicine and traded rooms. My new roommate was Charlie Plants, a farmer from Wisconsin, and it is because of him that most of my grandkids came to be; but that comes later in the story.

College classes were easy. In football I, as a defensive nose guard, was up against the starting center who was a senior and he couldn't keep me out of his backfield.

On Thursday nights, all the students went to Shady's Bar and drank beer and played cards. They had a ping pong table in the recreation area of the dorm and between my winnings at cards and ping pong; I always had beer and gas money. And to top it off, there was always someone with a guitar so we could sit around and sing songs together. Everyone treated each other as an adult and an equal. No tough guy stuff or no cliques; we were all one happy family, so to speak. It was truly great!

Then one day as I was walking into the library, a tall beautiful blonde was walking out. She looked just like Doris Day and I said, "Hi Doris." She acted like she hadn't even heard me and just walked on. She was the most beautiful woman I had ever seen in my life and I couldn't get her off my mind.

A week or so later my roommate asked me if I wanted to go home with him for the weekend. He didn't have a car and said that if I wanted to come along, he would furnish the gas. His dad's farm was in Ladysmith, Wisconsin, and I thought it would be fun, so I said sure. A few days later he said a couple of girls wanted to ride along and he wanted to know what I thought. I said I thought it would be more fun with just the two of us. He said one of the gals was a tall blonde and a real looker. I changed my mind, "OK, let's let them come along."

Was I ever surprised when the tall blonde turned out to be the one I had called Doris in the doorway of the library. Her real name was Irene Lunde, and she was from Conrath, Wisconsin. We talked a lot, and I arranged to pick her up first after the weekend.

When I picked Irene up, after meeting her parents we decided to take a walk in the woods.

What a walk it turned out to be. Her folks lived along a creek and there was a beautiful woods next to their home. On our walk I fell into a swamp not once but twice. Each time I got up laughing and making fun of myself. Later she told me she was really impressed with the fact that I could handle something like that.

On the way back to college she sat next to me and I put my arm around her shoulders. She told me later she wasn't impressed with that maneuver at all.

On the ride back she was trying to find out how old I was, because she was a senior and she knew I was a freshman. I told her I had gone to trade school before starting college and that I had worked for three or four years as an apprentice plumber. Both true, but both misleading, because I went to trade school while still in high school and I worked as an apprentice only during the summers.

I had learned never to ask a girl on the next date while you were still with her on the previous date. This wasn't a date, but I applied the lesson. The day after I got back to school, I called her and asked her out. To my surprise, she said yes. I later found out she was mad at herself for saying yes and even thought about trying to get out of going. Thankfully, she didn't.

I took her to a movie, and then we stopped and had something to eat. I just sat there and watched her eat. I was so lightheaded that I could hardly stand it. I kissed her goodnight at her door, and I floated back to the dorm. When I got to my room, I was in a daze and stood there looking at Charlie. Someone came into the room and opened the door and hit me in the head with it and I didn't even notice. I had never felt like this in my entire life. Just the thought of her made me feel like I was floating on air.

I saw her the next day washing cars for some school fundraiser. She was in jean short shorts that had been cut off and the legs were all ruffled. She was magnificent! She was more beautiful than I had even remembered.

We went dancing and danced very well together. We went on walks, we played cards, we met in the lounges and sang songs together, and we were at the library together a lot. I think she worked there.

She introduced me to the pinochle club or some such name; it was a group of mostly senior guys who knew how to have a good time and did a lot of singing and I fit right in.

We made a few trips to her parent's home and played cards with her folks. Her mother told her that she was sure she was going to be seeing a lot more of this guy from Minnesota.

But I never took her to the park where all the students went to neck. Then one night she asked me if she could drive, and I said sure. She drove us to the park and said, "As long as you never took us here, I thought that I would." WOW!

I don't remember if the Fizzy hunt came before she drove us to the park or after, I just remember the day. I asked her if she and her girlfriend Pat wanted to go on a Fizzy hunt with Jim Peterson and me.

She said, "What is a Fizzy hunt?"

I said she would have to come along and find out.

I bought a teddy bear that I named Fizzy and hid him high in a tree with a note and a poem in his paws. Then I laid out a blanket in the woods with a picnic basket and a bottle of pink champagne on it. We took the girls on this elaborate hunt ad-libbing all the way. Jim was great at it. I guess we both did OK.

At places we had to blindfold the girls; at other places we had to watch out in order to not be attacked. Finally after due suspense, we came to the tree where Fizzy was hiding. I climbed to the top and grabbed him.

The poem went something like this:

> "This may sound dizzy
> But I am a Fizzy
> __ ___ ___"

I can't remember the rest of the poem, but the note told where to find the blanket and said something about teaching someone how to love again. Irene had recently ended an engagement, and said she was never going to fall in love again. Perhaps that was the day she decided she could love again.

I don't remember taking her to Shady's but she was usually there when I was there. I always played euchre, and I always seemed to win. She would often watch me play. One time after she watched me win once again, she said, "You are so lucky."

I said, "I am so lucky that I could beat you nineteen out of twenty times cutting the cards."

She said, "No way."

I asked, "You want to bet?"

She said, "No one can win nineteen out of twenty cuts."

I said, "Are you positive?"

She said, "Absolutely!"

I said, "I'll tell you what I am going to do. I'll bet you that I can win nineteen out of twenty cuts and if I can't, you can have my car for the weekend. But if I win, I win a pair of your panties."

"No way!" she said as she blushed.

I said, "I thought you were positive. Positive means you can't lose."

By this time all her girlfriends were telling her to make the bet.

With a little more friendly teasing, she finally gave in and said it was a bet.

I shuffled up the cards and cut, and each time I cut a card higher than hers. I did it exactly nineteen out of twenty times.

She and everyone else were amazed.

"How did you do that?"

"I am just lucky."

"No way."

"Come on, how did you do that?"

"I am not telling."

"Come on tell me."

"No."

"Then if you don't tell me how you did that I am not paying."

"And if I tell you will you pay up?"

"Maybe."

"OK, a maybe is better than no panties."

"You see this deck. Euchre is the only game they play here and in euchre you only use the nines on up. They are all worn from being used, but all the rest of the cards are brand new from never being used. I just made sure I cut a nine or higher every time. You just cut the cards."

I remember losing the one cut when I cut a queen, and she cut an ace. But even being assured of a nine or higher each time, my nineteen out of twenty was a real long shot. I think the Big Guy wanted me to win that bet because it saved our relationship, but that comes later in the story.

"I am not paying! You cheated!"

I just smiled.

Around Christmas time I asked Irene if she would come home with me for part of the Christmas vacation and she said she would think about it. By this time we had been seeing a lot of each other and were doing most everything together.

Then she dropped the bomb. She wanted to see the guy she was formerly engaged to over Christmas. I was upset and asked her not to. She said she was going to see him, period the end.

I said, "OK, then it's the end of us."

I was really hurt, and I was having a real hard time, but I was trying to convince myself that it was really over. If she didn't love me, what else could I do?

I wrote the poem *Honor*.

After Christmas she called me up and told me she would like to see me again. She said she had bought me a Christmas present, and she wanted to give it to me. I told her that I too had a present for her, so I guess we could at least get together and exchange presents.

I don't remember where we met, but I remember she had a pair of brown Bermuda shorts on. When I opened the present she gave me, I thought at first that she had given me an empty box. It was a black jewelry case that I still have today. I had never heard of a jewelry box for a man, much less seen one. I think she saw the blank look on my face and told me what it was.

I smiled with relief and thanked her.

After I gave her my present—I have no memory of what it was—she gave me one more present. In a beautifully Christmas-wrapped little box was a pair of blue panties. They were brand new, of course, and had never been worn, but my heart melted on the spot. I took her in my arms and said, "I love you so much."

That was our true beginning, a pair of panties that only the Big Guy could have made it possible for me to win.

Shortly thereafter I asked her to go steady, and she said at her age going steady meant that we were engaged, so I said, "OK, so we are engaged."

About a week later she said, "When are we going to get married?"

I said, "Married! What do you mean get married?"

"When two people are engaged, they usually get married," she replied.

Oh man, wow, I really had not taken my thoughts that far. Really!

Once I let my mind go there, we started talking about it in earnest.

If we were to be married—and I knew I wanted to be, because no man could have ever been more in love—then I had to start making plans. I knew that I would have to quit college, quit football and get my plumbers license.

I knew how to support a family. I knew how to work and I knew that I was going to be the head of my family and I was going to be the provider for it.

I invited her home to meet my parents, and they were not impressed because they had blinders on. I was their oldest, and only a year ago I was still a little boy. Now I wanted to get married, and to a young woman three years older than myself.

At the time they thought she was robbing the cradle, and they didn't trust her.

I am not sure what Irene's folks thought, but I knew they didn't like Catholics. This wasn't going to be easy.

In time, her folks learned to put up with me and my folks learned to like Irene more than their own son. She was very special.

During our engagement we talked about religion and our faith a lot and we prayed together like I have never before prayed with anyone. It seemed so natural and so perfect. Perhaps because of this feeling of oneness and of our deep love for one another, she said she would take instruction to become a Catholic.

We talked often about what we each wanted out of life and marriage. Children, a home, and financial security were a few of the things. I told her, kind of jokingly, that I wouldn't marry her unless she learned to play bridge, and she just smiled and learned how to play.

She also had some friends and relatives who told us that if you wait until you can afford to get married, you'll never do it. If you love each other and you both have your good health, you can take on the world together. And we did!

During that time, I also told her I wanted to be the head of my family, but if she could allow me to be so, she could get most anything she wanted just by asking.

Over twenty-four years of marriage she demanded nothing and asked for little—she just gave and gave and gave.

We both realized that two people can be so in love that they can't really see things clearly, so we thought we should be separated for at least one month before we got married. This would allow us time to be sure we were both really comfortable with our decision.

She said she wanted to go spend a month out east with her brother after she graduated, so that would give us our month. The only problem was that by then the wedding invitations had been sent out. It was not until several months after we were married that we told each other that we both had felt, after our month's separation, that perhaps we were making a mistake. I am so grateful neither of us let those feelings get in the way.

We were married on July 28, 1962, at the Catholic Church in River Falls, Wisconsin. On our honeymoon, we went to the Wilderness Retreat Lodge on the Arrowhead Trail, in northern Minnesota. We portaged into Stump Lake for a night or two and camped out on an island.

Our first home was in a fourplex in Bloomington, Minnesota.

Irene got a teaching job, and I was becoming a plumber, working for my father. Within a year we bought our first home at 5540 West 104th Street in western Bloomington.

All my buddies were still single, so I went out of my way to make friends with other married couples like Mike and Peggy (Friendshuh) McDermott, Paul and Joyce (Friendshuh) Kessler, and George and Shelly Friendshuh.

About a year after we were married, we decided to start a family and soon Luke was on the way.

Grandfather's Quote

One of God's greatest gifts, when two become one

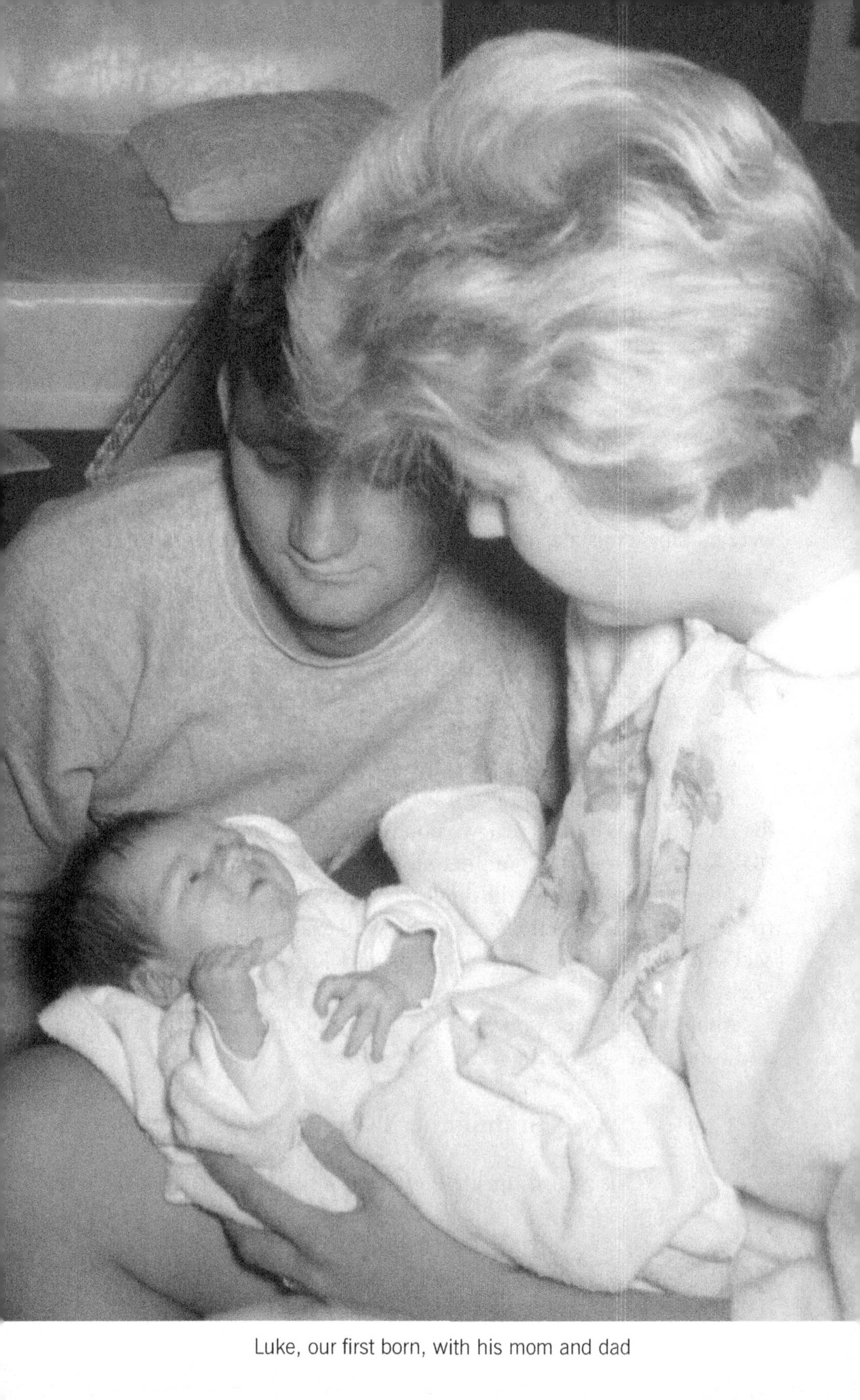

Luke, our first born, with his mom and dad

9

Luke

Luke was born on September 30, 1964.

Irene and I believed our unborn child could sense his father's presence and even become accustomed to his voice. We both knew he felt his mother's emotions so we would often lay in bed and talk to him or even sing him a song. He was a quiet child in his mother's womb and moved around very little, and when he did move, it was like a stretch or just getting more comfortable. When he arrived he did so with a loud cry, but he soon settled down and confirmed the calm, quiet nature we sensed before his arrival.

We were registered in the parish and had been going to church on a weekly basis at Nativity of Mary in Bloomington; Luke was baptized there on October 18, 1964, with my brother Jay and my sister Janet as his godparents.

When Luke got a little older, we were concerned because he did not roll over as soon as expected and he seemed to be a little slow in his development. So we took him to a doctor and discovered he had a congenital hip problem. The doctor put him in a cast that was harder on his mother and I than it was on him.

Except for the itch that needed to be scratched, that is. We spent a lot of time reaching into the cast to lightly scratch him. After the cast came off, we had to put him in a brace each time we put him down to

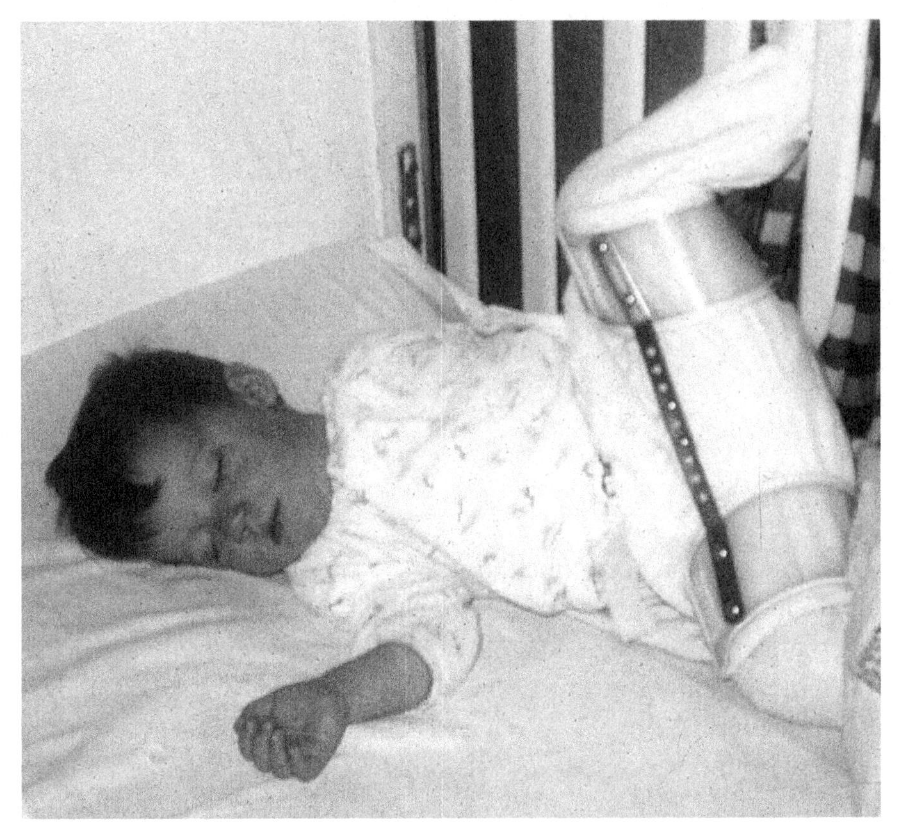

Luke with brace he had to sleep in

nap or at bedtime for about three months. He just went with the flow, and the brace didn't seem to bother him that much.

Before he was a year old, we made a bed for him in our pickup and headed for Alaska.

Luke was the oldest, so he was the first to stay out all night alone in the pasture where you could not see any lights or buildings in any direction. He was only six years old at the time! Luke was a good student in grade school and a better one in high school, and he was able to get along with anyone, even his brothers. He was always willing to pitch in and was a lot of help building our homes in Colorado and in Cannon Falls. He also became a very good handball player and started college on a handball scholarship in Butte, Montana, and finished up at Saint Cloud, Minnesota.

I leave here with something Luke wrote as he was raising his own sons:

ODE TO MY FATHER

Written by Luke

As I struggle through parenthood, I have come to appreciate more and more how well Dad raised us. I remember discussing with Tim how we never had the "need" to "fit in" and where did that come from? Is it our innate independence or was it that we were so secure in who we were within our family—we already had somewhere we belonged and fit in—that we didn't need to find it outside of that? We decided it came from our family.

I think it is one of the things about my personality that I value most. Dad did such a good job of making us feel good about ourselves that we didn't need that support from anywhere else. I can only hope that I can get close to doing the same for my kids. It is a high standard that I feel like I am not meeting much of the time.

Thank you, Dad!

Luke, you are one special human being who did a great job of raising your three sons. You have exceeded your father in every way, and that is how it should be.

Thank you, Luke!

Grandfather's Quote

The most important responsibility you will ever have in your life will be that of raising your children.

Luke enjoying life

10

Alaska

It has often been said about me that I was born two hundred years too late. I am sure that if I was born in another time and place, I would have been a mountain man. Now and in 1964 I could just dream about it.

Shortly after Luke was born, Irene and I started doing things with my cousin George and his wife, Shelly. Often times when we got together, the discussion got around to the possibility of moving to Alaska. The more we talked about it, the more we all wanted to do it.

The idea would be to go up to Alaska and each get a job as a plumber and then sometime in the future start our own plumbing business. We also had heard that you could still homestead land there, and we were going to look into that possibility.

Talking about it was one thing, but when it got it right down to the doing of it, George and Shelly just couldn't get themselves to pull the trigger. As for Irene and I, we were going to give it a try.

Soon our home was sold, and I bought a new three-quarter-ton pickup and a 45-foot mobile home that we were going to pull over the Alaskan Highway.

Luke was less than a year old so I built a crib in the cab of the pickup, tied our canoe on top, hooked our mobile home behind and headed down the highway.

We did not know a soul in Alaska, I did not have a job lined up, and we only had $1,500 in our pocket. But with our home being pulled behind us, we were off on an adventure of a lifetime.

Irene and I had often talked about it and both agreed that as long as we had each other, our good health, her teaching certificate and my plumber's license, we could try anything.

I can remember driving and staying behind the wheel for up to sixteen hours at a stretch and thinking I could be an over-the-road truck driver. The sixteen hours had several short stops to feed and care for the baby, but I never once asked Irene to drive.

The Alaskan Highway was 1,500 miles of gravel, but it was the best gravel road in the world. It had a milepost on each and every mile throughout its entire length. The Milepost magazine I had purchased, told you about approaching steep grades, sharp curves or interesting stops that could be made along the way. It also told me to put plastic covers over the headlights to keep them from breaking while driving on all that gravel.

I remember we made one stop where we hiked in about a mile to hot springs we were able to soak in. I also remember that I only passed one large truck on the entire 1,500 miles.

When we made our first stop after traveling on the gravel for a while, we went back and examined the mobile home. The cupboards had come open, and there were things spread all over the floor. It was a disaster, and Irene cried.

Somewhere along the gravel stretch we blew a tire on the mobile home, but fortunately we found a replacement in some small town. It did cost us more than a day and a half though.

I do not remember a single night along the way, but I am sure we must've slept in the mobile home. When we got to the Alaskan border, the highway became paved, but it was much worse than the gravel. Frost heaves had made the blacktop roll up and down like a roller coaster track. We hadn't traveled on the blacktop for more than a day when we came upon a mobile home that was cracked right in half.

Once we were in Alaska, not a single vehicle passed us by in the opposite direction without the driver waving to us. I found out later that no one in Alaska would drive by if you were in trouble on the road. No one locked their homes or cabins either. If you got caught out in the weather, you entered the first place you found, leaving as much firewood as when you got there. Even though every tenth man in Anchorage had a .44 pistol on his hip, it was the friendliest place I have ever been.

When we got to Anchorage, we could not find a nice trailer court to live in, so we settled for a rat trap and got our name on a waiting list for a very nice court.

When I went to the plumber's union and looked into getting a plumbing job, I was very dismayed to find out they had three waiting lists. To be on the list with the first priority, you had to be an Alaskan resident and have lived in Anchorage for at least a year. The second priority list was for Alaskan residents who had not been in Anchorage the required amount of time. The third list, which I was put on, was for nonresidents. If you were on this list, you could only get a job in the outback and you were not allowed to bring your family with you. Not only did we have a one-year-old baby, but Irene was pregnant with Tim and no way was I going to leave my family.

I looked into what it would take to get my master plumber's license, and then I tried to find whatever work I could to support my family.

Within a month of our arrival, a place opened up in the very nice trailer court. We moved there and made friends with our immediate neighbors, Gene and Mira Clinton. We also registered and became members of the closest Catholic church.

My first job was helping a contractor hang sheetrock. Then I helped him paint soffits. I wasn't very good at it, and paint was constantly dripping on my face and down my neck. I believe it was the worst job I ever had.

During this time, I began looking into the possibility of getting homestead land from the Federal government. I found out that once Alaska became a state, they were allowed to claim several million acres of Federal land and take title to it. Each year thereafter the state could select several million more acres of this Federal land, leaving that much less that could be homesteaded. A new highway had been staked out between Anchorage and Fairbanks. The state had used up their entire allotment for the year, but federal land was still available for homesteading along this highway. As soon as the first of the year arrived, the state would claim all the land along this highway and it would no longer be available to homesteaders.

It was at least mid-September by the time I found this out, so I had to act fast. I acquired the proper topographical maps and located a beautiful 160 acres right on a lake and only one or two miles off the new highway.

We could homestead this 160 acres and all we had to do was pay a $25 filing fee. Then we had to live on the land for eight months of the year for three years or for two years straight. During that two or three years we had to build a cabin, clear 20 acres and plant it with some kind of crop. After fulfilling all those requirements, the land would be deeded to us free and clear.

Now the only problem was that this land was fifty miles from the nearest road and the new highway was not projected to be completed for several years.

I tried to persuade Irene to consider homesteading anyway. I assured her I was very capable of delivering our second child in the bush, but she would have none of it.

These unreasonable women. Smile!

When winter set in there were no more construction jobs, so I started selling Britannica encyclopedias door to door. I will always remember my first sale. It was very cold out, and there was a lot of snow on the ground. I knocked on a doorway and a couple of friendly Alaskan residents invited me in. They told me they were not interested in buying any encyclopedias, but they offered me a hot cup of tea and we visited for a while. Once they heard my story, they asked me if I had sold any encyclopedias yet. When I told them no, they suggested that perhaps I could give them the spiel just for practice. I did just that, and they wound up buying and becoming our close friends.

The pickings were still rather thin, but fortunately Gene Clinton had introduced me to several of his friends who played poker. We played on a weekly basis, and for at least a three-month period, I won enough to buy groceries for my family.

The money was still scarce enough that I decided I had to sell our canoe to help tide us over. In so doing, I met a remarkable man and his six-year-old son. They had come to Anchorage from their remote homestead to buy supplies. They read my ad and came to buy the canoe, but they gave me something much more valuable than their money.

It was mid-September, and it was fairly cold outside, but this young boy had only moccasins and a breech cloth on. I got to visiting with his father and he told me about this incident that happened last winter, which I had every reason to believe was absolutely true.

Their homestead was over thirty miles from the nearest road, and it was the young boy's job to bring in the firewood each night. One night when the father had come in from the trap line, the firewood had not yet been brought in. It was mid-winter, and the snow was more than waist deep, and it was dark outside all but four hours each day. When the father told his son to go gather the firewood, the boy was sitting in front of the warm stove and didn't want to go. Dad told him again to bring in the firewood, and the boy just shrugged his shoulders and his father lost his temper.

He got angrier than he should have and he yelled at his son that if he didn't want to carry his weight around here that he could just leave. The boy had never seen his father lose his temper like that, and he got up, dressed, went outside, put on his snowshoes and left.

His mother just looked on in astonishment, and his dad said, "Don't worry, I'll go after him."

The father took his time getting ready, and he had to follow the snowshoe trail for over a mile before he came upon his son. The boy had started a fire and was warming his feet over it when his father asked if he could join him.

The two of them talked for a while, dad apologizing for getting so angry and the boy apologizing for not doing his job. They accepted each other's apology and snowshoed home together under the Northern lights.

How many twelve-year-old kids, let alone a six-year-old, can walk on snowshoes, build a fire and stay out all night in the bush alone? Not many. I made up my mind right then and there that my boys would be able to do it by the time they were six.

Shortly after selling the canoe, I began studying for my master plumber's license test. I took the test and passed it with flying colors. I now was a master plumber and could start my own business.

We also sold the trailer and moved to an apartment and shortly thereafter moved to a small house next to where Gene and Mira had moved.

My first real big break as a plumbing contractor came about thanks to Irene. She was sitting in a restaurant and heard a contractor complaining about his plumber. She told him about me and gave him our phone number. He called and offered me the opportunity to bid on a full-service gas station. I had never worked on one before, but how hard could it be? I remember putting together the bid and trying to guesstimate the hours it would take and then doubling the hours. I got the job.

I bid the total material and labor at about $5,000 and figured I would be making $25 an hour. When it was all said and done, I made nothing on the material and had worked for about five dollars an hour.

When he asked me to bid a second service station, I doubled my bid and got the job. When he asked me to bid a third service station, I increased the price again by an additional 50%. He told me I was no

Some of the waterfowl that I shot in Alaska.

longer low bidder, but he liked my work and if I quit raising my prices, I could have the job. I took it, but now I was so busy that it was hard to keep up.

I called George back in Minnesota and told him if he came to Anchorage I would take him in as a partner. A short while later George and Shelly joined us. As a footnote, when I left Alaska, George and Shelly stayed and are still there today.

There were lots of adventures, hunting trips, and I even bought my first piece of real estate while there, but I will leave all of that for other stories.

Sometime during that first year, a new contractor friend of mine invited us to go to church with him. For the first time in my life, I would attend a church on Sunday that was not Catholic. I went partly because of the man who invited us. He was a very successful contractor but seemed to have no money, so during one of our conversation I asked him why. He shared with me that he had been a contractor in Texas before moving to Alaska, but had gone belly up. Most people in his position would file for bankruptcy, but he refused to do so. He was going to pay what he owed. He told those who had money coming from him that they would get paid, but it might take a while. And he was still paying them off years later. Now that was my kind of man, so when he invited us to attend church with him, we accepted.

Not only had I never been to a Sunday service in a non-Catholic church before, I had never been to a church so small. It seemed like everyone there went out of their way to welcome us. It was a good feeling, which I remembered for a long time.

Tim was born on January 15, 1966, and baptized in the Catholic church a week or two later with George and Shelly Friendshuh as his godparents.

We now had two boys in diapers, and I always seemed to be working or away hunting. I was loving every minute of it, but I am sure Irene felt a little bit abandoned.

Then came the letter. My father was going into the hospital to have a hip operation and was not sure he would be able to continue running his plumbing business. He offered to sell me the business for so much money a month and nothing down. It was a phenomenal business opportunity, but I really didn't want to take it.

When I talked about it with Irene, I realized how unhappy she was in Alaska. She really wanted me to take my father up on his offer so we could move back to Minnesota.

Contrary to what some members of my family may think, I did not do things unilaterally. I loved Irene very much, and her happiness was extremely important to me.

We talked some more, and I made her a proposition. I would give up my Alaskan business and move back to Minnesota if she would consider agreeing to a future compromise between Alaska and Minnesota. We agreed that when we could afford it, we would buy a working cattle ranch somewhere out west.

We moved back to Minnesota.

Grandfather's Quote

If you've got family and you are all in good health, nothing else matters, so follow your dreams.

Irene on Alaskan canoe trip

George Friendshuh and Gene Clinton on one of our bear hunts

11

Alaskan Bear Stories

To set the tone for the bear stories I actually took part in, I will tell you an Alaskan bear story that is often told in the far North.

> It seems these two outsiders were going to go on a fishing trip in Alaska. It was a trip where you got to your destination by bush plane and there was an old Alaskan sourdough who joined them. The sourdough had a .44 on his hip, and the outsiders asked him if he was going to shoot those fish.
>
> When the plane got to the riverbank where they were to land, the bank was full of bears fishing in the river. The pilot buzzed the bears, as he always did, and all of them ran off but one. This big male stood on his hind legs and swatted at the plane each time the pilot buzzed him. It took several passes before the bear finally ambled off into the brush.
>
> When the fishermen finally got into the river, the sourdough had difficulty casting for his fish, because he had an outsider standing next to each of his arms.

Most outsiders are not familiar with the enormity of these large brown bears. In the Anchorage airport, a full mount standing on its hind legs was eleven feet from the floor to the top of his head. His paw measured twenty-four inches across. It was like standing next to something right out of the dinosaur age.

Gene Clinton and George Friendshuh. In the background, the very small boat we used to cross the open ocean.

These bears were usually found on Kodiak Island or along the southeastern coastline and were often referred to as Kodiak bears. The grizzly bears that were found in the interior were considerably smaller and were usually called just grizzlies.

The first couple of times I hunted interior bears, I never came upon one. Finally, George, Gene and myself planned a bear hunt along the southeastern coastline. We would be hunting Kodiak bear and black bear.

We drove as far as we could and then loaded all our gear into a small 19-foot boat. We had to cross an inlet that was perhaps four or five miles wide to get to where we were going. With the boat loaded with all of our gear and food, it rode rather low in the water. On the crossing, we got very close to several whales and thought nothing of it.

When we got to the other side, we hit our prop on a submerged log and lost it. We did not have a backup prop and could have been in some serious trouble, but as luck would have it, just then a large old military boat came by. We flagged the boat down and explained our problem. They were going back to port and would be returning shortly thereafter. They agreed to take us along only if all of us would go, so we left our small boat and climbed onboard.

We got back to port with no incidents and were able to buy a couple of props, so that we had a spare. On our return trip, the killer whales appeared once again. The boat we were on had to be at least ninety feet long, and yet this boat went way out of its way to avoid the whales. We were told these whales often times come up underneath boats, or would swat their tails against the side, and had killed many a fisherman.

We got back to our own boat at low tide, and it was high and dry about a half mile away from the water. We were let ashore and were able to walk back to our boat and put on the new prop. We unloaded our gear and set up camp.

From the water's edge, you could glass the mountain sides, which were absolutely full of black bears.

We only had a few days, but we really wanted to shoot a Kodiak or brown bear, so we spent the first few days right along the coast. We saw several fresh tracks that were over a foot wide and were obviously made by a Kodiak bear, but we never did see the bear that made them.

Finally we decided to go after the black bears we could see on the mountain. I don't even remember whether George or Gene shot the bear, but I helped them skin it and we packed the meat and hide back to camp.

The shooting of that black bear and getting it back to camp took most of the day. We only had one more day to hunt, and although I glassed several black bears on the mountain, I was never able to get within rifle range.

Me and Gene preparing a meal on the bear hunt

When we'd loaded all our gear back into our boat, the weight of the bear meat and hide had its effect. The boat, which I was driving, rode even lower in the water than it had been on the trip over.

When we were still quite close to shore, several killer whales suddenly appeared. They were within a hundred yards of us, and it is the first and only time any of us ever got into an argument. George was not a good swimmer, and he wanted me to beach the boat. I refused. I veered away from the whales, but the shoreline was very rocky and I did not want to get too close to it.

Soon the whales increased their distance from us, and everyone settled down. When we could no longer see the whales through our binoculars, we started out once again and got back without further incident.

On that trip George had been using a 30-ought-6 (.30-06) automatic. It must have got salt water in it because it jammed a couple of times. That incident had a direct bearing on me not getting a grizzly trophy on a future hunt.

I was hunting sheep with Gene and I was using George's 30-ought-6 automatic which had jammed on our bear hunt. We had packed in close to twenty miles, with each of us carrying 50-pound packs on our back. We were after Dall sheep, and although we had spotted several on distant peaks, we were never able to get within rifle range.

On our return, we decided that each of us would walk on opposite sides of a steep valley in hopes of doubling our chances of seeing sheep on the return.

I had been hiking for three or four hours and came to a large clearing. I could not see Gene on the other side, but there was something on my side, far below me. It looked like it was a brown bear, so I decided to see how close I could get to it.

As I got a little closer, I could tell for sure that it was in fact a grizzly. The grizzly season was currently not open, but going towards him would not make my walk back any longer. I decided to see how close I might be able to get.

When I got within about seventy-five yards of him, the largest moose I had ever seen came out of a clearing about a hundred yards below the bear. As the moose trotted across the clearing, the bear turned and stood on his hind legs and watched the moose pass.

Without thinking of the consequences, I took that opportunity to cut the distance between the bear and myself by more than half.

When the bear finally heard me and whirled around, I was within forty yards of him. The wind was in the right direction so he could not smell me, but he certainly saw me. The hair on the back of his neck stood up just like a dog's will do when they're angry. He started swatting his front paws at the sky and shaking his head.

He was at least eight feet tall, and his head was enormous. I remember how small his eyes seemed and how they appeared to be a dark turquoise in color. His hide was worn right down to the skin, and he would not have made a very good bear rug.

Because bears often attack people in Alaska, you were allowed to shoot them at any time if you felt you were in danger. I also knew—just like when you cut the head off of a chicken and it continues to run around—you could blow the heart right out of a grizzly and he would still have time to kill you. At this close range, to be sure of stopping this bear, I would have to break one or possibly both of his shoulders. I also knew I had in my hands the same rifle that had jammed on George a short time before. I could not be sure of getting off more than one shot.

To this day, I still wonder if I was smart or if I was just a little afraid. Either way, I decided not to take the chance of trying to kill the bear.

By now, the bear was swatting the air even more ferociously and foam was coming out of his mouth. I decided to try and talk him out of charging.

"Back off, big boy."

As soon as he heard my voice, he took two large lunges towards me. I raised my rifle and held it on a shoulder. I did not fire.

The bear once again rose to his hind legs and started swatting at the air. I just held my ground with my rifle aimed at the bear.

I could hear my heart beating, and after what seemed like an eternity, the bear took a couple of steps backwards.

I remained silent.

The bear retreated even further. When he got to about the distance where he had first noticed me, he dropped down on all fours and lopped in a wide circle around me.

I noticed that the hair on the back of his neck and along his back had laid down. A bear's eyesight is not very good, and I am sure he could not tell what I was when he was upwind of me. As he circled and got downwind, he smelled me for the first time. He stopped abruptly and the hair on his back stood straight up for the second time, then he turned and ran away at full speed.

I missed my chance at a terrific head mount, but perhaps I am here today, sharing all these stories with you, because I made the correct decision.

Grandfather's Quote

Perhaps a man's true trophies are the sum total of each of his day's memories.

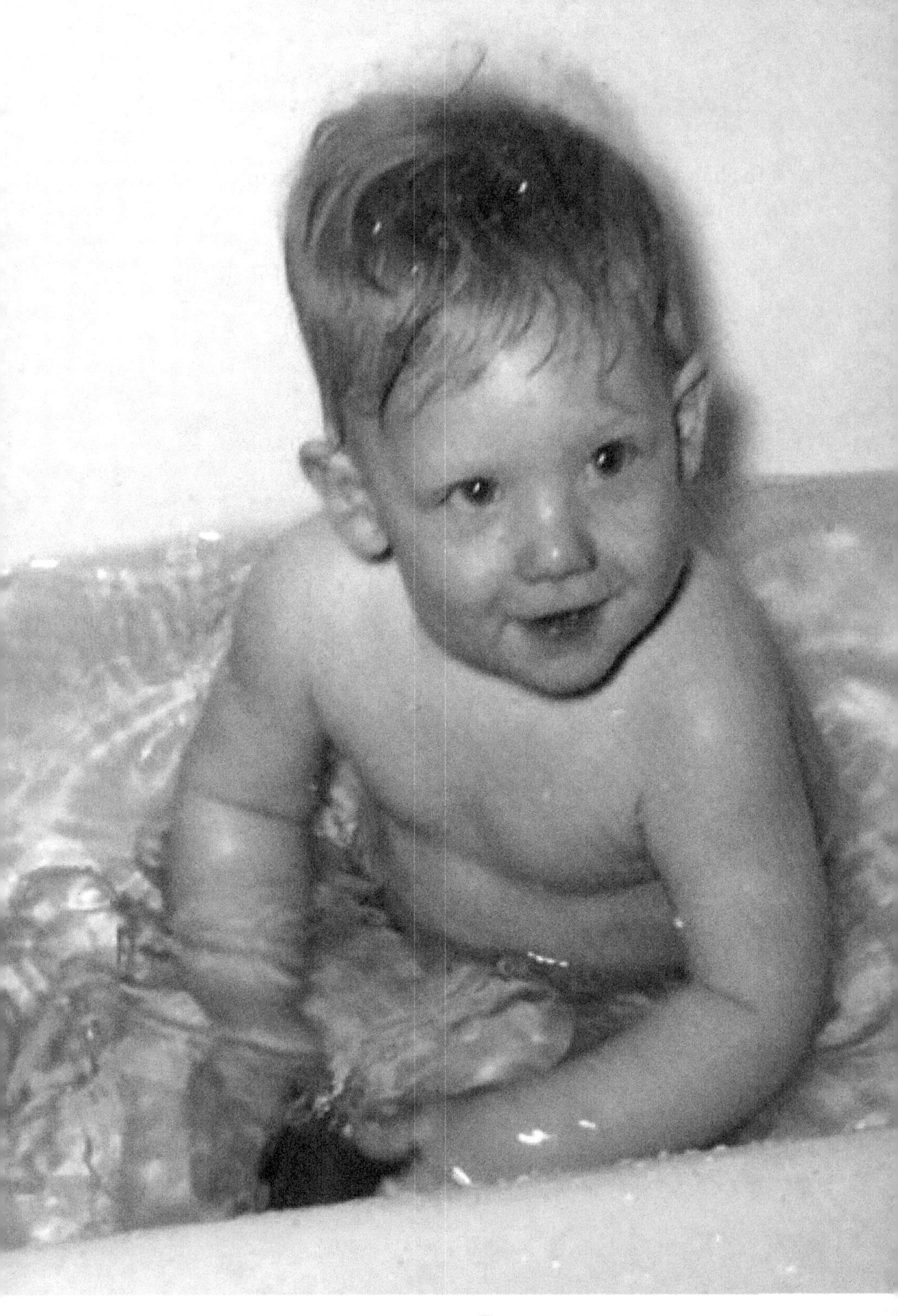

Tim

12

Tim

Tim was born in Alaska on January 15, 1966.

When Tim's mother had carried her first child, Luke, he was calm as can be in her womb. When she was carrying Tim, he was always on the move and would often kick her very hard. It was so different from her first pregnancy, which resulted in a boy, that she was sure she was going to have a girl this time.

No, just a Tim!

When Luke was one, you could set him on a dock and he would sit there and perhaps stick his finger in the water. If you put Tim on the same dock, he would run off the end and plunge into the lake without a second thought. Luke played quietly on the kitchen floor while Tim was always banging or throwing something or making loud sounds of delight or anger. We used to call him Bumper Car, because when he was in his walker he would bump into anything and everything. He went off the stairs without even slowing down. We put a chair in front of the stairs and he moved the chair and once again went head over heels down the stairway. We put a gate on top of the stairs and he tore the gate down and went head over heels for a third time. We finally put in a very heavy-duty gate, and this kept him from a fourth fall.

When Luke was playing quietly on the floor with his toys and Tim was still in his walker, he used to delight in running over Luke's toys.

When Tim was about 18 months old, he challenged me for the first time. We never put our knick knacks up, but rather chose to teach our boys that they could not touch them. Tim came to the coffee table and put his hand on a knick knack. I said no. He pulled his hand away and looked at me and touched it once again. I said no much louder this time, and once again he pulled his hand away. When he put his hand on it a third time, I tapped the top of his hand with my fingers and said no yet a third time. This time he looked at me with a look of defiance and touched it again. Now I slapped his little hand so it must have stung a little, and he pulled it away and with a tear in his eye. Then he actually made a face and touched it yet again. This time I really slapped his hand hard, and he went away crying.

When he was older, we moved back to Minnesota and had a large sandbox. Tim used to eat sand while he was playing in it.

Because of Luke's quiet, calm nature, he and Tim used to get along quite well. It was when Matt came on the scene and loved pushing Tim's buttons that things got a little out of hand.

Tim was always the one wanting to be the first to do something adventurous. When we built calving chutes so the boys could ride calves, Tim had to be the first to try it.

In Colorado, he was the one willing to go gather horses at 4 AM in the dark, and he was the one that came along and wrangled when I took hunters out.

Grandfather's Quote

Who we are is a gift from God. Who we become is a gift from our parents.

Tim on a family canoe trip in the boundary waters

Our log home that we designed and built

13

Our Log Home

We bought forty acres, sold thirteen of them to pay for the rest, cleared the brush, paid to have a driveway put in and designed a log home. The land was exactly three miles straight north of New Market and about three miles west of Interstate 35W in Scott County, Minnesota. The home started as a walkout basement with two bedrooms, a kitchen, a living room and a fallout shelter. It sat overlooking a four-acre marsh just east of the house. When I had the basement dug by a D8 Cat, I paid extra to have a dam built where the marsh emptied into a sort of spillway. Within a year we were living on a four-acre lake and had found a log company to make the logs for the home we had designed.

We helped lay the blocks, and we put our own cap (the floor joists for the main floor covered with felt) on the basement and sealed the roof. Now we had to get financing in order to build the rest of the home. I went through all the normal channels at the bank, but in those days no one had heard about log homes. No bank was going to lend me the money on a log home. Following our own path was not as easy as building a house like everyone else.

Well, it so happened that Cliff Jerback owned the Community State Bank in Bloomington and he hunted deer with my father and I. After spending a couple of years living in the basement, I was on our annual

Luke, Tim and Matt in the loft of our log home

The fireplace was the family gathering spot

deer hunting trip and told Cliff I couldn't get a loan. He told me to come see him when I got back in town.

Instead, when I got back, I went to the bank and met with the normal mortgage officer. He told me things were even tighter now, and that I had absolutely no chance of getting a loan at this time, especially on a log house. I mentioned that Cliff had asked me to come in so he agreed to talk to Cliff, but he assured me there would be no chance of getting the loan. A week later I got a call and got the loan for my log house. It taught me a valuable lesson in life—if you want something, go to the top—and it really helps if you have some sort of in with those at the top.

The logs were shipped in, and Irene, the boys and I put up the home. I did almost everything myself—I even made the doors—and couldn't wait to get done. We had to be done in order to get the mortgage, so I kept at it every night after my forty-hour week and every weekend. Irene's dad came and helped for a couple of weekends, as did my father and some of the other tradesmen. Soon it was all finished except for the soffit on the south side of the house. I called the bank inspector and when he came out, he noticed the unfinished soffit but passed it anyway. After he left, Irene asked me when I was going to finish it. I said in July, but I didn't say in what year. About eight years later I finished the soffit, in July, just before selling the house, and that has been my MO ever since.

Grandfather's Quote

You can take the easy path like everyone else, or
you can take your own path and follow your dreams.

Matt and Dad

14

Matt

Matt was born on June 2, 1967 and baptized a couple of weeks later with Gene and Lynn Friendshuh as his godparents.

When he was born, we were living in a house in Burnsville, Minnesota. Before Matt was two years old, we moved to our basement home in Lakeville and became members of the beautiful Catholic church in New Market. They welcomed us like we had been welcomed in the small church in Alaska, and I loved taking my three and soon to be four boys to Mass. We sat in the front row so they could see what was going on.

As a baby Matt almost never cried, and he always seemed to be smiling. Before he was even two, he thought he had to keep up with his two older brothers and he did a darn good job of it. He was already helping with the dishes.

He was also tough as nails and would wrestle or play tackle football with his two older brothers when he seemed half their size.

When Matt was little, he used to suck his finger. His brothers sucked their thumbs, but Matt was a finger boy.

For a while I even tried cow poop on the boys' thumbs and Matt's finger. They just washed it off and went back to sucking. Nothing seemed to work, so I gave up. I figured they would grow out of it with age. The older two did at a fairly young age, except for when they were sleeping, but Matt didn't want to give up that finger.

From the time that he was old enough to roughhouse, he was right in there with his older brothers. Even though he was absolutely as tough as his older brothers, his mother and I worried about it because he was so much lighter. I cannot remember him coming to me and saying, "My brothers are picking on me."

Then when his brothers started football, I bought pads for Matt so he could play too. He was in third grade and a lot smaller than his brothers, but man, could he tackle! He had absolutely no fear of getting hurt, and had the mentality every football coach looks for, but he still could occasionally be seen with his finger in his mouth.

I used to say that if he ever played college football, when they introduced him, it would go something like this: "And at 220 lbs, playing defensive end, Matt Friendshuh"—and this huge end would come running out of the tunnel. I would act out him running out of the tunnel with his finger in his mouth.

It made quite a show, and we all laughed about it.

To this day, I cannot recall when he stopped. Maybe it was soon after my little skit. All I know is I have never seen him do it as a young man, and the memory of my tough son with his finger in his mouth is very special.

Postscript:

I like to think he just had so much self-esteem, and the finger tasted so good to him, he just didn't care what others thought. "smile"

When Matt was still quite young, he ripped open his leg on barbed wire while riding his bike. We rushed him to the doctor, and he had a lot of stitches put in. The doctor said that this boy was sure to grow up and be a doctor because Matt watched with interest all the while the doctor was stitching him up.

When Matt went out in the back pasture, he had just turned six. He stated that now that he was six, he should be able to go. Luke was six years and ten months old when he first went, and Tim was six years and eight months old. Matt was six years and a few days old when he

Matt and his finger. Conrath, Wisconsin

did it. He was tough, but I was a little worried so I let Matt take the dog along. I watched him with binoculars from a distance for the first hour or so. Matt did just fine getting the fire going and being on his own.

Matt was the only one of my sons who didn't finish college, but he was as successful as any of his brothers.

Grandfather's Quote

Give your child the gift of self esteem and he or she will have a great journey through this life.

Luke, Tim and Matt

15

Good Friends Mike and Sue

When my father first became a plumber, he worked for Earl Blaylock at Blaylock Plumbing in Richfield, Minnesota. Earl had many children, and Mike was his second son. Mike and I were in second grade together at Assumption School, but I have little or no recollection of him other than as a very quiet kid with a butch haircut. The next time I remember seeing him was at Dunwoody Trade School, where he and I both were going in order to get our plumber's license. We visited a little and then I went off to Alaska. When I got back from Alaska, I looked him up and invited him and his wife over to play cards. That was the beginning of a very close friendship. Mike and Sue loved playing cards, and they were both super athletes. They also had four sons, each almost the exact ages of our four sons. Mike was a hunter to boot, so we had a lot in common.

We started playing bridge together once a week at alternating homes, but when we discovered that the gals liked visiting too much we changed the game to hearts. Mike was one of the best athletes I have ever known. He was a fast-pitch softball player, a good golfer, an excellent broomball and volleyball player, and he introduced me to the game of handball. His wife was on the world championship women's softball team and was an even better athlete than Mike.

We did a lot together with our families, including bringing all the boys to most of our softball games. We had Fourth of July picnics, went to the lake and of course were always at one another's home in the backyard. Once a year Mike, Sue, Irene and I would hire a sitter and go on an adults-only weekend vacation. We started that even before all our kids were born because I remember two back-to-back memorable weekends. On both, we had rented a cabin on a lake and brought along an eight-gallon keg of beer. We both had kegs in our homes in an old refrigerator and kept frozen mugs in the freezer. We all loved our keg beer and drank a lot of it, so it was just natural to bring a keg along on our vacations.

Over the years we did a lot of hunting together. When the boys got to be old enough to join us, we started going deer hunting on Lost Lake in northern Minnesota. You can read more about that here in my deer hunting stories.

Mike and I also played on the same men's broomball team, and I believe we won it all. I am sure Mike was instrumental in helping me get the couples softball league started in Bloomington. In those days most of the women were nowhere near as athletic as they are today, so we played with a 16" softball. The guys could not wear gloves, and all outfielders had to stay behind a chalk line 30 feet behind the bases. Each team had to have five men and five women and alternate the batting order. If a pitcher walked a man, the women behind him also walked. Ability-wise, our team really had six men on it because Sue was that good of a player. We had a distinct advantage and won most all of our games. After several years the competition got better, and we started to go to weekend tournaments, bringing all the boys along of course. We only had ten people on our team so that all could play all the time. If someone got hurt, we just played with eight. If a woman got hurt and had to sit out, a man also had to sit out. Then of course there was always the after-the-game keg party at Mike's or my place. Great years and great memories!

Mike also took me below the bleachers at Carleton College in Northfield, where they had a handball court and introduced me to the game of handball. Wow, I was immediately hooked!

In keeping with following my own path, I was soon planning my own court. I figured out what material I would need, priced it and went to Mike and two of his brothers, Dave and Wally, who also played handball. All three agreed to loan me $1,500 each, interest-free in return for unlimited use of the court. They also agreed to help build it. We dry-stacked 12" blocks 20 feet high and put block bond on both sides. Using five-gallon buckets, we dumped concrete in every fifth core and I built a pole barn over the top. When it was done, we had a locker room, a four-man shower, an observation area with an old refrigerator and of course an 8-gallon keg of beer.

The court allowed my wife to play racquetball and my boys to learn to play handball. It was also the beginning of couple's volleyball on the handball court. Boy, were Mike and Sue good at that! Soon we were going to couples sand volleyball tournaments and even one large "wallyball" tournament, which you played in a handball court and could ricochet the ball off the walls. The tournament was held in St. Paul and there were eight teams. Our team consisted of Mike, Sue, Irene and I. Most of the other teams played with five or six players. We played a round robin and beat every team, but the tournament was to be decided by a championship game between the two best teams in the round robin. The team with the second best record, who had only lost to us, originally consisted of four guys and two girls. When they showed up for the championship match they played with five or six guys and no girls. My spikes and Mike and Sue's unbelievable digs and setups were a great part of our winning ways, but it was my powerful overhand serve off the walls that no team seemed to be able to handle. In the championship game they just managed to keep my serve off the floor as it bounced off the first player and sometimes even the second, but thereafter, they were able to do something with it. We gave it a valiant effort and barely came up short as the five or six guys were too much for two couples.

Just before moving to South Dakota, we were told Mike, the superb athlete, had MS and there was nothing that could be done about it. When Irene and I heard this, we were so shocked that we both sat down and cried. Then we prayed and prayed some more.

I will never forget the last time Mike competed at any sport. He and Sue were at our home with the handball court in it, and Mike had to be helped down the stairs in order to get on the court. He really wanted to play, so we helped. He seemed to be unsteady on his feet until the ball was served, and then he was Mike again. He moved with grace, and he played like the Mike of old. After playing most of a game, seemingly unsteady between points yet moving with grace during play, he dove for a save and lay spread out on the floor. The ball was kept in the air, reset for a spike that ended in a point, but Mike did not get up. We helped him off the court, and he was never to compete again.

Shortly thereafter, I moved to the ranch in South Dakota. Mike came out several times to hunt turkey, but he was failing and it broke my heart.

Over the next twenty years Mike got to the point where he was bedridden and could only operate things through a puffer. Sue, who as a young child lost her father to World War II and had taken care of her failing mother in her later years, was now taking care of Mike. During the time she was caring for Mike, she got her counseling degree, was there for her boys and was a caring grandmother.

I am sorry to say I was never there for her. I visited Mike only once during the many years he was bedridden and I did not even go to his funeral. I was living on a ranch over a 10-hour drive away, but there was the phone and I did not call him or her enough. Yes, I was going through one of the most difficult times of my life, which you will read about later, but I greatly regret not being there for them.

Truly a poor decision.

As I write these words and relive these memories, I realize how close Mike and Sue were to me.

I wish that I had been there for them in their time of need.

It was Sue, this very beautiful woman both inside and out, who had first shared with me the phrase, "I hope that my friends can love me, in spite of me."

Now I can only hope and pray that she can, somehow in her heart, find forgiveness and love me in spite of me.

Grandfather's Quote

True friends are some of the greatest gifts that you will ever have in this life. Value them, cherish them, hold on to them and be there for them.

I wonder if Mark is asking his bear a question?

16

Mark

Mark was born on December 4, 1970.

Like Matt, he too grew up quickly. He had to, with three older brothers, and once he started talking, he never seemed to quit. At a very young age, he started asking questions, and the questions just kept coming.

When he was about four years old, I was driving somewhere with him, just the two of us. He started asking questions.

"Dad, where did that baby calf come from?"

"It came from its mother."

"What do you mean?"

"The calf was inside its mother's tummy and came out."

"How?"

"It came out through the cow's vagina."

"How did it get in there?"

"The bull put semen in the cow and it combined with the cow's egg and a calf started being made."

"Why?"

"Because that is how life starts."

"Why?"

"Because that is how God made it happen."

"Why?"

"Because God wanted to share and so he created all living things."

There were a few more questions and answers in there, but you get the idea. Then at some point there was a short pause and another question.

"Who would win a fight between a lion and a bear?"

And so it went until I ran out of patience because *he never seemed to run out of questions.*

Without me fully realizing it, Mark spent a lot more time with his mother than with me. I always wanted to take my very young boys along whenever I could, but their mother was tired of being alone. So she used the excuse that because Mark was so much younger, he should stay with her.

The first summer right after his mother and I were apart, Mark came out to spend three months with me on the ranch.

Both his mother and I just assumed he would want to finish out his high school years at St. Thomas Military Academy like his brothers had done. However, when I told Mark I was going to sail the South Pacific for a year, he said, "No, you are not. All these years it has been you and my three older brothers, and me and Mom. Now it is my turn and I am staying on the ranch with you."

I said, "If you do, you will have to work your butt off and it will be your job to do all the grocery shopping and cooking. I will do all the dishes and house cleaning."

He said, "You got a deal."

Thus began a special relationship. I actually got closer to Mark than any of his three older brothers because the two of us shared a small trailer and worked together on the ranch every day. We became good close friends. I treated him as an adult, not a teenage son, and he filled the part.

One of my best memories was with Mark. I had taken him back to college in Helena, Montana, and we were playing some table tennis on campus. A very good Asian player asked to play me. During our play, I was moving all over the floor and returning slams. A bunch of kids who were watching started laughing and saying, "No way." I asked Mark what was going on and he said they did not believe I was his father. They thought I was his brother! Man, did my head swell! It wasn't because of my young looks, it was because of the way I could still move.

But my favorite Mark story happened years after he was on his own. I always told my sons that the most important responsibility they would ever have in their entire lives would be raising their children. And to do it properly, one of the parents needed to be in the home until their youngest child started preschool. Nothing is more important, not the second car or the bigger home or anything else for that matter.

Mark didn't get married until after he had received a law degree, had practiced as a private attorney and was teaching law at Moscow University in Moscow, Idaho. I am sure he was making close to, if not over six figures when he married a doctor from Germany. When she got pregnant, he called me and said he and Sandra had talked it over and because she made a thousand dollars a day, he was going to be the stay-at-home mom. A year later, Sandra told me that when she came home, the house was clean, dinner was on and the baby's diapers had been changed. Twelve years and three girls later, their youngest is going to be starting preschool in the fall and Mark is talking about going back to work.

Mark and Sandra got it right and I couldn't be prouder of them.

Grandfather's quote

The most important years of your child's life are the first three or four. You need to be there for him, not some daycare.

Irene and me in Hawaii

17

Hawaii

I had always wanted to go to Hawaii, but I was not interested in doing it as a tourist, so we did it our way.

It was 1971 or 1972 and my dad thought I was crazy. We had young kids, a new business and not a lot of cash but boy, were we glad we did it when we were so young.

On the flight to the islands the stewardess took a liking to us and kept giving us free champagne, and we weren't even in first class.

When we landed, Irene was not feeling so well. We had planned to not even leave the airport on the tourist island of Oahu, but Irene wasn't looking forward to getting on another plane.

Our plane was pre-booked, so within an hour we had to get on another plane and fly to Molokai. I chose Molokai as our first island to visit because it was the most rural of all the islands.

We had agreed we would visit four islands: Molokai, Maui, Hawaii and Kauai. On the first night on each island we would stay in a motel. The rest of the time on the island we would camp out.

After we landed in Molokai, a cab took us to our motel. On the way he stopped at a pineapple field and got us a pineapple or two. He had a large machete for slicing them up and we ate some of it right on the spot. It was the best pineapple we had ever tasted!

The motel was small but nice and right on a large sandy, almost completely deserted beach. It had no screens on the windows and didn't seem to need them.

The next order of business was to rent a car. Before this trip I had never owned a credit card, but I found out that even with a $5,000 cash deposit, you can't rent a car without one. Luckily, I had done my research and found this out before the trip and had acquired my first credit card ever.

Once we had the car, we would be on our own for the next two or three days. On the first day with our car, we picked up a hitchhiker who was living in a pillbox on the beach. He had been living there for several years and told us where all the locals ate and hung out. He also suggested we should go to the east end of the island in Halawa valley and camp there.

After spending a little time with him, I can't remember how he put it, but he said something like "Do you want a joint?" and I had no idea what he was talking about. He pressed a little further and figured out how square we were and dropped it. Later on the trip, on a different island, we were once again offered drugs through the same kind of question and we figured it out and said no thanks.

When we went to eat at the place that our pillbox friend recommended, we found out the two of us could eat all we wanted and have a glass of wine for less than $6.00. That even included the tip. On our last night on the islands we decided to eat at a tourist spot and we had less food and it cost us over $35.

After buying groceries, eating breakfast and dropping off our new friend, we drove to the east end of the island. There we set up camp on the beach in the Halawa valley. Early the next morning after breakfast over a fire, we hiked up the valley, following the stream coming out of it. We went through what were obviously old irrigation ditches along the hillside, and we went through a very thick bamboo forest. About an hour in we met a couple of girl hikers who were lost, so Irene rested while I showed them the way to the beach.

When I got back to Irene, we continued upstream until we came to a beautiful waterfall and a small pond. We took a dip in the very cool water.

I had written all about this trip right after it had happened, but lost the notebook. I am now writing this again over forty-three years later, so all my facts might not be accurate. I cannot remember anything more about Molokai.

When we went to the next island, Maui, we rented a four-wheel-drive jeep. We were told we couldn't go on certain roads, so of course I sought them out. At the end of one very rough road, we came to a small cove with about one hundred feet of sandy beach. The waves came crashing in and Irene refused to go in, but I had to try it. I remember thinking "What a spot to put a cabin on your own private beach."

At that time there was no decent road going along the south side of the island, but there was a rough four-wheel-drive road and we took it. About an hour or more in, we came to a set of corrals along the road where a bunch of ranchers were having a ranch rodeo. We stopped and visited and watched. They were not very good at roping, but they were having a ball.

When we got to the east end of the island, at what was called the Seven Sacred Pools, we took a well-worn path in as far as most tourists do. At the end of the path a chain-link fence and a sign advised us to go no further. We went around the end of the fence and continued following the stream.

After about a half hour of walking, I came around a corner and there was a young girl standing on a large rock by the stream stark naked. I backed up, turned around and asked Irene if the naked girl had seen me. When she replied yes, I asked her, "So what is she doing?" Irene said, "Nothing, she is just continuing to stand there." I said, "Well, if she doesn't care, neither do I." I turned around and we kept on walking. I said "Hi" to the very beautiful naked lady as I walked past her and she just said "Hi" back. Just a few days on the islands and I had been offered my first illegal drugs and saw the first live naked woman in my life other than my wife.

Some local had told me that in order to get to the last pool I would have to swim upstream through some tight canyons. When we got to that point Irene had had enough, so she stayed put while I dove in the river, fought the current and continued on. I had to climb up at least one waterfall and hike a long way through a very thick bamboo forest, but finally I got to the last of the seven sacred pools.

On this island we also met a couple who were living on a sailboat and got to know them a little. They normally made their living by taking tourists sailing, but I told them we didn't want to be on a boat with a bunch of tourists. I also told them we were camping because we didn't have a lot of money. Finally they said, "What the hell, would you like to go out?" We spent half a day sailing and they taught us how to be of some help. And of course we stopped and swam out in the ocean far from shore. All in all, a great time.

I remember very little about the big island other than all the spectacular flowers around Hilo, touring the volcano, swimming on a large beach (pictures of which I still have) and touring the Parker Ranch. I was fascinated by the history of it. I knew I wanted to ranch someday, and it was fun thinking of the possibility of doing it on one of the islands.

What I remember most about Kauai is the miles and miles of deserted, beautiful sandy beach with no one else on it but us. You could look out across the ocean at the forbidden island. I remember thinking that I could swim to it. One day I ventured far, far out and then thought, "Four kids and a wife, I had better not try." We also went to where scenes in the movie *South Pacific* had been filmed, including the one where they were sliding down a waterfall on their butts and swimming in a crystal clear pool. There was a natural slide and a concrete one made for the movie, and we tried both. We also went to some spectacular overlook and actually went to one touristy thing where we were able to sit and listen to Hawaiians playing Hawaiian music.

What we noticed most at the tourist spot was how almost everyone was old and could not have done any of the things we were able to do. We talked about how glad we were that we were here when we were so young. Being young and in good health, we were able to climb Phallic Rock, swim in an underwater cave and do many other physical things.

Irene did restrain me in one instance. We had gone to the top of some waterfall that was 150 feet high. A sign there said for a Hawaiian to become king, he had to dive off this falls. That was enough of a challenge for me. I told Irene I was going to go check out the depth of the pool at the bottom of the falls to see if it was safe to dive. She finally put her foot down, and I wisely honored her wishes.

One of my last memories was on Kauai. We were going to hike into some wilderness area and camp. Several hours in, we came upon a tent on an otherwise deserted beach. Just as we were getting there, a guy comes out of the tent with nothing but a short t-shirt on. It quit at his waist and Irene just moved behind me and said, "What is he doing?" I responded that he was brushing his teeth in the ocean. Then he came up to me and introduced himself, then he stepped around me and introduced himself to Irene. When he left Irene said, "Let's get out of here" and I said, "No way, I want to see if his girlfriend comes out."

That's about all I remember over forty years later, but I do recall that when we got home, I heard Irene telling one of her women friends about the guy, and I overheard her say, "And it was tan too!"

One last footnote. After we returned, Irene stopped wearing a bra on several occasions, so all these hippie people we met had some effect.

Grandfather's quote

Do it your way no matter what
other people may think or do.

18

A Basketball Challenge

Among the contractors that I worked with I was known either as the cowboy, because I often wore a cowboy hat, or as the jock, because I was always playing some sort of sports.

One of those contractors was a painting contractor named Larry Schmidt. He was a good friend of mine. He had a young college kid working for him named Brad. Brad was a starter on his college basketball team, and Larry was always bragging about him.

Larry knew I played a lot of basketball, and one day at lunch, he teased me about how Brad could kick my butt in a one-on-one game.

I acknowledged that "Brad is probably a better player, but in a one-on-one game, I can hold my own."

"No way! He would kick your butt."

"I don't think so. I think I can handle myself with most anyone one-on-one."

Larry says, "I'll tell you what. If you can beat Brad in a one-on-one game, I'll crawl into the Legion Hall on my hands and knees and buy everyone there a drink."

"And if Brad wins?"

"Then you pay me $25."

"You've got yourself a bet."

We set the game for after work the next day.

Word got around and there must have been ten other construction guys there to watch.

The game was played to 11, counting by ones, and you had to win by two points. If you made a basket, your opponent got the ball. If you took a shot and the ball touched the backboard or the rim, your opponent had to bring it behind the free-throw line before he could shoot.

Brad was at least ten years younger than I was and he was a very good ball player, but he was shorter and didn't have near the heart.

I controlled the boards, and when the dust had settled, I had won 11 to 8.

Larry just shakes his head, then he says to me, "Do you wrestle?"

"I've never wrestled in the ring if that is what you mean."

"Well, I'll bet you five dollars Brad can pin you in three minutes."

"Is Brad a wrestler too?"

"He wrestled in high school and a little in college, but come on, you just won your bet, so give me a chance to win one of my own."

There was a wrestling mat on the floor in the corner of the gym.

I would guess that I outweighed Brad by ten or fifteen pounds, but I knew very little about college or high school wrestling. Once in high school, someone had shown me the starting positions, and I had wrestled for maybe a few minutes.

After about two minutes, it was absolutely obvious to everyone that there was no way Brad could pin me. The problem is, I got overconfident and decided I could pin him.

I was in complete control and had him in kind of a hammer lock in front of me. I wanted to roll him over, so I rolled over backwards and wound up on top of him.

As I rolled over, Larry slapped his hand on the mat, and said, "Pinned!"

Larry says, "It's over. You lose."

I jumped up and said, "What!"

He said, "Both of your shoulders touched the mat."

I cannot remember being more angry.

"He did not pin me!

"I was in control! I was trying to pin him. I thought you had to pin someone for three seconds."

Larry says, "No, you just have to pin someone for the count of one."

"He didn't pin me. I just rolled over."

Larry says, "What are you, a sore loser?"

Brad says, "He's right, Gary. In high school rules, that's a pin."

"Well, I didn't understand the rules. Let's do it again."

Larry says, "No way. Just pay up."

To this day, I am not sure if they were right, but I gathered my composure and paid him five dollars.

Then we went to the Legion bar, and Larry did crawl in on his hands and knees, and he bought everyone there a drink.

Grandfather's quote

If you are going to compete, compete
with all that is in you.

19

Wolf Hunting in Canada

When I was a young man, cold didn't bother me at all, and I was fascinated with winter camping. I kept track of the temperature and one night, when it was supposed to get down to 40° below zero, I took my goose down sleeping bag and slept out in the yard.

It's true—ask Grandma about it. She'll remember because she thought I was crazy!

There is a great book out there for those of you who want to know more about enjoying the wilderness in the winter. It is called *Paradise Below Zero* by Calvin Rutstrum.

I also have always been fascinated with wolves, so one winter I planned a wolf hunting trip on the Minnesota-Canadian border.

I had a lot of difficulty finding anyone willing to go along on this adventure, so I had to settle for someone who was unproven. I had never taken a trip with him before and didn't really know how he would hold up in the wilderness. That can be a very dangerous combination.

I don't even recall his name so for this writing, I will just call him Bob. He was a contractor that I did plumbing for. One day over lunch I was telling him about wanting to go wolf hunting and he seemed very interested. One thing led to another, and the two of us finally agreed to spend a week on a wolf hunt.

I wanted to go with just snowshoes and skis, but he would only agree to go if we took a snowmobile along. My choices were to go alone, to not go at all or to go with him and take a snowmobile. I decided to try it with him.

I had read a lot about winter camping, and I knew the snow would be very deep at this time of the year on the Minnesota-Canadian border. I also knew the lakes would be windswept and the snow there would be wind-packed, hard enough for a wolf to travel without sinking in. I don't even remember the exact place we went. I do remember talking to some conservation officers and finding out where a very high concentration of wolves were located.

I sent for some maps and made a list of supplies, and the two of us made tentative plans for the trip. We had to cover five or ten miles before we got back to a series of connected lakes. Once we got to the lakes, the snow was sure to be packed much harder than in the timber. Those conditions would make travel for the wolves possible and travel for us much easier too.

Once we got to where we were going to leave the vehicle, I knew right away that we were in trouble. The snow was so deep that when we stepped into it, we sunk almost to our armpits. It was obvious to me that the snowmobile would be almost useless. I wanted to leave it behind, but Bob would have none of it.

In order to use the snowmobile, we had to break trail with our snowshoes. The snowmobile's only value was that it carried most of our gear. As you can imagine, the going was very slow. Breaking trail with the snowshoes was very difficult. The man in front could only walk for a few hundred yards, and then the man on snowshoes behind him would have to take the lead.

Even though it was very hard work, the wilderness itself was awesome!

When the snow is that deep, it insulates all sound and when you stand still, you are surrounded by the sound of silence. Even the crunch of the snow under your snowshoes and the sound of your heavy breathing are muffled by all the snow insulation that surrounds you.

Then all of a sudden, out of the stillness, you will hear the sound of what you think is a rifle. Another tree has split from the tremendous cold.

I was still at that stage in my life that was summed up by the phrase "pride in the hard way," and I loved it!

When we had spent fully half of our daylight hours breaking trail, it was time to go back for the snowmobile. It only took about an hour to walk back over the trail that had taken us over three hours to make. When we got back to the snowmobile, we loaded all our gear onto the sled behind it and started out. We soon discovered that the snowmobile could not stay on the snowshoe trail and when it got off the trail, the machine bogged down hopelessly. We sank in the snow above our waists and it took us a lot of time to get the snowmobile and sled hauled back on the packed snow. We had to take off half the load and make two trips.

If we had come without the machine, we could have traveled much lighter. But my partner insisted on the snowmobile which allowed him to bring a lot more gear than I would have liked.

Over the years, the one thing I have learned about the wilderness is that you let her dictate your schedule. You must bend with her ebb and flow or you could break. And you must be prepared at all times to be at the mercy of her whims. Yes, we had planned to get to our campsite on the first day, but I knew we were not going to make it. We might not be able to return on the snowmobile and get the second load before dark, so I wanted to take all the gear necessary to spend the night on the trail. Bob argued with me and insisted we were going to be able to make the second trip. He was bothered by the fact that we weren't keeping our schedule. I insisted we bring the sleeping bags and some of the food on our first trip with the machine.

We had so much trouble staying on the trail that it was dark by the time we got halfway to our destination. Bob was grateful that I had insisted on bringing the food and sleeping bags.

I remember digging down to the forest floor in the snow. I was on a slight ridge under a pine tree, and it was only three feet down to the ground. I lined the bottom of my pit with pine boughs. We ate a cold dinner and went to bed. The temperature was 35° below zero.

In those early days, I always slept nude in my sleeping bag. At the crack of dawn, I climbed out of my bag and got dressed and built a fire. I waited until the water was hot before I woke Bob. We ate a cold breakfast along with hot tea, and then went back to get the rest of our gear. We made the trip back with an empty sled in about 15 minutes.

By the end of the second day, we reached our destination on the shore of the first of many in a long chain of lakes. We soon discovered that despite the below-zero temperatures, the lakeshore was all slush. You could walk across it fine on snowshoes, but the snowmobile got bogged down in it. Hallelujah! Bob agreed to shut the machine off and we never used it again until the day we left.

We made a comfortable camp that even had a tent and a small camp stove. The camp stove was very smelly, and after the first night, Bob couldn't keep it working. That too pleased me greatly.

I do not remember a whole lot more about the trip, other than the temperature never got above -10°. I also remember I set up a self-feeding fire with birch logs. Green birch made the hottest and longest lasting fire, but pine coals could not get green birch logs to burn. Instead, I had to start with small green birch sticks, and add bigger sticks, then small logs, into the pine coals. Once birch coals were created, green birch logs would burn.

I also learned on this trip not to sleep nude in a goose down sleeping bag. Even in those very cold temperatures, a person tends to sweat at night, and soon the goose down becomes wet. Once down is wet, it is about impossible to dry out in sub-zero temperatures. After the fourth day, I could no longer stay warm in my sleeping bag. After this trip, I had Irene put snaps on a wool blanket I put inside the goose down bag. Unlike the goose down, when the wool got wet, it was very easy to dry out, even in sub-zero temperatures.

We agreed to sleep during the day so we could be up all night, sitting motionless, looking for wolves. But in those frigid temperatures, we had to move every hour or so to warm up. We often heard them and saw their tracks but not one time did we see them. I am sure they saw us.

I also remember making homemade ice cream, and several hours after eating it, getting sick. I do not believe my sickness was in any way caused by the ice cream, but rather by not being able to stay warm while I was sleeping.

I don't even recall the trip out, perhaps because of the way I was feeling. I do remember my great surprise shortly after our return. Ron Sara, an outdoor writer for the Minneapolis Star and Tribune, had been camping within 20 miles of us at exactly the same time we were there. He wrote an extended article about his experiences, and they were almost exactly the opposite of mine. He wrote that the only time he could stay warm was when he was in his sleeping bag. In my case, the only time I was cold, after the first three sleeps, was when I was in my sleeping bag. I remember him saying he could not bare his fingers for even a short while, and yet I did all sorts of camp chores with no gloves on. Perhaps this was because I knew you had to eat a lot of fat to thicken your blood in order to help stay warm. I also knew the value of drinking lots of liquid in the form of hot tea. Plus, our birch fire truly gave off warmth, unlike what a fast-burning pine fire will do. We also had large rocks behind us that reflected the fire's heat that was in front of us. Whatever the reasons, I do remember my surprise at his article.

After reading his article, I wrote him a long letter telling him about my very different experiences, but I got no response.

Grandfather's quote

Achieving each and every goal you set is not what matters. What you learn and experience along the way is where the true value lies.

20

The Cadillac Dinner Story

In the early days of running my plumbing company, I got to know other contractors on the job. We sometimes played golf, softball or cards, and they often called me either the cowboy or the jock.

One year, Northfield had a stag event called the Cadillac dinner. It was mostly for contractors and their employees. One hundred guys paid $100 for the dinner, and in the past, a chance to win a Cadillac. Because Cadillacs had gotten so expensive, the grand prize that year was $4000 cash, and $100 to nine other ticket holders.

Most all of the contractors I worked with were going, and on the day of the dinner, I kept telling everyone that I was going to win. That evening before I left, I also told my wife I was sure I was going to win.

The entire evening, I kept telling everybody I was absolutely sure I was going to win.

Now the way that they decide on the winner is like this: Each ticket holder writes their name on a ticket and deposits it in a box. The MC draws nine tickets out of a box, which are all losers. The 10th ticket drawn wins $100. Also the 20th ticket, the 30th ticket and so on, until 99 tickets have been drawn. The one ticket left, the hundredth ticket, wins the $4000.

After the dinner was served, the MC got everyone's attention and started the drawing.

I happened to be sitting up close to the stage where the MC was doing the drawing, and as usual, I was wearing my cowboy hat. I had had a few beers and was razzing those around me about the fact that I was sure to win.

The MC kept drawing the tickets, and I kept talking about being a shoo-in to win. The fewer tickets that were left to be drawn, the more confident I became.

But on the 86th ticket drawn, they drew my ticket, and I was eliminated.

An electrical contractor and friend of mine named Jet was sitting right across from me and he was still in. I told him I would give him $500 for his ticket.

"Come on, Jet, sell me your ticket.

"I'll give you $500 for your ticket. They could draw you next and you get nothing.

"Put a sure $500 in your pocket.

"Somehow I'm going to win this thing, so you know you can't win, so you might as well sell me your ticket."

"Five hundred big ones."

The MC drew another ticket and another.

"Jet, you better sell it to me now or they will draw your ticket and you'll get nothing."

But Jet kept debating on whether to sell or not, and on the ninety-second draw, they pulled his ticket.

For the first time all night, I was quiet.

When only four tickets were left, the MC called the last four ticket holders up to the stage to explain the rules. If they all agreed, they each could take away $1000, but if one of them did not want to split, then he would have to draw another ticket.

One guy refused to take the split. The MC then asked the other three if any of them wanted to sell their ticket. And then he looked right at me and asked, "Hey cowboy, do you want to buy a ticket?" He must have heard me bragging all night about the fact that I was going to win.

"Sure," I said. "I'll buy a ticket."

"How much will you pay for a ticket?"

"I'll pay $500 for a ticket!"

The MC turned to the three. "Cowboy here will give you $500 for your ticket! Do any of you want to sell?"

He got no response, so he tried again.

"If I draw your name, you'll get nothing. If you sell your ticket to the cowboy here, you are assured of $500.

"Last chance!"

When once again he got no response, another ticket was drawn and now they were down to three.

"Alright you guys, do you want to split the $4000?"

The same holdout who refused the first split said no again.

"Cowboy, do you still want to buy a ticket?"

"You bet! I'll pay $500 for a ticket."

He turned to the other two ticket holders, "Cowboy here will still give you $500 for your ticket. If you don't take it, and I draw your name, you get nothing.

"Look what happened to the other guy. He didn't sell and he got absolutely nothing.

"Last chance! $500 in your pocket, what do you say?"

One of them, a young kid, couldn't take the tension and broke. He took my $500 and left the stage.

I was now back in.

The MC drew another ticket.

It was the ticket of the guy who would not split.

The MC looked at me and said, "That was the best $500 you ever spent. You've just won $2000."

I said, "No way. Draw the ticket."

"Wow! Cowboy here says to draw another ticket."

The MC reaches into the box, draws a ticket and looks right at me and says, "You could've had $2000."

A long pause.

"Now, you have $4000!"

I felt bad for the guy who wanted to split every time, so I told him that if he would not be offended, I would like to give him $100. And I did. I also bought a lot of drinks that night, but it was worth every bit of it. When I finally got home at about three a.m., I walked into our bedroom and started laying out $100 bills on my wife's tummy.

An absolutely true story.

Grandfather's quote

Always remember, you make your own luck in this life.

This is how I like to cook my dinners.

Rented 40-foot Morgan sailboat

21

Planning to Spend a Year on the South Pacific

I had daydreamed about sailing the South Pacific, so I decided to take a shakedown cruise with my family. If all went well, we would put everything else on hold and our family would spend one year sailing the South Pacific.

Luke was a junior, Tim was a sophomore and Matt was a freshman. I asked Luke to study celestial navigation, Tim to study diesel mechanics and Matt to study radio operation. I learned all about sailboats, and the terminology used on them.

I don't remember just how I did it, but I found some ads where people were renting their sailboats out. Then I found out how to line up a captain with experience.

I leased a 40-foot Morgan sailboat and lined up a captain for a two-week cruise in the Bahamas.

I even bought an old van so we could drive to Florida in comfort. We drove almost straight through and met the captain at the Miami residence of the sailboat owner. We had to sail from Miami to the Bahamas, which was scheduled to take most of the afternoon and the entire night. I told the captain that I wanted him to teach us all he could in the first couple of days so he could then be just an observer.

The sailboat had a diesel engine that powered all the electrical systems. All its navigation equipment was very modern, but it was powered by electricity supplied by the diesel engine. The lights and refrigerator were also run on electricity supplied by the diesel engine.

I was disappointed that the captain was relying upon the engine rather than just relying on the sails, but he said we needed to do so for the crossing. A few hours after sundown, the diesel engine quit, and we could not get it running again. The captain wanted to turn around and go back. I said, "No way, this was perfect!" Now, we would have a real test of the skills we would need to sail the South Pacific. I informed the captain that Luke had studied celestial navigation and he would navigate us to our site. The captain was skeptical but agreed to proceed, in part because some of the navigation instruments could be operated for a short time on batteries.

We sailed, with no mechanical support, the rest of the way to the Bahamas.

For many hours we saw nothing but stars and water. When the sun rose, Luke took a celestial fix on the Sun. When we finally sighted land, the captain could not believe it. Luke had put us within one mile of our exact location. He continued to navigate for us on the rest of the trip and the most he was ever off was a little less than five miles.

We all paid attention to what the captain was teaching us and it was quite easy to sail on open water, but sailing into a port was another matter.

When we sailed into the island where the port of entry was, we anchored and the captain went ashore to handle the affairs of entering a foreign country. Before he left, I asked him if we should move the boat because I noticed the tide going out. I knew if we didn't get out of there fairly soon, we would be aground. Maybe the captain was in a hurry and got careless, or didn't think I knew what I was talking about. He walked away saying don't worry about it.

Sure enough, the tide went out and we went aground. Now we were stuck there for several hours until the tide came back in. An interesting side note is that several Bahamian children just laid on the beach and watched us the entire time.

The time lost to the tide would have been acceptable, but during that time, we all went beachcombing and Irene stepped on a sea urchin. She hurt her foot quite seriously, and it bothered her for the rest of the trip. Having a sore foot and cooking in a kitchen with no lights, no fans and no refrigeration was not much fun. In retrospect, I wish I had assigned a rotation whereby all of us guys took an equal shift in the galley.

We as a family took over all the sailing duties soon after leaving the port of entry. I can specifically remember the first time that we sailed into a port without the captain's help. It was difficult, but it was fun and gratifying to know we could do it.

We did have a small dinghy on board with a 10-horse outboard motor. It got us out of trouble a couple of times. Once on our way into port, we were having trouble navigating through lots of other vessels with only the wind. The dinghy bailed us out.

Once we were becalmed in the middle of the ocean. We could not see land in any direction and there was absolutely no wind. We were enjoying the day, and all of the boys and I went snorkeling. Some dolphins came fairly close to us, and we were really enjoying ourselves. Then Matt dropped his mask to the bottom. Even though we could not see land in any direction, it was only about 20 feet deep. All of us were so intent on searching for the mask that we lost track of the sailboat, and the current had moved the boat away from us rather quickly. The next thing Irene noticed was that her entire family was in the water over a half a mile away from the boat. The captain had to put the dinghy in and come get us. No big deal to any of us guys, but it kind of shook up the boys' mom.

Another time Irene got pretty shook up was when we were anchored just outside of the inner reef along a deserted island. All but the captain swam to shore and had a great time exploring the deserted beaches and a little inland on the island. We lost track of the time and, when we tried to swim back to the sailboat, the tide was going out. It was very difficult getting back. Mark, being the youngest, was just barely able to make it. Irene was the only one of us who did not have fins along. She was losing ground and being pulled out to sea. I swam back after her and she put her arms around my neck, and then I turned and tried to swim to the boat. There must have been strong currents involved too because I could maintain my own, but I was barely making any headway.

The captain saw what was happening and told Matt to let out more anchor rope so the boat could get closer to us. When the boat got reasonably close, the boys threw the dinghy over the side and I was able to get to it. About the same time, Matt came to the end of the anchor rope—which had not been tied. I don't remember if he lost hold of the rope and sails had to be hastily put out or if everyone on board hung on to the untied rope.

In either case, no one could be worrying about us when the boat was about to go on the reef. I got Irene into the dinghy, but it was harder trying to make headway pulling her in the dinghy than it was with her on my shoulders. I dove to the bottom and tried to dig the dinghy's anchor in the sand. I remember figuring if I had to I could just climb in the dinghy and let the tide and current pull us out to sea. The boys could sail around all the reefs and pick us up on the open ocean. No big deal. Before that happened, they secured the anchor and someone was able to throw me a life preserver on the end of a rope. I exerted a monumental effort and managed to get to it. End of story.

To me, this was just another adventure and learning experience. To Irene, it was one more reason why she didn't want anything to do with sailing in the South Pacific.

Disregarding warnings that it was not safe to anchor by ourselves near deserted islands, we did so anyway. (There had been instances where modern day pirates had killed all aboard and stole people's boats.) Most nights we spent anchored out of sight of any other boats or lights of any kind. I always slept on deck, while the captain and the rest of the family slept below. I never could figure out why I couldn't get the boys to join me topside. Maybe my memory is failing me, and perhaps they did join me a time or two or even more often. I do remember how wonderful it was, sleeping under the stars. There were always enough ocean breezes to ward off any flies or mosquitoes, and the starry heavens were spectacular. Each morning I was awake before the sun broke the horizon. The first thing I did was dive in the water and swim to shore. I hiked along the deserted beaches for a while and then swam back to the boat.

The water in this area of the Bahamas was the warmest ocean water that I have ever been in. I felt like I was jumping into a warm bath tub, and I loved it.

I remember a couple of other adventures on this trip. One was the only cold day that I can remember. We had all our sails out and were running with the wind. All of us had our rain gear on. The seas were very rough, and we were being soaked by the seawater and the rain pouring down from the sky. I thought it was awesome and exhilarating, but I am afraid Irene may have looked at it a little differently.

I also remember losing the prop on our outboard motor and hiring a Bahamian to take us in his speedboat to Walker Cay. One of the boys and I rode along. It seemed as though he was going 90 miles an hour across the ocean. It was a lot of fun and one more adventure.

The trip was too soon over, and it was obvious Irene would never agree on an extended sailing trip anywhere, let alone crossing the Pacific. There was no way I would take such a trip without her, so it would be over 24 years before I went sailing on the ocean again.

Grandfather's quote

Experience your own adventures, not the adventures of others in some book or movie.

I lost my hat so I used leather rawhide.

22

Facing a Grizzly with a Knife and a Rock

The Bear and Elk Story

When I was younger, I was a man who enjoyed swimming upstream just for the pleasure of it. I had a saying, "Pride in the hard way." Many other men did not like going hunting or canoeing with me because I was always pushing the physical envelope.

When I lived in Alaska in 1965 and 1966, I spent many days with a pack on my back chasing after Dall sheep and grizzly bears. I slept where evening would find me. I actually had a few personal encounters with bears and heard many other bear stories, so I was not a complete *cheechako,* an Alaskan name for tenderfoot.

In one of my hunting experiences in Alaska, I met a homesteader who was living on a homestead over fifty miles from the nearest road. He knew I was after a Kodiak bear and said he could show me where one was. He guaranteed me the bear would make the Boone and Crockett record book. All I had to do was to pay him $1,000. If it didn't make it, I owed him nothing. NO THANK YOU!

I don't mind having someone show me the lay of the land or give me some advice, but I wanted to earn my trophy.

When I went after my first elk, I wanted to do it myself. If I had to do it over again, or for those of you who would rather not use a guide, I recommend you get someone to pack you in, and pack you and your game out. Let them tell you about the country and give you some advice. If you do it entirely on your own as I did, you will need several days to familiarize yourself with the country. And the horses will add to your work and take away from your hunting time.

I was still living in Minnesota at the time of this, my first elk hunt, and I wanted to hunt an area as remote as possible. After extensive research, I chose the Bob Marshall wilderness area of Montana. I called the ranger there and asked him if I could hunt in an area completely away from all other hunters, and he said that I could.

I have been on many hunting and fishing trips into the wilderness, so I was very familiar with the kind of gear and outfit I would need. I will say here that the most important thing you can take with you is the right companion. I chose Rick Buss, a contractor friend of mine. He was an athlete and outdoorsman, a man who could handle the rigorous type of hunting I so enjoyed.

Rick was newly married, and when I talked to him and his wife, she was somewhat concerned. I assured her Rick would be in the best of company. If any accident should befall him, he could have no one better to care for him or get him out. If I had stopped right there, I would not have gotten in trouble, but I added something partly in jest. I told her that I had planned this trip for too long so if by some misfortune he were killed, I would just put some dirt over him and finish my hunt. I would bring the body out when the hunt was over. She did not take that too well, but fortunately Rick was still able to go.

I knew a rancher in Sheridan, Wyoming, and we hauled two of our horses that far the first evening and laid over there for the night. The next morning we borrowed two of his horses and drove from there to Hungry Horse on the northwest side of the Bob Marshall wilderness areas. From Hungry Horse we drove about 55 miles of gravel to the Meadow Creek trailhead. We spent the evening in the parking area and figured we would start out at the crack of dawn.

On the ride in I was really shocked, surprised and disappointed by the well-used trails along the river. They even had emergency battery-powered telephones at different places. Most all of the side trails were marked with signs, like street signs in a suburb. What had I gotten myself into? Several hours along the trail brought us to the Helen Creek trail, marked by a street sign. It was the one the Ranger told me would take us back into an area that was very remote. I still had my doubts, but the further we got away from the main trail, the more the trail we were riding on began to fade.

We each were riding a horse and leading a packhorse behind us. I was told I could not count on enough grazing for our horses, so one horse was carrying over 250 pounds of high-protein horse pellets. I didn't have a lot of experience packing horses up to that time, and found out that a horse carrying dead weight gets tired more easily than a horse carrying a much heavier man. Perhaps the horse being from Minnesota had something to do with it. After about eight hours on the trail, he just laid down on his stomach. We unloaded the horse and spent the night right there.

The next morning, on our way up the mountain, we came to a place where the trail was only about thirty inches wide and dropped straight down several hundred feet. On the upper side of the trail was a very steep embankment. The horses kept walking on the outside of the trail, giving me quite a view of the drop-off. It made me a little nervous. Actually, if I had thought about it, it was the safest place to be. If the horse had gotten too close to the embankment, on the uphill side, he could have bumped his pack and perhaps gotten pushed over. It was my first experience with narrow trails and horses and steep drop-offs.

We had some very good topo maps, got to where the maps showed the last spring, and decided to make camp there. We were at about 9,000 feet, and the rim of the mountain was perhaps another thousand feet up.

We set up our camp and staked out the horses. We then scouted on foot, because the last thousand feet up did not appear as though a horse could even make it. We could not find any water further up the mountain, so this became our permanent base camp.

In order to get to the top of the mountain by daylight, we had to get up at three a.m. We had to water the horses and stake them out for the day, eat breakfast, and then start our climb. By the time we got to the

The look of a mountain man, and how I see myself

top we were soaked in sweat, but we carried extra shirts so we could change into a dry one after our climb.

I had learned in Alaska that you can learn new country much more quickly from the mountain tops. Once on top, you could walk the hogbacks and cover a lot of country.

Our aim was to spend as much time as necessary just getting to know the lay of the land and trying to find where the elk were. We always stayed out until dark caught up with us, wherever that may have been. The first few days we stayed together. By the time we walked back to the mountain peak above our camp and climbed down in the dark, it was very late.

We had to take care of our horses each evening, dry out our clothing and prepare and eat dinner. It was usually 11 p.m. by the time we crawled into our sleeping bags.

Moving our picket line for the horses each day and trying to get them enough feed was a job we would rather not have had. We could not ride the horses along the mountain peaks we traversed by foot. A horse between our legs would have saved a lot of walking, but we would have had to be well below the peaks. A man on foot and on top of the mountain can cover more country than a man on horseback lower down.

About the third day out, upon returning to camp, we discovered we were missing a horse. The next day Rick went back up the mountain while I went looking for the horse. When I finally caught up to him, he was down the trail past the sheer cliffs. I had only brought headgear for the horse, so I had to ride him bareback. By this time I was comfortable enough with the horse and the trail that even bareback riding along those sheer cliffs didn't bother me.

The country was magnificently beautiful and we were truly alone. We saw no sign of other hunters and many a morning we looked at the valley below us, completely socked in by clouds. We smiled about the hunters who must have been there and couldn't see a thing. On the morning of our ninth day at about 7 a.m., I heard an elk bugle. I followed the sound for over an hour and got on a mountain top where I could look down below and see several bull elk among a large herd.

They were well out of rifle range and it appeared that they were just leaving the grassy open meadow for the timber. I just watched them with the binoculars. When they had all disappeared into the timber, I left and went to see if I could find Rick. I found him, and the two of us got back to the spot during the late afternoon. We climbed down the mountain a ways to put us into gun range should the elk come back out at dusk. We put the sun to rest, but they never reappeared.

The next morning we were back at that spot right at sunrise. The elk had come back to an open meadow below us, but they were now lower down than before. They were once again out of range. An interesting footnote was that Rick, although only thirty feet from me, never heard any elk bugling and I could hear them like they were sitting in my lap. The mountains will sometimes do that to you. I assumed he was hearing and seeing the same thing I was, and he was not.

Once again I watched the elk move out of the meadow and then crawled over to Rick. He was very surprised. He hadn't seen or heard a thing. We made a very long, quiet descent, putting us within three or four hundred yards of the meadow they had disappeared out of, and we waited all day. The elk never returned.

Rick was really disappointed, having not seen or heard anything. He told me that when we went back, he was going to be my shadow.

The next morning at daylight, Rick was right by my side and we both could see and hear the elk. There was one very big bull among the herd, but once again they were even lower than before and we estimated the range to be about 700 yards. The rifle I was shooting was a 264 and it was right on at 300 yards. The angle of descent was over 45 degrees.

I had to decide how high above the elk to put the rifle's crosshairs.

We both knew we could not move any closer from where we were without being seen, and I felt confident in my rifle. I braced myself on a rock and held the crosshairs right on the top of his back. When he moved into a position that presented a broadside shot, I squeezed the trigger. He took two steps behind a pine tree and either fell to the ground, stopped, or turned and walked directly away because he never came out the other side.

I told Rick that if I had missed, it was because I had not held high enough. He wanted me to help him shoot his elk, so he shot and then I shot. Both of us were now holding about a foot above the elk. In just a matter of seconds they disappeared and none we knew of were hit.

Rick stayed there and marked the pine tree that my bull had stepped behind and I worked my way down the mountain.

On the way to where I had shot the elk, I had to go through some very heavy timber and found myself face to face with a small bull elk. He was less than thirty yards away. I could see nothing in my scope but hair, but because he was so close I felt quite confident and took the shot. There was blood all over and I took off my scarf and marked the spot of impact. I trailed him for a short time, then went to where I shot at my first elk. I did not want Rick to leave his observation point because of the shot I had just taken.

Rick stayed put even after hearing my shots. He directed me to the tree, and there was a magnificent bull shot through the back bone. Assuming no human error, the bullet had only dropped three or four inches.

By the time Rick got down to me, I had the bull gutted and skinned and was caping him out. As soon as that job was done, we went back to my scarf and started tracking the other elk. We spent most of the rest of the day and finally had to give up for lack of blood.

In order to get my elk off the mountain, we had to pack him back to the top and then along the ridges to a big rock slide. From there we could slide down to the bottom of the rock slide, a place our horses could get to.

Each leg of our journey took three round trips by each of us. We took one quarter each on the first two trips, and on the third trip I packed out the rack and Rick packed out the cape. We got everything to the top of the mountain and made our first two round trips to the top of the rock slide. We had left the rifles at the top of the rock slide

Me walking back to camp

on the first trip. When the second trip was completed, all four quarters were there.

Upon returning for the cape and rack, we found the cape missing and a few bear tracks in the snow.

It was now very close to sunset and there was no time to go back for the rifles. I told Rick I was going after the bear. I had waited too long and worked too hard to have some damn bear steal my cape. Rick had a few choice words about my sanity and said he would wait right there.

There were just enough patches of snow that it allowed me to follow the trail quite easily. I was not too far down the mountain from Rick when I first saw the grizzly. I put my knife in one hand and grabbed a rock with the other.

I yelled, hopefully loud enough for Rick to hear, "I see the bear." When I yelled the second time, "It's a grizzly," another bear stood up behind the first. Rick had a few more choice words about my sanity, and I proceeded to go after my cape.

From my long experience in the wild and my experiences with bears in Alaska, I knew if the bear is not cornered or is not protecting its young, the biggest bluff usually dominates. I knew a forty-pound wolverine could back a thousand-pound bear away from a fresh kill just because he acts so furious.

I started yelling at those bears at the top of my lungs in my meanest voice, and I do have a loud, deep, mean voice.

For the second time in my life I saw the hair stand straight up on the back of a grizzly and it certainly got my attention. The bears were standing on their hind legs, swatting at the air and foaming at the mouth.

I kept slowly moving towards them, swatting at the air and trying to sound meaner than them.

I got close enough to where I could start throwing rocks at them, and on the third rock I hit one of the bears in the head. He dropped on all fours and headed down the mountain with his companion right behind him.

I went over and grabbed the cape and put it around my neck and started up the mountain. When I got back to Rick out of breath, I said, "Watch my backside."

Rick's eyes got big, and he said, "What do you mean, watch your backside?"

I said that you don't take anything away from a grizzly and that they would be back.

We had to go through some heavy timber on the way back to the rifles, and it brought some anxious moments.

We got back to the rifles with no further sign of the bears. It was definitely twilight now.

We each tied two quarters together, and I put the rack on my back and carried my rifle in my hand. I was holding the rope tied between the two quarters and I let gravity pull me down the rock slide.

Rick had the cape on his backpack and his rifle in his hands and was doing likewise with his two quarters.

About halfway down the mountain we came to two 8-foot cliffs. I dropped all four quarters over the first cliff and climbed down. When I looked up at Rick looking over the cliff, a grizzly was less than three feet behind him.

I yelled, "Rick, jump! There's a bear!"

He jumped down, and now we were looking up at two grizzlies looking down at us.

It was a cloudy evening, and we were still several hours from camp. If we were going to shoot these bears, we had to shoot them at the same time and we had to make sure we killed them both. I didn't really want a wounded grizzly coming after me in the dark, and I thought we should just try to scare them away.

Rick agreed.

I fired three shots, one so close I was afraid I had hit the bear's nose, and they acted like nothing had happened. I told Rick I couldn't figure this one out, but I was not about to give up my cape.

I would share my elk meat though. So we lowered the four quarters over the next cliff and left it. We climbed down ourselves and proceeded down the mountain. I figured we could return in the morning and get what was left of the elk meat.

It was now so dark I could not see the fingers on my hand, but I was sure the bears were back up the rock slide dining on elk.

Wrong!

The bears could not climb over the cliffs, and when they circled them, they came out below the elk meat and picked up our trail instead. The first thing we heard was the deep breathing of two very close grizzlies. Rick jumped forward and bumped into me and knocked me down.

I scrambled to my feet, yelling and trying to sound mean, while scratching at the same time below me at loose wood that was there. We were now at the bottom of the rock slide, and there was a lot of loose wood. I built the fastest fire that I have ever built in my life.

We had not seen the grizzlies up to this point, but you could continually hear them walking or breathing.

By this time Rick's anger was worked up and when I asked him if I should consider giving up the cape he said, "No way!"

I said, "Tangling with a bear is one thing but I don't want to tangle with your .30-06 so be careful."

One footnote worth sharing is that, whenever I watched a movie where the soldier was on watch knowing Indians may be sneaking up on his camp, it often showed him as falling asleep. I thought that was very unrealistic. How could a man in imminent danger fall asleep on guard? Now I know how. Push yourself to the limit for twelve days on very little sleep and then try to stay awake by a campfire with grizzlies circling you.

We took shifts staying awake and the bears never came into sight.

About 2 a.m. on my watch, I could tell the bears were getting restless and just as I woke Rick, the bears came in on a charge. We both fired shots in the air and yelled as loud and as mean as we could. I grabbed a burning stick and threw it at the now very close bear. When he turned and ran, I ran after him, making very loud, angry noises. I did not go very far and was never out of the firelight, but it was far enough.

My first elk

We never heard the bears again, and about an hour later the cloud cover began to break. We found a large pine tree, and I climbed up it and left the cape there. We then went back to camp by the light of the moon. When we returned with the horses the next day, there was no sign of the bears and the elk meat was missing. I followed the trail and found all four quarters buried and partly eaten. Obviously, when we had at last driven the bears off, they had backtracked and found their elk steaks.

I asked Rick that morning if he wanted to go get his elk. I already had mine, so I felt this was his choice. He said, "No way, let's get the hell off the mountain."

By the time we cleaned up the meat a little and got it securely packed on the horses, it was past noon but we started out anyway. I knew we would be riding in the dark and would have to go over those narrow trails by the steep cliffs in the dark.

When night truly descended, I could not even see the ears on my horse's head, but I knew from experience the horse could see. The only real danger would be a spooked horse, so we sang songs to alert any wild creatures to get the hell out of there before we arrived. Hey, if my singing will drive away people, it certainly ought to drive away little wild creatures. Our horses did a super job of getting us off that mountain, but I did not appropriately reward them. In fact, I got in the most serious trouble of the trip upon reaching our vehicles.

I was tired and could not untie the rope from my pack horse—which was tied to the tail of my wife's horse—so I cut his tail off.

To show you how much trouble I was in, I will tell you what my wife related before the trip. She imagined if we didn't return on time that she might have to call the ranger at the Bob Marshall Wilderness area.

In her little scenario, she asked the ranger about her horse and he asked her in return, "How did your horse get here?" She would answer, "Oh, my husband was missing too."

My rack was not a Boone and Crockett one, but the taxidermist had never seen an elk head as big as mine. This old bull had lived long enough that his rack was starting to get smaller. The bears had torn the lower lip of the cape and eaten off one ear, but my taxidermist found another ear and did a good sewing job. Now I have something much more important than a Boone and Crockett trophy. I have an experience of a lifetime, and a story that I can pass on to my grandchildren.

Grandfather's Quote

Though I walk through the
valley of death, I fear no evil
because I am the meanest sounding
son of a bitch in the valley.

Rick and me on the way home

Entrance to our 7 Arrows Ranch and beginning of our six-mile long driveway

23

Colorado

When Irene and I left Alaska in 1967, we agreed we would compromise between Alaska and Minnesota, and someday we would own a working cattle ranch out west.

The problem was by the time we could afford a ranch, we were living on our own 200 acres, on the shores of our own private lake, and in a log home we designed and built ourselves. We had our own private handball-racquetball court, we belonged to an athletic club and we drove a Cadillac. Needless to say, Irene was not thrilled about giving all this up and moving to some remote ranch out west. But she did not stop me from looking or tell me she had changed her mind and would not move.

I started looking for ranches, but for each one I found, Irene found some reason not to go there.

We did look at one ranch in Klamath Falls, Oregon. I went out first and had Irene fly out and join me to look at it, but that's another story.

When I found a ranch in Westcliffe, Colorado, and took Irene out to look at it, she said she was willing to try this place. I knew I could not have a working cow-calf ranch at these high elevations. I would just have to find something else to do for a living.

Westcliffe was the best-kept secret in the entire state of Colorado. It parallels the beauty of the Grand Tetons in Wyoming, and the amount of wildlife there was phenomenal. I decided that I would be a guide and outfitter and take people on hunting and fishing trips in the mountains. Heck, I figured that was even closer to what I always wanted than running a cattle ranch.

Irene's only stipulation was that we try it for a couple of years, and I would look for another place if she was not happy there.

I agreed.

Westcliffe is at the base of the Sangre De Cristo Mountains and was too high for rattlesnakes or mosquitoes. Sangre De Cristo means the blood of Christ in Spanish. The mountains got their name because when the sun rises, the snow on the peaks turns pink. As the sun gets higher in the sky, the pink appears to slowly move, or flow down the mountain. The Spaniards said it was the blood of Christ flowing down the mountains.

The snow remains on the 14,000-foot peaks eleven months a year, and the constant breeze coming down the mountain keeps it cool all summer long. Summers are not only cool but short. Usually even the valley gets a heavy snow by the middle of September, and snow often remains until mid-May. It even snowed a little on the Fourth of July when we were there.

The air always seems to be fresh and clean. Each summer afternoon seems to get a 20-minute shower that makes everything feel brand new and alive.

The Catholic church there was much smaller than even New Market, perhaps having only a dozen or so families. The priest was an older man and understood the weather at those elevations. He was often surprised that we had managed to make it to Mass in spite of the weather and roads. He kept assuring us that it would be okay to have a home service.

When Irene agreed to move to Westcliffe, we were still contemplating which of two ranches we might buy. Now, I never made a unilateral decision, but Irene was always trying to please me and I was very good at talking her into things.

I should have known better than to buy a ranch that was ten miles from our nearest year-round neighbor and had no electricity or telephone. But it sure was spectacularly beautiful. The 480 acres bordered the San Isabel National Forest and sat at the base of the mountains, the beauty of which was out of this world. It was mostly timbered, in the middle of elk, bear and lion country. Just to the west of the ranch was Music Pass and a series of mountain lakes among the 14,000 foot peaks. Over the pass about an eight-hour horseback ride are Colorado's Great Sand Dunes. Among the peaks themselves were the highest, most dangerous caves in all of Colorado, the Spanish Caves.

The ranch had a small five-room cabin, an old outbuilding, a good spring, some small corrals, and exterior fencing around it.

We sold our place in Minnesota, which I never seemed to have much difficulty doing, and packed up for Colorado.

I first went to Westcliffe with Todd Aldrich, a handball playing buddy who had a young man named Duke that worked for him. Duke later agreed to help us move to Colorado and stay for a while.

I bought a British Land Rover station wagon that we could fill with our belongings, which Duke would drive to Colorado. We put our Honda on the back of my one-ton flatbed truck and filled it with more of our belongings. Lastly we had a 3/4 ton pickup that we pulled a horse trailer behind. The front half was packed full of belongings, and the back half carried two horses.

With Irene, Duke and I all planning to drive, we packed in the four kids, two horses and a dog and headed down the road.

For the second time in our lives we were heading to a new state with no job lined up, no friends or acquaintances there and Irene trusting her man to make it all work. But this time we had a steady source of income from contract for deeds on land that I had sold prior to moving.

The first time we had pulled our home behind us to Alaska. This time we were moving to a small five-room cabin with no electricity or running water, and with the intent of building a new home.

Arriving on our ranch after driving up our six-mile long driveway.

Original cabin and bunkhouse

On the trip out there, the Land Rover overheated, and Duke did not immediately shut it down. The engine blew up, and we had to leave it and all of the belongings that we had in it, in some town in the middle of nowhere. Within a month, we returned and towed it back to the ranch.

The driveway to our new ranch left the highway 16 miles south of Westcliffe. Then we drove on our six-mile-long driveway to get to our cabin. I had to break a lock on a steel gate about a mile from the cabin in order to get by. When we got to the cabin, it too was locked, and I wound up breaking a small window and having Mark, our smallest boy, crawl through and let us in.

There was a small outbuilding or shed, the ruins of another one, and of course we had an outhouse. There was a spring about a quarter of a mile up the mountain that flowed a gallon a minute.

Within the first week the boys and I built a triple set of bunk beds, a new set of corrals, and ran a water line from the spring down to the cabin. I purchased a propane tank and propane hot water heater that we set up outside of the cabin. We also built an outhouse that was truly out. You could sit on it and see miles down the driveway. You had plenty of time to get your pants up if someone was coming.

I also bought a stock tank that we could take baths in. Irene always got the first bath. As a guy, if you were lucky you got the second bath. If you were unlucky, you got the seventh bath. The rotation changed each time, and needless to say, when you were in the last three positions you usually just skipped your bath.

At first we took our baths outside. Even in the summertime, at 9200-foot elevation, the temperature almost always got below 50° once the sun went down, so most of our baths were taken in the daylight.

Irene would always let us know when she was about to take her bath and we all found jobs to do away from the cabin. No one was allowed to return for at least a half hour. Then one day during her bath time I heard her scream. I ran back to the cabin and up rides a neighboring cowboy. I threw Irene a towel and met him before he got up to the beautiful and embarrassed blonde in the horse tank.

Outhouse

The family bathtub for the first year. Matt, Mark and Tim

What can I say? If I were out checking fence line, rode up on a ridge, looked down and saw a beautiful blond sitting in a horse tank, I would have to ride down to say howdy too.

That was the end of the outdoor baths. The bathtub got moved inside.

Soon we owned a generator, and our washer and dryer were moved into the room with the bathtub. I wired the cabin up with a few outlets and lights, but I hated the sound of the generator so much that we usually went to bed when the sun went down. Duke soon left us and all four of the boys were in a small bedroom only eight feet square.

Irene and I had our own bedroom. We had the living room and a small kitchen, along with what was now turned into a laundry bathtub room.

Irene didn't like the outhouse much and would not go there without taking the dog along, but we never did get a toilet in the cabin.

It wasn't very long before we purchased a CB radio. Most everyone in the valley had them, and soon we were part of the network. You could call someone who had a landline and ask them to make a call for you, and they always seemed happy to oblige.

Irene applied for a teaching job at the school and the boys joined 4-H. Even in the summertime the school would have dances and there we got to know more of the people in the Valley. They were the best dances that I have ever been to before or since. They weren't for middle schoolers, high schoolers or adults. They were for the entire family. Most of the Valley families came. If they had infants, they put them on blankets. A family member or neighbor watched them while mom and dad were dancing. All country-western music, all family, and all fun.

At one of these dances I remember getting only one dance in five because I had to share Irene with each of her sons. Halfway through the evening a couple came over and introduced themselves. They had been watching and noticed our predicament. They had four daughters about the same ages as our four boys, so we introduced them. From then on the boys danced the night away, and I had their mother to myself.

At the ranch our days began at sun up and by the time it was getting dark we were finishing up the dinner dishes. The cabin was so small that if you wanted any time alone, you had to take a walk outdoors. If it was your night to do dishes, you were still in on all the conversations. We truly interacted as a family and I loved it.

We had a battery-powered radio, and many evenings after dishes, cards and family conversations, we would listen to Mystery Theater on WCCO radio all the way from Minneapolis, Minnesota.

Before long, we started building our new home. Within a year we moved in. But the time spent as a family in the small cabin was one of the most enjoyable times of my entire life.

I am not sure that my best friend and partner felt the same way. In fact, on our first Christmas, our new generator went out. We had no electricity and no Christmas tree lights. Irene told me that since she lived in the middle of nowhere for me, I ought to be able to bring her electricity no matter what the cost. I agreed. Before our new home was completed, I paid $20,000 and brought in electricity.

Shortly after starting our new home, my dad, my brother, Brent and a friend of his named Mark Hoagland (Hoag) came out for a visit. Before they left, I tried to get my brother to agree to come spend a year with us on the ranch and help us build our new home. However, he had a girlfriend back home and was not about to leave her, but Hoag said that he would like to come back and spend a year with us.

We turned a portion of our outbuilding into real nice living quarters for Hoag. We were, once again, seven.

I found out what was required in order to become a professional guide and outfitter and I easily fulfilled all the requirements. From my first trip at age 15, to my time spent in Alaska, through all my time spent hunting or fishing, my entire life had prepared me for this. The written exam and whatever else was required was a breeze, and soon I had my professional guide and outfitter's license.

About this time I made friends with Gary Zigler, who owned and operated Bear Basin Ranch. He also took people river rafting on the

Arkansas River. Within a short time he had me occasionally captaining rafts shooting down the Arkansas River.

We purchased several more horses and started taking people on riding trips in the mountains. The boys were my wranglers. They would catch and saddle horses and go along on the trail rides. On one occasion, we took about eight or ten girls who were all in high school. They were so impressed with my sons, and even though the boys were several years younger, they wrote letters to one another for some time afterwards.

When the boys weren't helping me, they were often hiking in the mountains. They liked to go fishing in a stream behind the ranch.

On one memorable occasion the boys took a young lad from out of state, who was about their age hiking in the mountains and lost him. Fortunately about an hour and a half later, a cowboy rode up over the hill asking us if we had lost someone. Then there was the time that my brother, Jay, came out to visit. He had never ridden a horse before, so we put him on Digger. We assured him that this horse was absolutely foolproof. Then we rode up the hill just north of the headquarters and as we crested the top, a silver streak flashed by, followed by the sound of the jet. The plane could not have been more than 100 feet above the top of the hill and even seemed to have come from below it on the other side. Digger turned around and ran full blast back to the corrals. Jay managed to hang on, but needless to say that ended that city boy's riding days.

The summers were full and pleasant, but winter could be quite another matter. Several months after buying the ranch, we found out that our mountain was called Blizzardeen because of the severe winter storms there. One time we got three feet of snow in a 24-hour period. Any winter day that the sun shined, which was most of them, the temperature would get up to 50°, but at night it could often be 30° below. The temperature could make eighty degree swings within a 24-hour period. What that did to the snowdrifts was remarkable. They would thaw during the day and freeze at night. Soon they got so hard you

Luke, Tim and me with neighbors, beginning new house

Our new Colorado home

could drive a 4-wheel drive over the top of rolling snowdrifts twelve feet high!

The wind could blow up to 100 miles an hour. One time while Irene was outside, the wind snapped a pine tree in half fairly close to her. The tree was over eighteen inches in diameter. She came in crying and I asked her what she was doing outside when the wind was blowing like that. She told me the wind was always blowing, and she just didn't pay any attention to it.

One Sunday we were going to Mass and got stuck about a mile down the driveway. The wind was so strong that you had to bend way over to brace yourself against it as you were walking uphill back to the house. Mark was the youngest and was having a lot of trouble, so I put him on my back and carried him to the house. Irene had not followed, so I went back to get her. She was kneeling in the driveway, exhausted. I asked her why she had quit and she told me that she was just too tired to go on. I asked her what she would have done if I hadn't been there to come back and get her. I took her hand and helped her back to the house.

Then there was the time when the whole family was in town except for Irene, and we got hit with a big snowstorm. The driveway was impassable for several days, and Irene was snowbound by herself. When she couldn't stand it any longer, she called the neighbors on the CB and asked them to reach me and let me know she was cross-country skiing to the highway.

When my appendix burst, Irene had to drive me almost two hours to the nearest hospital, and she had a flat tire along the way. It would not have been unusual for a long time to pass before anyone else came along, so she just changed the tire herself. You learned very quickly to be self-sufficient living in the remote valley, but everyone considered themselves neighbors and were truly amazing. It reminded me of the people in Alaska—old school people who are always more than willing to help each other out.

When the whole family got sick while still living in the cabin, the people who owned the motel in town heard about it via the CB network. They insisted we all come to town and stay there so we would have constant heat and indoor plumbing.

When the boys first started school, we realized it would not be a good idea for them to be let off the bus at the end of our six-mile long driveway. I talked to the sheriff and with his approval Luke at age twelve began driving the Land Rover to the highway, and then the boys got on the bus. The Land Rover had a CB in it, so if there was ever any problem, they could call the house or even a neighbor. And the bus driver made sure the Land Rover started before he left them.

Once the boys started school, they made many new friends, including the Bray boys. It turns out that their father was a contractor and soon our entire families became good friends. Don, their father, helped me on more than a few things while building our new home.

There were many hunting, cave, and bear adventures in them there mountains, but I will save those for another story.

Irene was unable to get a full-time job teaching and the boys and I were enjoying this type of life so much that we didn't realize how miserable she truly was until I received the letter. Hey, that sounds familiar.

Riding home in the rain. Matt on the ground, Tim, Mark, Luke and Mom

The letter this time was from the father of a friend of mine. My friend had been killed in an automobile accident. His father wanted to know if I might be interested in buying the athletic club his son had built.

In Alaska, Irene and I had talked about building an athletic club. I even went to a banker and asked about borrowing money to do so, but was turned down. Now over ten years later we were being offered one at what seemed to be a very reasonable price.

No way were I or the boys ready to leave this man's paradise. But when I saw the change that came over Irene with just the possibility that she might be able to move back to Minnesota, my heart was moved. I can still see her standing in the bedroom in the loft as the glow came over her while I read the letter.

She hadn't said anything about moving, but we had agreed on a two-year trial period. When I saw her light up like a Christmas tree, I realized this was my Irene. Over the next few days, as we talked about it, I realized how truly unhappy she had really been.

What could I do?

We had a family meeting and told the boys what we were thinking and reluctantly got their approval. That approval was partly obtained because I promised that someday we would also own property in British Columbia. I never did fulfill that promise, and to this day I still feel guilty about that.

It seems that whenever I break trail, so to speak, a friend follows and then when I leave the friend stays on. After I moved to Colorado, Todd Aldrich followed and the two of us, along with new friend Ed Yaklich, even built a handball court in the town of Westcliffe. It was the highest handball court in the nation elevation-wise, so we called it the Supreme Court. After I left, Todd stayed on and eventually became mayor of Westcliffe.

Grandfather's Quote

Follow your dreams wherever they may lead,
for life's journey is over in but a moment.

24

Spanish Cave

A Family Adventure

When we lived in Colorado, we lived on a remote ranch at 9,200 feet elevation. The highest, most dangerous caves in Colorado were higher than that, and about five miles away. The entrances to the caves were covered by snow for all but four to six weeks a year.

I had been to the caves a few weeks before I took my boys. In order to get into the caves you either rappelled 150 feet down a rope at one entrance or entered through a much smaller opening that did not require a rope. I figured the older three boys could handle and enjoy the trip. At the time, the boys were about 12, 11 and 10.

In our tack shed we had fifteen saddles and bridles for the fifteen horses we had, and each of us had our favorite horse. We allowed the horses to run free on our lower pasture, which contained about two hundred acres, but we had trained them to come to a whistle. Once gathered and saddled, we rode across the ranch and into the San Isabel National Forest. We crossed a large valley and rode up what is called Music Pass. If you rode over the top and down the other side, you would come to the Sand Dunes. But we veered off to the north before reaching the top of the pass. From there we rode the horses as close to the caves as we could. We tied the horses on a line and made the grueling hike up another thousand feet or so to the entrance of the cave. We all had flashlights and started into the cave on our hands and knees.

Soon we were at a spot that you could only get through by dragging yourself on your belly. It took a while to get in, and when we finally made it, we were dirty and full of mud.

Marble Cave was large enough to hold a small house, and it had writing all over the walls. I have never understood that sort of thing, so we didn't leave our "Friendshuh was here" with a date like many others did. We spent a lot of time looking for other passages, but never found one. As we explored for several hours, I told stories about how the caves got their name from the conquistadors who supposedly had hidden gold there. I told them how some of the old-timers say that at night you can see lights on the mountain by the caves. These lights were supposed to have been the lights used by the ghosts of the Spaniards.

All in all, it was a grueling 14-hour day, full of excitement and adventure for my sons. I just didn't know how much of an effect it had upon them until that night.

One of the older two talked in his sleep continuously. The other one kept yelling out something, and must have yelled at least nine or ten times throughout the night. Matt walked in his sleep several times, and once even walked right past us out the front door. Luckily we were awake and could turn him around and head him back to bed.

These caves caused yet another sleepless night. Some time later I had gone to the caves by myself or maybe with Hoag, and we had run into a couple of cavers there. They had long hair and looked like hippies. We talked a lot about the caves, and afterwards I invited them back to the ranch. Irene didn't really mind a couple of extra mouths to feed at dinner, but when I offered them a place to sleep I hadn't noticed her reaction. It was not until we went to bed when she asked me what I really knew about these two guys. Then she asked, "What if they are a couple of crazies and slit our or our children's throats during the middle of the night?"

I have always trusted people, but her concerns caused me to lose a little sleep myself that night.

Grandfather's Quote

Life should be an adventure even for the very young.

Me heading into the mountains

25

A Colorado Guide and Outfitter

Before moving on to the athletic club I will tell you about being a Colorado guide and outfitter and a few other stories about our time in them there mountains.

There were several things about being an outfitter that I really loved.

I could buy horses, tack, binoculars, guns, ammunition, and all the other things that every hunter loves buying, and it was all tax deductible.

I learned to love the mountains. The high elevations didn't bother me or Hoag, the young man living on the ranch, at all. We could put a client on a horse, and either one of us could hike up the mountain faster than the horse carrying the client and his gear.

Hoag turned out to be a great wrangler, and my boys were great help. And the boys learned a lot about living in the outback.

Some great stories came out of living as an outfitter. For instance, Hoag was good help, but he did lose some clients one time. It seems that Todd Aldridge, a friend from Minnesota, had told some of his friends that if they drove out, I would take them elk hunting. They never called or asked beforehand. They just showed up one day. There was no way that I could take them, and I told them that Hoag was not a guide yet.

Me taking a pack horse into the mountains

I did offer to help them out by renting them a couple of horses and told them that Hoag would go with them up the mountain. He could show them the lay of the land and stay with the horses while they went hunting.

That evening Hoag came riding back to the ranch after midnight, woke me up and told me that he lost the hunters.

"Lost the hunters! What the hell does that mean?"

"I took them up the mountain and stayed with the horses as they went off looking for elk. They were supposed to come back before sunset, but they never did. Just before the sun went down, I built a big fire and fired a few shots but got no response. When it got dark, I made the fire even bigger and fired a couple of more shots in hopes they would find me. Finally, when it became obvious that they were not coming back, I rode back to the ranch."

"Well, there is no sense going up the mountain in the dark. Go to bed and I'll get you up about an hour before daylight."

The next morning the two of us rode back up the mountain, and it wasn't long before we found the two anxious hunters.

They were really glad to see us and explained that they had always heard that if they got lost that they were to stay put. They had very few matches and were lucky to get the fire lit on their last one. By keeping the fire going, they were able to stay warm through the night.

I think they were a little overwhelmed by it all. They decided that they had enough of elk hunting and headed back to Minnesota.

The best outfitting memory that I have is when my father and most of his brothers came out to the ranch to hunt elk. A few of their wives came along, but they came to see the ranch and visit.

On one of the mornings, I got my father into a whole herd of elk just before daylight, and Hoag put Uncle Claud on just the right elk trail. My father took a couple of shots and missed, but in his defense, it was still rather dark and the elk were in a little fog. Claud, on the other hand, had a whole string of elk come down the trail. First there was a cow, followed by several other cows and calves. After 15 or 20 elk passed, a nice spike bull appeared. We had neglected to tell him that the big bulls usually came last. By the time 20 elk had passed, he was so excited he shot the spike as soon as he saw the horns.

They were only there for a few days, and none of them got any other shots, but everyone enjoyed themselves. We had elk meat in camp, played lots of cards, told lots of old stories and just enjoyed being family.

The outfitting story that had a major impact on me for the rest of my life began on a warm fall morning.

We were taking some hunters from Minnesota on their first elk hunt. Tim wanted to go along, so I took him out of school so he could help Hoag wrangle. We had our gear packed up the night before, but as usual we had to gather the horses in the dark the next morning.

We headed out when it was still pitch black, so I did not notice that Tim only wore tennis shoes. Yes, it was nice and warm, but he knew better than to head up into the mountains that rose to over 13,000 feet with tennis shoes as his only footwear.

When we got over Music Pass, Hoag put up the tent and gather firewood while Tim handled the horses. The hunters and I scouted for elk.

In the mountains at over 12,000 feet, the weather can change very quickly. By noon it was obvious that a winter storm was moving in. Before dark, the temperature had dropped from above 60° to well below freezing and the snow had already begun.

That night the mountains dumped so much snow on us that the tent came down. One of the hunters was a personal friend of mine. He was a banker, and this was his first time ever in a tent. He still talks about it today as being the worst night of his entire life, and he says that no one will ever get him into a tent again.

By morning, everyone was wet, cold and miserable, and it was still snowing. I wanted to build a large fire and get everyone warm, but the hunters were afraid and wanted to just get off the mountain.

We saddled horses, packed the gear and headed down the mountain. It was a little over a two-hour ride back to the headquarters, but by the time we were halfway there, Tim, my toughest son, had tears in his eyes. He told me he could not feel his feet. The hunters were really cold, and a little scared. I knew that they would not want to stop while I built a fire to warm his feet. I should have insisted, but because they were friends and I knew they were in no real danger, I did not force them to do the right thing. Instead, I just took Tim's tennis shoes off and put his bare feet under my shirt and in my armpits.

It didn't take very long for Tim's feet to get warmed up to the point where he could put his tennis shoes back on, and he got back to the headquarters with his feet no longer hurting. But my body temperature had dropped so low from having two ice cubes under my arms that I could not get warm. I walked the rest of the way, which took over an hour, and I pushed myself as hard as I could, but I still could not get warm. When I got back to the house, I got into a hot shower and still did not warm up. I was shivering uncontrollably as I crawled into a bathtub full of very hot water. It took several minutes for me to finally warm up. And I was left with a physical and/or mental handicap.

In the past, cold did not bother me. I had even slept out on the ground when it was 35 below zero. But ever since that incident, I cannot take the cold.

I do not know whether it is my body or whether it is a mental thing. All I know is that once I start to get cold, my body seems to shut down and just start shaking.

There were many other outfitting stories, including some where the clients thought that they knew more than I did, but that didn't bother me much. The thing that did bother me about being an outfitter was that most of the people who came to hunt elk were not wealthy men. They were all guys from the construction trades that I had gotten to know over the years. I knew that for them, an elk hunt was perhaps a once-in-a-lifetime event. I also knew that the odds of getting an elk in our area for the general public ran about 25%. I figured with me as their guide that their odds were about 50%. But I felt really bad for the 50% that I was unable to get an elk for. I also knew that there were areas in Colorado where even the general public's success rate was over 90%. That made it real hard to take my friends' money and encourage them to hunt with me. I found myself sending them to the public areas, where even without a guide they had a better chance of success than hunting from my ranch with me. If I ever do it again, I'd want to be an outfitter in an area where I could almost guarantee my hunters some shooting.

I liked being a guide and outfitter, but I loved living so close to the wilderness. Ten miles from my nearest year-round neighbor, no phone, no TV, no human sounds other than what we ourselves made and the sharing of this lifestyle with my sons.

Grandfather's Quote

I love not man the less, but nature more.

Bear cub in tree just outside of our garage

26

Colorado Bear Stories

We had many encounters with bears in our short time in Colorado. Once we even had a bear cub climb a tree within six feet of the house. When he came down, we chased him into the garage and tried to close the door, but he got away.

Then there was the time we took a horse carcass and dragged it across the ranch. We left it in a spot where we could keep watch in hopes of being able to shoot some coyotes. All four boys and I were there early the next morning and Matt spotted a golden-brown black bear approaching. From that time on we called Matt "Eagle Eye" because he was the best of all of us at spotting game at a distance.

Once a neighboring outfitter came up to the house and asked if he could pass through the ranch while taking his Texas client after a bear. He even asked me if I would come along and help him out, so I did. His dogs were hot on the trail of a black bear, and his client could not maintain the pace. He had walkie-talkies and gave me one. I stayed with his client as he followed the dogs. Soon he gave me a call to tell me the dogs had the bear treed. I was to get there as soon as I could. As I got very close to the sound of the baying dogs, his client was absolutely exhausted. I told him to take a rest and I would go over the next rise and see what I could see. When I crested the hill, I saw the dogs barking at the bear. The guide held a long stick and occasionally poked the bear's rump to make sure that he stayed up there. The guide looked absolutely bored and asked where his client was. I told him "just back over the hill" and he asked me to go get him. When I brought his client over the rise, the guide really put on a show.

"Oh wow! Look at the size of him!"

"Hurry, I am not sure I can keep him up there much longer!"

The guide was frantically hurrying to and fro and excitedly telling his client to be sure of his shot because "we don't want a wounded bear on our hands."

The dogs were running around baying at the top of their lungs, and the guide was jumping up and down with excitement. The client was trembling so much that I doubted that he could hit this big target only twenty feet away.

Boom! The crack of the rifle sounded, and the bear dropped out of the tree like a ton of bricks. The guide frantically grabbed all the dogs to keep them from biting the dead bear. The hunter hugged the guide and kissed the dogs and frantically shook my hand. He seemed so excited that I was afraid he'd piss his pants.

Heap big bear hunter! He paid $1000 and shot a bear out of a tree.

They didn't even want the meat—they took just the hide and left the meat to rot. I returned a few hours later and salvaged most of it. It turns out that bear meat is really greasy, and we had trouble eating it all, but we didn't have any trouble giving away what we couldn't eat.

The best Colorado bear story involved Tim and his 4-H pig

The boys were in 4-H and I lent them the money to buy their animals, feed and whatever else was needed. They were to take care of their animals and then sell them at the county fair. After they paid off their debt to me, whatever was left would be their profit. The idea was to teach them something about business.

Matt and Luke each decided to buy a sheep and Tim bought a pig. The only problem was that Tim's pig thought that he was a sheep. He would not eat any grain and he ran around the mountainside with the two sheep eating grass. Needless to say, as it got close to County fair time, he was a pretty thin and scrawny pig.

One day when Tim got home from school, he could not find his pig. After spending some time looking, he came upon its half-eaten carcass not too far from the house. He was pretty upset, but he went back and asked his mother if he could take the rifle, sit by the carcass and shoot the coyote that had killed his pig.

I was not expected home until after dark, and she was not comfortable with Tim taking the rifle out alone, so she agreed to go along with him. Just about the time the sun was going down, a bear came out and started dining on what was left of the pig. Irene would not let Tim shoot the bear.

Kids get pretty attached to an animal that they've had for a while, so Tim not only lost money, he also lost an animal friend. By the time I got home, all of this had sunk in, and he even had tears in his eyes as he told me the story.

The next morning, Tim and I were hidden near the carcass before daylight. Even before the sun rose, the bear came back to finish what was left.

Tim took careful aim and killed himself a bear at the age of twelve. He was so excited that he was no longer upset about having lost the pig or the money he might have made.

To top it all off, the townspeople heard about the ranch kid who had lost his 4-H pig to a bear. They bought him a new one, which was roly-poly fat like a pig should be.

At the county fair, Tim's new pig brought at least five times more money than his original pig would have brought.

We had Tim's bear made into a rug, and Tim made out like a bandit. He wound up with a pocket full of cash, a bear rug and a great story.

Grandfather's Quote

Often times life's disappointments can turn out to be blessings, so take what comes and enjoy the ride.

Broadside, one of the games I invented

27

Inventing Games

While living in Colorado, I thought about starting my own business of making and selling board games.

I don't know where my love of them originally came from, but I do love to play board games. As a child, I played Monopoly and many others. As I got older, I realized that few of them were really good.

When I was first married we had little money, so we often got together with other couples and played board games. I usually suggested new rules in hopes of making them more competitive or enjoying it more.

Soon I decided to make my own games. But what would make them good? I decided that elements within them needed to change, like the seasons or the economy. The game should require strategy but allow those who are not so competitive the opportunity to play without getting blown away.

The first three I made were *Decision,* which was about the stock market; *Deception,* about World War II naval warfare; and a horse racing game. I made the boards and the pieces, and then I wrote a set of rules. The rules were the most difficult part because they had to allow a new player to learn to play it.

Soon I was bringing *Deception* to work with me, and playing the game with other businessmen after work. I was doing plumbing work out of my father's buildings and he had several other tenants. The owners of an electrical shop and a carpet-laying shop would stay and play the game with me for several hours after work. In this game, all the players placed the ships of their navy throughout the board. Each player had two aircraft carriers, three battleships, five destroyers and several tankers, all of which could not be moved. They also had a movable submarine and a movable destroyer. No other player could see their submarine, and no other player knew where it was until it shot torpedoes at one of their ships. It was a great game, as evidenced by the fact that so many businessmen devoted so much of their time to it. But it was a war/strategy game, not a family game.

Because of the response I got from other players, I decided to send the games off to Parker Brothers and Leisure Dynamics. I got a nice rejection letter from Parker Brothers and a personal interview with Leisure Dynamics. At the interview they took me in their back room and showed me another horse racing game that was almost exactly like mine. They said that happens a lot. They told me that they wanted me to go home and invent a game for preschoolers that was fun, exciting and educational. I did just that.

Each child sat looking at a wall, so to speak, and they couldn't see the other side of it. On this wall were several steps going up the wall at a forty-five degree angle. They had a marble that they could put on one of the first three steps. Their opponent did the same on his side of the wall. Now each player pushed down a lever on one of the three keys attached to their opponent's steps. If there was a marble on that step it fell into a chute, rolled to the bottom and rang a bell. If they pushed a lever and no marble fell down, they knew the marble had to be on one of the other two steps. They also drew cards that gave them an extra push on a lever or made them skip a turn or some such thing. The first one to the top was the winner. The game was rejected.

The other main thing that I learned from both companies was that if they took one of your ideas from one of your games, they owe you nothing. They only had to pay you for your game if they accepted it in its entirety. You had to sign a contract to that fact before they would even look at your game.

The thought of playing games for a living was very appealing to me and I thought about asking them for a job, but that would have required living in a city or suburb. I was not willing to go there.

I invented several more games just for the fun of it, and I still have most of them. When I was in Colorado, I actually gave serious consideration to hiring several teenagers and starting my own game company, but I never pulled the trigger on it.

Broadside was one of my better games and after publishing my first children's stories, I decided to try and find a company to make the parts for it. I was willing to invest up to $50,000 to produce the game. I even talked to several retail game shops who agreed to carry it for me. The board of course would be easy, but the forty-five little sailing ships the game required were much more of a problem. I even talked to a couple of Chinese companies but couldn't get it done.

(Please forgive me for getting a little ahead of myself by sharing what follows here.)

Years later I was introduced to the game *The Settlers of Catan,* the first game that I ever played that was better than any of mine. It was a game I couldn't improve on. Actually I did come up with a two-player version that was much better than any other out there, but my confidence in my own games was completely undermined.

Bottom line, I almost certainly will never spend the money to get any of my games out there. Although my submarine game *Deception* could have real possibility with a computer's ability to keep track of all the submarines on the board. But maybe someday one of you will enjoy playing some game that I have invented.

All of the above was written years ago. In 2018, a couple things changed. First, Paul, one of my grandsons, graduated from college and decided to come and spend a month on the ranch before starting his career. It turns out that he is as big a gamer as I am and he also is a computer wiz. We played several games of the games I designed. He and his older brother Jordan, who came to visit the ranch while Paul was here, liked my games and thought that they could easily be turned into video games. Jordan is also a computer engineer, and both thought my games could be a real success on the computer. So who knows, with the help of family, I may still get a game or two into production.

Grandfather's Quote

*Life, and business in particular, is a game.
Teach your children how to play games well and
they will do well in life and/or in business.*

Broadside treasure chest

Broadside game pieces

Building our underground house above the river. Luke, Mark and me

The house was underground, but had two stories of
glass overlooking the river valley below.

28

The Athletic Club and Our Underground Home

Once I found out Irene was not happy in Colorado, the opportunity to buy an athletic club fell into my lap so I got on a plane and went to check it out.

The athletic club was on Highway 52, just outside of Cannon Falls, Minnesota. A friend of mine who was killed in a traffic accident had built it. When his father wrote me a letter informing me about the accident, he also asked me if I would have any interest in purchasing it.

The club had three handball racquetball courts, a weight room with a full set of weights and machines, a whirlpool, three outdoor tennis courts with lights and a softball diamond also under floodlights. Along with all that, the large bar had facilities for serving food and a 3.2 beer license. A large observation area had a pool table and several tables suitable for playing cards or dining. A large basement storage area could be turned into an apartment.

I knew that I would not be happy living in an apartment along a highway, so while I was there, I checked out land prices and availability. I was delighted to find 200 acres along the Cannon River with over two miles of river frontage. It was on a dead-end road, and over half of it was timbered. The bluffs overlooking the river were about 100 feet in elevation, and the views were spectacular. All along the river was excellent cropland that I knew could be leased out. An old railroad bed

The boys and I built this underground house all on our own using oak timbers from our own land

View of our home from the air

ran at the base of the bluff through the timber and the signs of wildlife, particularly deer, were everywhere. The woods were filled with lots and lots of wild raspberries. And it was only five miles from Cannon Falls, and about seven miles from the athletic club.

I signed a purchase agreement on the land, contingent upon me buying the athletic club. Then I began negotiations for the athletic club.

Steve's dad wanted me to buy the entire thing, but he reluctantly accepted my offer for all but the softball diamond, contingent upon me being able to assume the SBA loan.

I had researched the books very thoroughly and knew the club was in trouble. But I also felt that I could turn it around if I were able to purchase it at the right price.

The SBA (Small Business Administration) people that I was working with told me they had never had an applicant read every word of over fifty pages of loan papers. Nor were they used to dealing with a buyer who was not using an attorney. I found several things in the loan papers, which would have to be changed before I would assume the loan.

I think they knew the club was in trouble and were extremely motivated to see me take it over. But they told me that they had never before changed anything in their standard loan documents. They did tell me that they would check with their supervisors and get back to me. I gave a little on a few problems, but when it was all said and done, they gave me just about everything I asked for.

I was now the new owner of the Cannon Valley Athletic Club.

Before I made my offer, I contacted a good friend who was a contractor, Don Pavic, about building an apartment in the basement storage area of the athletic club. He agreed that he could finish the apartment within thirty days and that I would not have to pay him anything until I had sold my ranch in Colorado. Now that is a true friend.

Forty days later we had packed up everything in Colorado and moved to Cannon Falls.

I am shocked that neither I nor any member of my family remembers anything at all about the move back to Minnesota. It is somewhat

Luke, me and Mark taking a lunch break while working on the house

understandable for the boys and I, because we hated leaving the ranch, but you would think that Irene, who was so excited to be moving back to Minnesota, would have some memories of the move.

In spite of leaving a super lifestyle in Colorado, there were some advantages to owning an athletic club. It was nice to have such an elaborate weight room and whirlpool always at your disposal, and the kids loved the pool table. Also, we could play handball, racquetball or volleyball on any of the courts at any time.

We found out over time that dealing with the public on a daily basis was another matter. The financial success or failure of the club was based on court time and memberships, so that is what we concentrated on. We did turn it into a money-making business.

We organized women's exercise groups, couples volleyball games, tennis leagues, handball and racquetball leagues, handball and racquetball ladders, special rates for slack times, duplicate bridge tournaments, and anything else that we could think of to bring the people in.

We lived on the phone. You couldn't just hang up a sign—you had to call people and invite them in. Then you had to call them weekly and remind them to be sure and come to exercise class or to the bridge tournament or whatever. We created innovative sliding membership pricing based on your mileage from the club. The farther away from the club that you lived, the cheaper your membership was.

Of course, we had to be active and participate in almost each and every event. I even played tennis for the first time in my life, and because of my natural athletic ability and my experience playing ping pong, I didn't do too badly. I even have a Bobby Riggs/Billie Jean King story.

We had one woman who was too good to play in the women's tennis league, so she played in the men's league. The first time I met her on the court, I didn't hand her flowers, but I did tease her a little. Then when I played her, I played close to the net and put spin on everything. All dink shots and spin. She became so frustrated that I was able to beat her. Needless to say in our second meeting, I got handed my lunch, but that first win sure was fun.

Irene or I were almost always behind the desk. We did hire one other gal to help us from time to time, but we put in countless hours.

The boys got up every morning before school and cleaned the entire club, and that was no small matter either.

We paid the boys good wages for their work and they were able to pay their own tuition for St. Thomas Military Academy, about $3,000 a year per student.

I even ran a couple of handball tournaments for cash prizes, one of which ended up during a snowstorm. Several handball players had to stay at the club overnight. The handball community still fondly talks about those tournaments.

It was one of the few times in my life that I lived somewhere that was not private. In order to be able to handle that, I took daily walks through the timber and farmland right behind the club.

That's where I began having my daily talks with the Big Guy, my father's fond name for our Heavenly Father. We had of course become members of the parish. The church was half way between old-fashioned and modern and the people were friendly.

We sold the ranch in Colorado about a year after moving to Cannon Falls. As soon as the ranch sold, we put in our standard (truly out) outhouse and began construction on an underground home. It was built on our 200 acres along the bluff overlooking the Cannon River. The boys were older now, and they were a lot more help than on our first two houses. They also helped clear a trail along the old railroad right of way, and put in more trails in other areas. Together we even created a real nice beach area on the river just below the house.

A card playing friend of mine, named Ed, also helped a lot more than he intended. He was a linoleum and carpet layer, and he put in all the linoleum and carpeting in the entire house. After he had completed everything, we invited him to dinner, and after dinner he wanted to play Gin. We played through the night and when Irene got up the next morning, our last game was just winding up. She liked his work

View of our home from the crop land along our two miles of river frontage

so much that she didn't even complain. She made us breakfast and after eating he left. Then she gave me a very strange look when I told her that I had won the entire job for free.

Ed's work just about wrapped up the entire process, and by then both Irene and I knew that running an athletic club was not for us. About two years after buying the club, we sold it for a nice profit. I then began buying and selling property once again, only this time I concentrated on lakeshore property. But here again, that is another story.

Grandfather's Quote

If you can dream it, try it. Life goes by in a heartbeat and way too soon your chance to follow your dreams will be over.

Me getting ready to stroke the ball

29

Handball and a State Title

In 1972, Mike Blaylock introduced me to the game of handball. I was twenty-nine years old and had never even heard of the game before then.

I could hit the ball to the front wall, but when it started wrapping around the walls, I couldn't seem to get my hands on it. I had a lot of trouble using my left hand. I loved it just the same, so much so that I built my own indoor four-wall court.

I got three of the Blaylock boys to put up $1,500 each and we all worked together and did most all of the labor ourselves. The court was made out of concrete blocks and was at the end of a 40' x 60' pole barn building. Off to the side of the court, in the rear, was an observation area, a locker room and showers.

Shortly thereafter I joined the Decathlon Club, and I started playing in handball tournaments. Most of the tournaments were local, but I also traveled to North Dakota, South Dakota, Iowa and Wisconsin.

Depending on the number of entries, you normally had to play one game on a Friday evening, two on Saturday and two on Sunday. In those first two years, I never made it to a Sunday. Then I went to a handball camp at Wake Forest College in Illinois. Five-time national champion Paul Haber was an instructor at the camp. When I returned, I spent the next three months or more doing everything with my left hand. I ate with my left hand, shaved, brushed my teeth, combed my hair, and anything else that you could do with one hand. I even studied the throwing motion of my right arm in the mirror until I could duplicate those same motions with my left.

Soon I started winning, but I always seemed to choke in the semi finals or championship matches. The ability was beginning to get there, but the mind was not.

I had heard that Rod Carew, a famous baseball player for the Minnesota Twins, had used a hypnotist to help him improve his hitting. I got an appointment with the same hypnotist, but it was a joke. It seems that I am one of the few people that he had ever known that could not be hypnotized.

Then I discovered the book *The Inner Game of Tennis*, and I really started working on putting my mind to rest. I got so proficient at it that the other handball players started calling me The Buddha of Handball. When the match started, my mind was completely stilled. I was at one with the ball and was unaware of anything else. I would not even acknowledge my opponent in any manner. It was said of me that if all the spectators were naked women, I would not notice a single one of them. I started winning tournaments.

That kind of mental concentration took an enormous amount of effort. It never did become easy for me, so I only called upon it in tournament play. At other times I played as hard as I could, but I was a different player. For example, I used to play Steve Sheppard at least once a week for several years, and he kept track of all of our matches. He won more than 85% of the time, and yet when I faced him in tournaments five or six times, I won all our matches.

Then I walked away from it all and moved to Colorado for two years. I did build a handball court there, but there were no other players except Todd Aldrich. Now Todd was a good player, but he never seemed to have time to play.

When I returned to Minnesota in 1979, Alva Rankin and I won the state B doubles championship. (About 1985, they changed the divisions to

Open, A, B and C, but in 1979, Open was still called A and A was still called B.)

In 1980, I lost to Grant Wiessner in the semifinals of the state B singles and wound up taking third behind Grant and Alva Rankin. I beat my good friend Steve Sheppard for third place.

In 1981, Grant and Alva had moved up a division, and I was seeded number one in the B division. The day before the tournament, I ran my thumb on my left hand through a table saw. I went to the doctor, and he wanted to graft skin off of my hip onto my thumb. This was a Thursday and the state championship tournament started the next day. I asked the doctor if we could wait until Monday to do the skin graft. He said that the graft could wait, but that there was no way that I could stand the pain of hitting a handball with that hand.

When the tournament started, I had to get permission from my opponents to cut the thumb off of the glove used on my left hand. The thumb was wrapped in so much gauze and padding that it was almost the size of a light bulb. At first, each of my opponents felt sorry for me and did not pick on my left hand. When it came to crunch time, they had no choice but to hit it to my left side. I would backhand the ball as often as I could with my right hand. But if I was forced to hit it with my left hand, I could not do it without extreme pain and more than a little moan.

I managed to make it to the quarterfinals, but by the time I got there, the competition was just too good to be beaten by a one-handed man. In 1982, I cannot remember exactly what happened, but on my way to the quarterfinals I beat a much younger and better player. In that match, I won a very long and hard-fought first game. In the second game, I gave it all I had and lost 21 to 20. I was shot, and I knew it. My opponent was 20 years old, and I was 19 years older and totally out of gas.

The tiebreaker was played to 11 points and my opponent was ahead five to nothing when he hit a kill shot in front of me. The shot was so close to the floor that normally it would be unreturnable. I dove belly first on the floor and got my hand under the ball for a re-kill. The referee asked me if I had gotten the ball, and I told him yes. He said, "Side out," whereupon I got the serve and could score a point.

My opponent went ballistic.

"No way he got that! Absolutely no way!"

The referee asked me again, "Did you get it?"

"Yes."

"Side out."

Now my opponent started yelling and swearing and I turned around to the referee and said, "Give him the point."

"If you say you got it, Gary, it is a side out."

My opponent is still yelling and swearing.

"If he wants it that badly, just give him the point."

"Six serving zero."

Before this incident, I had tried with everything that was in me to dig down deep and play another 11 points, but I was unable to do it. Now it was like my opponent put a hot poker up my posterior and from somewhere within, I gathered the strength to play outside of myself.

He never scored another point. I won the match 11 to 6.

After the match, I went over and talked to him. I told him that someday he was going to be a professional handball player, but that he had to know if I said I got the ball, I truly did get it. I told him how I was completely out of gas, and he saw for himself how his unsportsmanlike conduct motivated me to play like I did. I hope he learned the lesson.

The record book does not show me as one of the semifinalists in 1982, so I must have lost the next match in the quarterfinals. Perhaps I cannot remember the loss, because my mind was probably as worn out as my body.

In 1983, I had lost my number one or two seeding, but I still got to the semifinals. In my semifinals match, I won the first game. I was leading in the second when I dove for a ball and smashed my right shoulder on the wall. My shoulder was broken or separated. The pain was so great that I could barely move around, and I lost the match to Tom Walek, who went on to win the tournament.

I went to the tournament director and told him that I could not play for third place. He told me that Mike McGraw was so upset at having lost his semifinal match that he said he was not coming back to play for third place. The tournament director told me all I had to do was to dress, show up and go on the court. If Mike didn't show within twenty minutes of the starting time, I would be given the third-place trophy.

When it got to the starting time for the third-place match, my pain had eased considerably, but I could hardly move my right arm. I was dressed and on the court and was about ready to be awarded the third-place trophy when Mike shows up.

What's a fellow supposed to do?

A couple of years ago, I had played without my left arm, so now I might as well try it without my right.

Things were a little bit different this time though. My opponent didn't realize that my right arm was useless, and my right arm was normally feared by all my opponents, so he hit everything to my left side. I won the first game.

I cannot believe how unobservant my opponent was, because in the second game he continued to hit everything to my left side. Halfway through the second game, I had a three or four point lead when Mike's buddies in the gallery kept telling Mike to call a timeout. Mike finally called a timeout. When he stepped out of the court, his buddies told him my right arm was useless and to start hitting everything to my right side. He did just that, and I lost the match.

In that year of 1983, the state held the state doubles championships on a different weekend than the singles were played. I believe it was played the weekend before the state singles. I would be turning 40 in that year, so I was allowed to play in the Masters division. No way was I going to play in the Masters in the singles division. But I thought I would give the Masters doubles division a try if I could get an older player to be my partner. I believe that the total age of the two players had to equal 90 or even 95. I had been hearing stories for years about an older player named Rich Rawlings, and I heard that he was a great guy. I also heard that he now lived in St. Cloud, but I gave him a call anyway. I asked him if he would like to be my doubles partner in the Masters division. He agreed.

I met Rich for the first time about thirty minutes before our first match. I had never seen him play nor had he ever seen me play, but we really fit together well and we went on to win the championship. It was one of the most enjoyable tournaments of my entire career.

I was turning forty and my sons, who I had started teaching right after I built our own handball court, were now playing in tournaments of their own. What a joy that was to watch them play, and on occasion I even played against them or with them as my partner in doubles. Some of the best times were had playing outdoors on three wall courts

Luke watching me serve in an outdoor three-wall doubles game

and soon Luke was catching up with me ability-wise. And I went to the national collegiate handball tournament with Luke in Austin, Texas. The highlight of that trip was when Luke and I got on the court, in a cut throat game, with John Bike. He was soon to be a pro player, and he was noted for hitting the fastest ball in handball. I was there, and Luke hit it faster!

Another chance for a championship match for a state title

In 1984, I was now 41 years old, in an extremely large field of players, and I was not seeded very high. In order to win this state tournament, I would have to win five matches. I knew that I could beat any one of my opponents in a single match, but I was not sure I could outlast the younger players in a marathon tournament. So I devised a plan that is still talked about today.

I believe my oldest opponent was 35 years old, and most of them were in their twenties. I decided to win the first game, throw the second game and win the tiebreaker. That way, I would have to score only 32 points rather than 42 or 52 points.

My first match was so easy that I went on to win the first two games. In the next match, and in each match thereafter, I won the first game and stood there while my opponent served the ball and won the second game 21 to zero. Then I would go on to win the tiebreaker.

I had some tough first games and tie breakers on my way to the championship match. I had a tough match against Steve Sheppard, my friend who beat me 85% of the time in non-tournament play. Then I had to play Dave Rawlings, the son of my Masters doubles partner of the previous year. In fact, with his father's coaching, I was fortunate to win that hard-fought tie breaker 11 to 8.

My opponent in the championship match was Mark Warner from Rochester, Minnesota.

Mark was a 35-year-old anesthesiologist who I had played many times before. He was a left-hander and a very good player. Steve Sheppard and/or Jim May and I would drive to Rochester at least once a month to play with the players down there. I had faced Mark at least four or five times, and I had never won a match or even a game off of him. But this was tournament time.

I won the first game 21 to 4. The game was not as easy as the score indicates. I worked very hard at it, but I was so surprised at the large margin that I decided to try and win it in two games. In the second game, when the score was five to five, I realized that Mark had gotten it together.

I stood there and watched him serve out.

"Six serving five."

"Seven serving five."

"Eight serving five."

Mark turned to the referee, "This just doesn't seem fair."

"Just keep serving."

Mark won the second game 21 to 5.

For those of you who have never played handball or racquetball before, only the server can score and you only have to win by one point.

That tiebreaker was as tough a game as I have ever played. The score went back and forth, and both of us let it all hang out. There was dive after dive, after which we had to wipe all the sweat off the floor. There were at least one or two glove changes by each of us, and we both used our allotment of timeouts. There were no hand errors by either player, and each point had to be earned.

Soon the score was 10 to 10 with Mark serving, but I was in the zone and not even aware of the score. I have never been so focused before or since.

Mark served the ball as he always did, to my left hand, and it was almost an ace. I managed to dig it out and wrap it around the walls, driving him to deep court. He hit it to the ceiling and began the longest volley of the entire match. After what must have seemed like an eternity to the spectators, he hit one high and deep in the left corner. I was barely able to get it back to the middle of the front wall.

I had set him up for a kill.

Before he even got to the ball, I was charging frontcourt. If he had made the shot to either his left or his right, he would have won the match, but he killed it right in front of himself. I was right behind him.

"Hinder!" the ref called.

I flopped down on the floor on my back and just laid there catching my breath.

Mark grabbed a towel and started wiping the sweat off the floor. Mark had not complained because he knew that he had made a mistake by hitting it right back at himself and he had seen me get impossible balls before.

When the floor was finally dry, Mark served again. This time about four or five shots into the volley, I was able to drive a ball past him on his right.

"Side out."

There was no pressure, there was no nervousness, and most importantly, there was not a single thought in my mind. I just slowly bounced the ball several times and lobbed it high into the right-hand corner.

Everything seemed in slow motion. A new volley had begun.

Several shots into the volley, I made the mistake of giving Mark a left-handed shot off of the back wall. As he turned to follow the ball and began his swing, I swayed my body back towards him as if I were going to take a back wall shot myself. As he started forward, I started forward. As the ball left his hand, I was moving in the same direction towards the front wall. When the ball struck the front wall, about 6 inches from the floor, I was already diving towards it.

I was sliding on the floor less than six feet from the front wall when the ball struck my hand and shot back to the wall. It rolled out as a final kill shot. The crowd went wild.

I had finally won my state handball championship!

Grandfather's Quote

It is not the title or the trophy that matters,
it is knowing that you were willing to pay
the price that makes you who you are.

Handball players Luke, Tim, Mark, me and Matt with their trophies

30

The Freight Train

I truly loved Irene. I would've done anything for her. I thought of us as one. We grew together, and each year that I was married to her, my love continued to grow. She was so beautiful, both inside and out. She was soft-spoken, kind and giving and always trying to please. She was a good mother, and an even better partner. She hated confrontation, and she always trusted me to do what was right. She gave me a free hand to pursue my dreams, and there are very few women who would allow their husbands that opportunity.

She had just one fault, and ultimately that fault cost us our marriage. She believed her man would know how she felt from her actions, so no matter how she felt, she couldn't bring herself to tell me something if she thought it would cause any confrontation. And, like a typical male, because she didn't put it into words and spell it out right in front of my face, I was oblivious to it.

I really would have done anything for her. I thought that I could always make her happy. And I believed what she told me, not what her actions should have told me. Right up to the day before asking me for a divorce, she told me she loved me.

I left Alaska for her, I left Colorado for her, and I bought the white elephant house in Lakeville for her. I always sought her advice about the boys, and I supported her going back to school to get her master's degree. I don't believe I was a man who wanted to be somewhere else. I just was not willing to settle for whatever hand was dealt me. I believe I was a man who wanted to be in the right place for both of us.

In 1986 I found yet another ranch. This one was in Buffalo Gap, South Dakota. When she looked at it, she told me she was so glad we had finally found a place where we both could be happy. But she wanted to stay in Minnesota for a few months so she could finish up her master's degree in counseling.

We purchased the ranch, and the entire family made several trips back and forth during that summer. Come fall, the three older boys went off to college, and Mark went back to school at St Thomas Military Academy. Irene stayed in Minnesota with Mark to finish her master's degree. I went to the ranch.

This was the first time in our entire 24 years of marriage that Irene and I were separated for more than three weeks at one stretch. After the first couple of weeks of separation, I called her each and every night. She and Mark even came and met me in the middle of South Dakota and we went pheasant hunting together.

It just so happened that a month or so before leaving for the ranch, a friend of ours, Larry Blaylock, was just divorced or in the process of getting one. He had been coming over for dinner almost every night. He was having trouble holding it together and we were there for him. When I left, he continued to come. I trusted Irene completely, and during this time I never even gave it a second thought. But he and Irene became even closer friends, and she now had someone else she could lean on.

On December 1, 1986, I talked to her on the phone and she told me she loved me. I drove back to Minnesota the following day, and when I got there, she met me at the front door. Standing in the doorway, she told me she had been lying to me for a long time and that she no longer loved me. She wanted a divorce.

My entire life I have always thought that I was prepared for anything. I always tried to think of any possible situation, but I never once thought Irene would leave me.

I was devastated beyond all possible understanding.

I offered to sell the ranch and promised to live in Minnesota for as long as she wanted to. I offered to do anything that she asked me to do in order to save our marriage. I would have cut off my right arm to save our marriage.

It did not matter.

She told me she could not bring herself to tell me her love was dying until it was dead and gone. She told me her love had begun to die over ten years ago, when I sold our place in Minnesota and moved to Colorado. She told me I should have known and that all the signs were there for me to see. And most importantly, she told me once her love was dead, she could not bring it back.

She admitted that 80% of her classmates working on their master's degree in counseling were divorced women, and they all asked her why she was moving out in the middle of nowhere for me. She also had a very close male friend that she could lean on and go to for comfort and advice. I am sure the advice he gave her was to end the marriage because they are still living together.

To this day I find it very difficult to believe that when we went to two counselors and a Catholic priest, all of them told her the boys didn't matter, family didn't matter, and our vows did not matter. All that mattered, according to them, was that she be happy. Such was the thinking of counselors back then, and perhaps even now.

I would have given anything if her parents were still alive, or if someone, anyone, had told her she owed it to herself, to her family and perhaps even to God to try and work on getting her love to return.

During this time of counseling, I talked to several couples who had been married for a lifetime. Each and every one of them told me that during some period of their lives their love seemed to have died. In almost every case, when one partner told the other that their love had died, the other was taken by complete surprise. But because of family and their commitment, they worked together on bringing it back. In each and every case, they were able through lots of hard work to do just that. And when the love came back, it was stronger than it had ever been.

For the next month or so I was back and forth between the ranch and our home in Minnesota. I remember the first time that I was back at the ranch after being run over by the freight train. I could not sleep and I could not stop crying, so I called my friend Gene Clinton. His wife Myra told me that Gene was in Point Barrow, Alaska, and even though I told her nothing about what was going on, she sensed something was seriously wrong. Within an hour, Gene called me from Alaska. He even told me that the exact same thing had happened between him and Myra. He told me that they were separated for a while, but that they worked on it and worked on it until her love came back. And today, their love is stronger than it ever was.

I prayed, and I prayed, and I prayed some more. One time while praying when I was staying at my folks' house, I was really losing it when the phone rang and it was Dick Roxberg. I know today that the Lord had him call just then because he helped me pull it back together.

I was under more stress and pressure than I had ever been in my entire life. I could not sleep at all and the more that I tried to talk to Irene, the more she told me to just be quiet and leave her alone. I finally cracked a couple of times. Once I had put together a bunch of family pictures, wrote a poem and bought a bottle of champagne. When she rejected it all, I came unglued, and threw the champagne bottle through the window. On another occasion, I even started to do something worse.

I immediately stopped, but I was mortified at the thought that I could even think about going there. I cried and cried and begged for her forgiveness. When she remained silent, I told her all I wanted was for her to be happy and that if she wanted me to I would file for divorce.

That is exactly what she asked me to do, and I said if she would forgive me that I would do it.

I am so very sorry for not having been able to see all the signs that were right in front of me and for not being a better person. I am grateful for the time that I had with my best friend and partner, and I can only hope and pray that she has found her happiness.

It was many years later when I finally understood why my prayers could not be answered. There is one prayer the Lord cannot answer; He will not take away someone's free will. It was not within the Lord's power to bring Irene back to me, nor would I have wanted her back if she would not be happy. But I still love her—or the memory of her. Perhaps that is why things have been so unfair to any other woman that I have tried to make a part of my life.

I do not like the fact that the record shows that I filed for divorce. I would never have done so on my own. I only filed because I promised her I would, and I kept my promise.

One last footnote. I never could figure out which one of my distant relatives was a saint. One of them had to be, because it is said that God will reward his exceptional people for many generations to come. My entire life has been showered with blessings. It feels like whatever I touch seems to turn to gold, and heaven knows, I have not deserved any of it.

Even in my life's greatest loss, the Lord has given me great gifts.

In losing Irene, I was given Daniel and Jeanne.

Grandfather's quote

*There is one prayer that even God can not answer.
He will not take away another's free will, but if you
try to be the person He created you to be, even our
greatest tragedies can be turned into blessings.*

My brother Jay and myself in Remer, Minnesota

31

Deer Hunting

I grew up knowing that my father hunted deer every year in northern Minnesota. I remember watching him pack all his gear for the trips, and I can remember him coming home with many deer stacked in the back of his pickup. Getting stories out of my father was a little more difficult, but I did manage to get a few.

I couldn't wait to join my father's deer hunting camp, but just about the time I was old enough to go along, another hunter brought his son. The son made enough serious mistakes that the camp decided that no more sons could come along until they reached the age of 18. This young lad shot a rabbit and carried it around in his back pocket with the white tail bobbing up and down. A definite no-no in Whitetail country during hunting season.

In 1963, I joined my father's hunting camp. That was the first of many enjoyable years hunting with that group.

Joe's Hunting Camp

The hunting group had been started over 40 years before by a hunter named Joe, and all the hunters still referred to their group as Joe's hunting camp. When I joined the camp, they were hunting in Remer, Minnesota, near Goose Lake.

I packed all my gear on Thursday evening and reviewed my professional guide's manual, which showed in great detail how to field dress and care for a deer.

Half the group always left on Friday morning. That way, they could drive during the day and arrive in time to get the camp ready before the season opened. The last eleven miles of the trip was all on gravel and ended at the Goose Lake store. From there we had to go another mile or so on a field road, which took us back to an old two-story log cabin.

On the first floor of the cabin, benches sat along each side of a large long table. A sink, cupboards and a stove were on one side of the table. The other side had a washing area and the stairway going upstairs. At the far end of the table, opposite the only door, a 50-gallon drum served as a wood stove. Mouse shit was everywhere. Upstairs consisted of several double bunk beds, single bunk beds and beds in general. The cabin had no running water, but we had several large metal milk cans.

Usually about five or six hunters came up during the day on Friday, and the others arrived late Friday evening. Soon all the hunters were busy doing all sorts of odd chores. The first order of business was sweeping up all the mouse shit. A couple of other hunters took the milk cans to a flowing well that was a couple miles away on the shores of Goose Lake. They cleaned the cans and then filled them with fresh spring water. Other hunters were busy gathering and cutting firewood while some were busy washing all the dishes that had been stored in a couple of the milk cans.

With six guys pitching in, it didn't take very long until the cabin was shipshape. Then we all carried our gear in and unpacked it upstairs by our chosen bunk. As a newcomer, I had to take the bunk that was assigned to me.

When all that was done, someone brought out the cards and the drinks. With a couple of hours of daylight left, after being given the lay of the land and shown where the main trail began, I went scouting.

The country was very flat and heavily wooded with a lot of poplar, birch, oak, a few pine trees, and lots and lots of brush. The main trail started at Goose Lake, about a mile west of the cabin. It ran east through a clearing by an old abandoned cabin, then through more thick woods, and broke out into the second clearing where our cabin was. You could drive to the cabin. But going east, there was just a two-mile trail through the woods, which ended up at two large beaver dams.

When I walked east on the main trail for the first time, I could not believe all the deer sign. The deer seemed to use this main trail as their highway, and buck scrapes were all along it. I didn't worry about walking quietly because I wanted to cover as much ground as I could the first day to learn the lay of the land. I followed the main trail all the way to the beaver dams, and then backtracked to where Red's Trail left the main trail. I followed that around until I was heading back to the cabin clearing. Then I headed straight east through the woods. About a half hour before dark, I picked a large oak tree that was far away from everyone else's favorite stands and easy to climb. Perched up in the tree, I could get quite comfortable and have a great view overlooking the intersection of a couple of deer trails. I then cleared a little brush and made a small trail going straight north until it intersected the main trail. I wanted to be able to find my tree in the dark before the sun came up.

The only advice my father gave me about being new to the camp was to say little and listen a lot. And do more than my share of the work. Because I was new to the camp, at night after dinner I was expected to do all the dishes for the entire crew. First, I had to clear one end of the table so that the other hunters could play cards. I pushed all the dirty dishes to the other end and then started boiling water. When the dishes were all washed and dried, I joined the card game.

No one stayed up very late that first night because everyone was anxious to get out for the first morning's hunt. When the late crew arrived I was introduced, and shook each of their hands, but shortly thereafter everyone was in bed.

As we all lay in our bunks, we discussed where each of us was going to hunt in the morning and the other hunters shared a few more stories. I was told, for instance, that each time Paul shot a deer, he got so excited that on that night he would talk and walk in his sleep. A couple of guys didn't think it was too funny when someone else kept shouting, "Paul, stick 'em! Stick 'em, Paul."

The following morning the crew got up long before daylight, got dressed and came downstairs. They were all seated around the long table on the main floor.

The wood stove glowed at one end of the cabin and the smell of the mornings breakfast filled the room. We had pancakes, eggs and all the bacon you could eat.

After eating more than my fill, I was the first one to head out into the dark woods. No snow lay on the ground, and I could not see five feet in front of me, but the main trail was easy to find.

Any deadfalls or branches that might slap someone in the face were always kept cleared away from the trail, so even though it was very dark, walking was easy. The day before, I made a mental note of a large tree by a bend in the trail. I scraped away all the leaves with my foot to mark the spot to leave the trail. I also scraped all the leaves away in a line every ten or twenty feet so I could easily find the large oak tree I wanted to sit in.

I walked out that opening morning with all my clothes on. Even though my jacket and shirt were open, I still worked up quite a sweat. All the mornings to follow, and for all the years to come, I carried most of my clothes to my morning's stand. If you've got your clothes wet with sweat, it is impossible to keep warm. Cold was not the enemy—moisture was.

I had to climb my tree with my rifle in my hand—not a good idea—because I had forgotten my rope. By the time I settled in the comfortable crotch that I had tried out the day before, the first faint rays of light could be seen in the eastern sky. I had jumped at least two deer on my way in, but I only heard them bounding away. Now I was surrounded by silence.

Slowly my heart beat began to soften and get back to a normal rhythm and I began to notice how wet I had gotten from the walk in.

If the temperature had been much colder, the moisture would have been a real problem. Fortunately, it was only a minor annoyance.

All was still around me and only occasionally could I hear the rustling of the leaves as the wind gave out her gentle gusts.

I could barely see the intersection of the two deer trails that I had located the day before about one hundred yards from where I sat.

As the light penetrated the surrounding woods, at about 7 AM, life began to stir. A bird landed in the branches above me. Off to my right, a squirrel scampered across the leaves covering the earth. I jerked my head around for a quick look because I was not yet accustomed to recognizing the different sounds of the forest inhabitants.

My movement was instantly noticed by another squirrel in a tree about thirty feet away. He sat on his hind legs and began to scold me over and over again. The squirrel's constant chatter seemed like it would never quit, and I wondered if the deer knew that such a racket meant danger to them. I tried not to move a muscle in hopes that he would forget about me and cease his scolding. After what seemed like a very long time, the woods once again grew quiet and the squirrel disappeared.

An hour after my scolding, I found myself wanting to doze off. I figured if I fell asleep I would be abruptly awakened by hitting the ground at the end of a thirty-foot fall. I restrained myself from catching a quick wink. I heard no shots all morning and began to wonder where all the deer were. Then I heard what sounded like a whole herd of deer approaching.

They were there, four or five deer about 150 yards out, moving through the trees. My heart was beating so fast that I wasn't sure I could hold my rifle steady, and I couldn't get a clear bead on any one animal.

When I finally had a glimpse of an open side, I pulled the trigger and the silence was smashed by the sound of my rifle. Deer began running in all directions as I quickly slammed the lever on my rifle. I fired a second and third time at a large doe running away.

Then it was quiet again and no deer in sight. I tried to remember exactly where I had fired my first shot, but I could see no definitive landmarks and no sign of a fallen deer.

Slowly I began to move my head from left to right, scanning the timber before me. Then I saw something. At first I was not sure what I was looking at, but the more I stared, the more sure I became. I was looking at the head and neck of a deer. The rest of the deer was completely hidden from my view.

I tried to steady my rifle as best I could, holding on the neck of the deer and I slowly squeezed off a shot. The deer did not move.

I tried once more, only this time concentrating even harder to squeeze and not jerk the trigger.

Still the deer did not move a muscle.

I now tried to bring my knees up so that I could steady the rifle on them. I fired once again.

The deer was like a statue.

Now I moved so that I could lean my rifle on a branch, and once more I fired.

Nothing.

I figured that I must be missing because of the distance, so I held ever so slightly above the deer's neck and squeezed off another round.

I had not counted the shots that I had taken and was not aware that I had my last round in the chamber. I raised my point of aim slightly higher still and squeezed off my ninth shot.

I could hear the thud as the deer dropped like a rock.

Not until then did I realize how badly I was shaking inside. My heart was racing, and my adrenaline was on fire. I had killed my first deer.

I knew that I needed to wait for at least twenty minutes before going to the deer. If he was just wounded and heard or saw me coming, he would run off. With no snow, I might not find him. If I let him lay, he might bleed to death or stiffen up too much to run away, so I waited.

While waiting, I marked the spot where he had fallen and examined the route that I would take to get to him.

I checked my rifle and realized that I had used all nine shots.

I reloaded my rifle and took a candy bar out of my pocket and enjoyed its sweetness.

I stood in the tree's large branches, stretched, and took a leak from thirty feet off the ground.

When twenty minutes had passed, I made sure there was not a shell in my gun's chamber and climbed down to the ground.

Before I started walking, I put a shell in the chamber and located the big evergreen that I knew was just beyond where the deer had fallen.

When I got to the deer I saw that it was just a fawn and that it was deader than a doornail. I had slit its throat and snapped its spine with that last shot.

But now I felt like a real tenderfoot because without my rope, even this fawn was not easy to drag through the woods. I did not dare to carry him because in brush-filled woods like this, that could present a real possibility of getting shot myself.

When I finally got back to camp, no one else was there, but the fawn was small enough for me to tie up on the deer pole by myself.

I got a drink of cold water, found a rope to take with me and headed out once again.

I mostly moved the rest of the day, exploring the woods and its many trails. I kept a sharp lookout in the trees for any hunter who might be perched high off the ground. The couple of times I saw another hunter, I snuck off in the opposite direction.

About an hour before sunset, I found a place to spend the remainder of the day. I sat on a small knoll overlooking what I would, from then on, call Wolf Pothole, which became one of my favorite places. It was a solid evergreen woods with little or no brush, bordered by this little pothole with heavy brush on the other side. I could easily visualize a deer stepping out of the brush to take a drink. I sat on the ground leaning up against a large evergreen tree with an open view through the other evergreens to the pothole. Several trails came to the pothole from slightly different directions. I was at peace.

I did not move until it got so dark that I could no longer see the pothole. I didn't care that it was pitch black because I knew what direction the main trail was. I loved being out there alone. Many a night I did not arrive back in camp until an hour or even two after it got pitch black. Over the years it became my trademark: First out each morning and last to return each night.

Now however, I was still the new guy in camp and after dinner I had to do all the dishes for the entire crew again. No one even lifted a finger to help. I think they were testing me, but I must have passed because each night thereafter one or two of the other hunters helped me out. After the first year, I took my rotation with the other hunters who weren't cooking.

Everyone wanted to hear my story. I really got razzed for not having a rope with me, but the razzing was all done in a friendly manner. I also got toasted for getting the first deer in camp that year. Two other hunters shot deer that day, and all the hunters related their experiences of the day.

Before the cards were dealt I was told one of my favorite hunting camp stories which I will share with you at the end of this segment.

I hunted with Joe's hunting camp every year from 1963 to 1977, except for my years in Alaska. Those years were full of great memories and great stories, and before moving on I will share one of my favorite camp stories.

THE RABBIT

One year it was so cold that even with a fire in the cabin, the water still froze in the milk cans alongside the outside wall. Late one night, one of the hunters opened the cabin door to make a trip to the outhouse. There stood a rabbit huddled up against the slight warmth coming through the door. When the door was fully opened, the rabbit just sat there, as if frozen stiff. The hunter gently picked him up and set him down in the middle of the cabin floor. The rabbit still didn't move, just sitting there like a statue. Another hunter put about a half inch of whiskey in a saucer and put it on the floor in front of the rabbit. As the rabbit grew slightly warmer, his nose began to twitch a little, and he moved his ears ever so slightly. Soon his nose was sniffing the high-powered octane in front of him. Finally, he stuck his tongue into the booze and started lapping it up. The hunters stared in amazement as the rabbit drank most of the whiskey. Then he sat back on his hind legs.

Soon one foot began to thump the cabin floor, ever so slowly at first and then a little faster. Soon the thumping became a fast beat and then a racing clamor. By now the hunters who were awake were all watching this strange rabbit slamming his foot on the floor faster than seemed possible. The next thing they knew, the rabbit took off like a streak of lightning.

He ran around the cabin floor several times, and then shot up the stairs and ran right across the face of one of the sleeping hunters. The hunter came out of a sound sleep screaming as if someone had stabbed him in the ass.

The rabbit kept on running round and round and over and under the upstairs bunks, until the shocked hunters chased him down the stairs. After a few more rounds of the main floor, someone opened the door and the rabbit shot out into the cold night, sending snow flying in every direction.

One of the hunters remarked that the doe rabbits were sure in trouble that night.

Hunting in Wisconsin

Along with hunting during the rifle season in Minnesota, I hunted with a bow many winters at uncle AJ's cabin in Wisconsin. I even hunted a time or two with a bow on cross-country skis and slept under the stars wherever nightfall would find me.

Two deer hunting memories in the Wisconsin woods are also perhaps worth relating.

One was on December 30 and I was hunting alone on cross-country skis. I had packed along my sleeping bag so I could spend the night wherever I happened to be at the time. I figured there was no need for any cover because snow falling would not be a problem, but on that particular night it didn't snow. It rained, and it rained hard. I and my sleeping bag got thoroughly soaked, so I had to either start a fire in the rain or ski out in the dark. I decided to ski several miles along the logging road to the suburban. It very easily could have turned out to be the wrong choice because the rain soon changed to freezing sleet. By the time I got to the car, hypothermia was knocking at my door and the suburban didn't want to start. I got lucky, or my guardian angel was on the job. Just when I was about to give up and start a fire, the outfit kicked in. The warmth of its heater was a welcome relief. From that day on I always have carried a light rain cover even in the dead of winter.

The other story worth relating was when I was climbing out of my tree just after the sun set and broke my compass on the climb down. It was a cloudy night, and I really didn't know exactly where I was. I just picked a straight line and walked for an hour or two until I came to a road. When I reached the road, I knew that I had walked west when I should have walked east, so I had a choice to make. Walk about eight miles around by road or walk about four miles straight through the woods. I decided to take the short route and headed back into the woods. I came out the other side close to midnight. When I got back to the cabin, I was happy to see that my hunting partner was asleep and not up praying for me.

Deer hunting on Lost Lake

When my boys got old enough to hunt, my father had long since quit hunting. Joe's hunting camp had lost our hunting spot with the death of its owner, so I started anew. I researched areas of northern Minnesota and settled on Lost Lake. I checked out the area the summer before and the woods were great, with rolling hills, several lakes and a few swamps. One island in a small lake/swamp we soon called the Bank. The next year in 1980 I took Luke and Tim out of school for a Friday, Monday and Tuesday and had Hoag join us. We took the camper back into the lake and hunted from there. All I remember of that year was that I put Tim on a trail that I had scouted the day before (on Porcupine Hill). Tim later told us that he had sat for 15 minutes and got cold, so he put his long johns on; while doing so, a buck came within 30 yards. Tim saw him but was in a compromising position, and the buck ran off.

The following year I invited Mike Blaylock and his sons along. For some reason only Mike's son Paul was able to go. I brought Luke, Tim and Matt and we took our boys out of school for a week, loaded all our gear, and headed north. We had a wood-burning stove in the large Army tent for heat. We built bunk beds, so we had enough room for everyone, which over the years would include Mike and his three sons, and my four sons and me. We brought in all our food, with a propane stove for cooking, and drank water right out of the lake.

We had the area pretty much to ourselves and although we only got one buck, we had a great time and learned a few lessons. On opening morning on the way back to camp, Matt saw two bucks on the trail by Apple Hill but had no time for a shot because he was walking with no shells in the chamber. Lesson number one, when hunting always have a shell in the chamber.

The next day Tim missed a buck standing less than 50 yards from his stand. His scope was off because he had dropped it a day or two before. Lesson number two, don't drop your rifle and if you do, be sure to sight it in again.

On Thursday morning, Matt was following deer tracks in the snow and drove a spike buck to Mike just south of Deer Lake. Mike dropped him with one shot. We all saw lots of deer that year, but it was a bucks-only year and no more bucks were seen.

The third year at Lost Lake, in 1981, we had eight hunters in the camp and hunted for eight and a half days and got six deer.

In 1982, our fourth year at Lost Lake, we had 7 hunters and got 6 deer.

1983–Lost Lake. 6 hunters–6 deer.

I believe this was our last year at Lost Lake. Not sure why we quit there because six deer for six hunters ain't bad! Perhaps too many other hunters were closing in on us.

As for hunting at Lost Lake, "That's all folks."

Camp on Lost Lake

For more deer hunting stories, go to the Deer Hunting section under the "Ranch Stories" chapter.

Grandfather's Quote

To truly become one with nature you need to be so immersed in the present that there is not a single word thought in your mind.

Our tent on Lost Lake

Me at the county fair (2000)

32

A Cow-Calf Rancher

People have often said that I was born 200 years too late. More than once my own mother even said to this young man who would rather be in the woods than a five-star hotel, "Where the hell did you come from?" I did try once to turn the clock back by moving to Alaska to homestead. But the only homestead land was 50 miles from the nearest road. That was fine by me, but we had a year-old son, and my wife was pregnant. She wanted no part of it. These unreasonable women, <smile>.

When we left Alaska, my wife and I both agreed that a compromise between Alaska and the farmlands of southern Minnesota would be a working cattle ranch. Short of living in the Alaskan bush, I thought the closest lifestyle to living 200 years ago was being on a working ranch.

Actually, being a guide and outfitter was even closer, but living ten miles from my nearest year-round neighbor at 9,200 foot elevation was not an ideal choice for my partner. Bless her heart for giving it a try, but I had promised her if she didn't like it we would give it up, and I kept my promise.

Having given up living in the mountains and winding up back in Minnesota, I once again started looking for a working cattle ranch. That is, I started looking after trying out owning an athletic club and buying and selling land for a few years.

Home built in 1991. Did it all: footings, poured walls, carpentry work, plumbing, heating, electrical, stone work and more. Mark helped for three months. Took a year to complete.

Buck resting under a pine tree in our backyard

In my search, I found a 5,000 acre ranch on the Guernsey reservoir in Wyoming. It sounded perfect, except for the price. It was way too cheap, so I asked the realtor what the problem was. He assured me that there was no problem. I pushed him harder. I said that maybe whatever the problem was, that for me, it would not even be a problem. I just did not want to drive all the way out there and find out that it was something that I would not even consider. He again assured me that there was no problem, so I drove 12 or 13 hours to look at the ranch. I got there before the realtor and the couple who owned the ranch explained to me that the ranch bordered the Fort Laramie firing range. They said the cattle got used to it, but bombs were going off 24/7 during the summer. I was so pissed I told them that if I stayed until the realtor came I would deck him, so I left.

On my drive back through Hot Springs I stopped at all the realtors, a couple of bars and at the feed mill, and left my card saying I was looking for a ranch. A short time later, I got a call from Herman Perry. He was married to Lisa, formerly a Schroth, and he said that they had 5,000 acres for sale. I left the next day to see the ranch.

The first place he took me was in what we now call the North Pasture. As we looked down the cliff at the bowl and the rough land around it, he commented, "I suppose it is too rough for you?" I kept silent, but I was busting inside because I knew I had found my ranch.

Without all my real estate experience, the deal would never have been put together. The ranch had been part of the FO Butler ranch, and Rudolf Schroth had been a foreman on the ranch for many years. When Butler died, he left 25% of the ranch to Rudolf and 75% to Brookings State College. The College was not willing to buy Rudolf out so they sold their 75% to him with a two-year redemption period in case he ever got in financial trouble. Rudolf had a daughter, Lisa, and an adopted son, Frank, who was known as Hap.

When Rudolf and his wife passed away, Hap and his sister inherited the ranch. They would have lost the entire 14,000 acres in December of 1986, but by selling 5,000 acres to me in July they were able to pay off the note and save the 9,000 remaining acres.

Branding on the ranch (Mark holding front leg of calf)

Me in one of my Rangers

When I realized the value of the 640 acres along Highway 385, just north of Hot Springs, I told Hap and his wife they did not need to sell to me. I really wanted the ranch, but it did not seem fair that the college, which had been given a gift, was now trying to take more away from those who had been on the ranch all their lives. I told them they could sell eight 80-acre parcels along the highway and pay off the note. The time was very short however and I am not sure they believed me, so they went through with the sale.

I have looked for ranches in all the western mountain states and—if it were 200 years ago—there is no place I would rather be than in the Black Hills. But today there are no grizzly bears, and too few elk and the Black Hills are too tame. Irene liked that though and when she came out and looked at the ranch, she said we had finally found a ranch where we could both be happy.

Now I was on a ranch that would run up to 250 cows, living out of the back of my pickup with one electrical outlet and a phone hookup in the entryway of the root cellar.

Unfortunately, within a few months Irene had changed her mind and left me.

She got almost everything we owned, including all the Contract for Deeds that were going to be used to build our new home, buy machinery and a cow herd. I got the ranch. The next summer I was forced to sell the 640 acres I told Hap and Loretta about. I went to every realtor in town and they all said that I could not get $19,900 for 80 acres. It took me the entire summer, but I sold all eight 80-acre parcels myself for exactly that.

I soon bought a 45-foot mobile home, added a porch and moved in.

I got my first ten cows as payment for leasing most of my grass out to a neighbor. With the down payments on the 640 acres, I bought thirty bred heifers. They all had a little ear (Brahman) in them, but they turned out to be great cows. I also bought a horse named Loco, half Arabian and half Morgan. He was a super ranch horse; he could do all you asked and go all day. I even had a few "Man from Snowy River" rides chasing bulls on the side of the mountain.

Once when Matt was visiting, he ran Loco down the driveway and touched the reins to his neck to turn towards the trailer. Loco turned right out from under him. He flew over the top and landed in a heap on the ground. When you rode Loco, you needed to be aware that you were on a super sports car.

Actually, in those early years I used to live in the saddle. I had sixteen miles of exterior fence line to maintain, and the ranch was almost seven miles from east to west. I even gave thought to selling all my outfits (motorized vehicles) and just going to town once a month with a pack horse and buying groceries and supplies.

I learned many ranch lessons over the years, but the most important lesson was to be very gentle when working cattle. You can always tell a rancher and a good cowboy from the run-of-the-mill cowboy by how gently he works cattle.

Grandfather's Quote

If you are blessed enough to love what you do for a living, it will never be considered work.

My mother standing at the head of Big Spring Canyon, which is three miles long and all on the ranch

33

Jamie's Story

A couple years after purchasing my ranch in South Dakota, and a short time after Mark left for Australia, my brother Jay gave me a call.

It seemed that his son Jamie was in trouble in and out of school, and Jay thought that spending some time on the ranch might help straighten him out.

Jamie was 16 or 17 years old, and he was an athletic kid who loved to play cards and games. We hit it off right away. In a way, he was a young Jay.

The understanding was that he was to spend a month and that he would work for me on the ranch. I would pay him $25 for the month's work and furnish him with all the shells that he could shoot while hunting prairie dogs. He also could use the pickup once a week to go to town, but he never did.

Jamie was a very open kid, and we did a lot of talking. I told him about my arrangement with Mark when he was still living here. Jamie liked the sound of it, so we charted the same course.

We had to take care of our own cooking and cleaning so one person cooked and the other did the dishes. We shared the cleaning chores.

Our days began at 5 a.m. and we spent about eight hours on the mountain or doing other ranch chores. That way, even taking a half hour for lunch, we were done each day by 2:30 in the afternoon. Then we headed for the lake for our daily swim and cooling-off period.

I taught him to shoot a rifle, run a chainsaw, dig fence posts, drive steel posts and stretch wire among other things. During all this time I was right at his side, working as hard or harder than he was. I remember one time he looked at the blisters on his hands and said, "I've never worked so hard in my life. And I love it!"

We ran over a mile of new fence between what we now call the Dinosaur and West pastures. We cleared many old fence lines, rolling up all the old wire. We also cleared a trail from the bowl near Elm Creek to the top of the mountain. We named it Jamie's Trail, and it retained that name until a cowboy flipped a horse over backwards on it and it acquired a new name. It is now known as Horse Wreck Canyon.

Jamie was a great worker and became a good friend, but what we enjoyed most was each other's competitive nature.

I had invented a football game and every afternoon on the way home from the beach we would both say, "Are you ready for some football?!"

We played every afternoon and some evenings for almost two weeks. He was a very aggressive player who constantly threw passes. I was rather conservative and methodically drove the ball down the field. We kept track of all the games and all the scores, and neither of us could get ahead of the other. After two weeks and playing over twenty games, I think we were dead even.

Then things changed. Jamie had the ball on his own twenty-yard line, and it was fourth and one, and he went for it. He made the first down. Three plays later, it was now fourth and two, and once again, he went for it and made it. One more time on his way to a touchdown, Jamie was successful at converting a fourth-down play.

I do not even remember if he won that game or not, but I do remember that from that time forward, he would hardly ever punt.

With him not punting, the tables began to turn. I was now winning at least five out of six of all our games.

He never could recover from that. No matter how much I tried to reason with him, he would just have none of it. He basically quit punting, and quit winning, but he was unable to connect the two.

In our play, we were always bantering with one another.

"I am better at this and I am better at that."

"No way, I could kick your butt at that."

And so it went, in good-natured fun back and forth. We argued about who was the better softball player, ping pong player, football player, card player, risk player, monopoly player, and then we got to who was the better basketball player.

"Now come on, you might be almost 30 years younger than me, but you are a short runt."

"No way, you are an old man and I can run circles around you."

"Five Jamies might even be able to put up a good show against five Garys, but in the end, height would win out. In a one-on-one game, you wouldn't stand a chance."

"Do you want to bet?"

It was just a few nights before this friendly discussion began that we talked about his month coming to an end. I asked if he would consider staying on for the rest of the summer. He said that he would have to think about it.

"I'll make a bet with you! I am so sure that I could beat you in a one-on-one basketball game, that if you win, you can select your own prize. If I win, you will agree to stay for the rest of the summer."

"OK, if I win, you pay me $2000."

"Get real! I'll tell you what I'll do. If you win, I'll pay you $500, and you don't have to stay for the rest of the summer. But if you decide to stay for the rest of the summer, I'll pay you $100 a month in wages too. And if I win, you agree to stay for the rest of the summer, and I'll double your wages to $50 a month."

"It's a bet."

We had a new basketball, and we went to a basketball court at Coldbrook Lake.

We played the game by counting to eleven by ones, and you had to win by two points. If one player scored, the other player got the ball. If a player took a shot and hit the rim or backboard, the other player had to take the ball behind the free throw line before he could shoot.

He was 16 and I was 46, but I was over 6'2" tall, and I do not think he was even 5’8".

I took no chances. I would drive the ball to the boards and easily score. He could not shoot over me, and even with his quickness, he could not get around me. The game was soon over, and I had an 11 to 3 win.

I think in the end that he turned out to be the real winner. He got to stay on the ranch for another two months and I watched a young boy turn into a man.

Grandfather’s Quote

One's manhood can be most easily
found in honor and hard work.

34

Hunting for a New Partner

After the freight train ran over me, I was dead below the waist for over a year. That is how powerful the mind is. About a year and a half after the freight train, I told a friend I was tired all the time yet could not seem to sleep, and that I had a few other problems I can't remember now. My friend said I had all the signs of chronic depression.

I told him I didn't believe in depression, so I took stock of what he said and decided I needed to get out. I made myself go to a bar or a dance every weekend. Hot Springs didn't have much going on, so I drove to Rapid City a lot.

When the weekend came around, I usually didn't want to go, but I did not allow myself that option. I went. That was a really bad two or three months. I was meeting the kind of people that I didn't want to meet. They were always talking about getting wasted or bombed, and I even remember one conversation where they were bragging about spending last Christmas Eve in the slammer. That was enough for me.

I called an athletic club in Rapid and found out they had couples volleyball so I started going to that once a week. The problem was that I was in my mid-forties and everyone else was in their early twenties. Also, I didn't use my fist on saves but rather made them with an open hand. At first they let that go because this old man was doing a really good job of playing, but soon others complained and the refs started calling my carries.

I also joined a country western dance class, and that was kind of fun, but neither the athletic club nor the dancing led to any dates.

Back then they didn't have computer dating, and I didn't even own a computer, so I joined Country Connections. You posted a profile and read women's profiles, and then you wrote to each other. I got real good at that real fast and soon I was sending tapes rather than writing. A couple of different gals even called me the Garrison Keillor of South Dakota. I can't recall how long I did this, but I wrote or sent tapes to over one hundred women. I had twelve of them fly out to the ranch and spend a few days. I treated each one with dignity and respect, but I think it was too soon after my divorce and I never made a connection.

During that time, I wrote this poem and shared it with a few of them.

Somewhere

There is a whisper on a lonely breeze;
There is a message in its silent tune.
I know that she is there somewhere—
May I find her soon.
But if I search and search each day,
I'll not despair, despair, no way,
For I am something special.
There is just one of a kind
And I too
May be hard to find

The first to come to the ranch was a gal I called Sunshine. She was a real nice ranch girl, but she was the first and I definitely was not ready. We went dancing in Rapid City, and on the dance floor she said when we got home she was going to seduce me. When we got back to the ranch, she started coming onto me and when I sat down on the couch, she straddled my lap and started wiggling around. I hung my head. When she put her hand under my chin and lifted my face, she saw tears flowing down my cheeks.

Up to that point in my life, I had never even touched the breast of a woman other than Irene. I had been married to her for over twenty-four years, and I was not ready to go there yet.

She immediately stopped, got off me and went into the guest bedroom. We said little the next morning. I took her to the airport and she left.

Then there was the 28-year-old who had her own cow herd and bragged about how tough she was. So when we hiked up Rattlesnake Canyon to check water, I left her in the dust and she got pissed.

Then there was Matt's girlfriend's mother, who actually put off sailing around the world in order to come meet me. She was very well off. She offered to build us a new home and buy us a cattle herd and she was really nice, but for me there was no magic. I had felt so much magic with Irene, I just didn't want to settle for less.

Then there was Cherrie, the only one that I asked back a second time. My parents even met her that time. In between her two visits, I went to Colorado and met her parents. There may have been a little magic, or maybe it was because she was so beautiful, but she also cried at the drop of a hat and was very immature. I ended it.

That's all I remember before meeting Daniel's mother, but that definitely is another story. You can read it right after this chapter or jump to it now and then come back here if you are so inclined.

After Daniel's mother, actually shortly after I got custody of Daniel, I joined Country Connections again and met Evelyn. On paper, she was a perfect match. She even had gone on elk hunts with her former husband and cooked for all the guys. She was a great cook, and she made clothes. She even made Daniel's vest for his 16-month-old picture, and it matched the vest I had used for my other four sons perfectly.

Evelyn really fell in love with me. She spent several weeks on the ranch and made many visits, and I tried and tried. I liked her a lot, she was very good looking, and she would have made a very good mother for Daniel. But by now I had known love/magic twice in my life, and it was not there with her. I broke her heart and walked away.

Grandfather's Quotes

Life is so special when you are in love with your best friend. If the two of you can keep the magic, even after years of marriage, you both are really blessed.

35

Daniel's Mother

Gene Clinton was my best male friend in Alaska. When Irene walked away and I felt like I needed someone to talk to, I called him. A couple of years later Gene had moved to Denver, Colorado, and one night he gave me another call. He thought that I should meet this girl he used to work with in Alaska. She was moving to Denver and a short time after she arrived I drove to Denver and the four of us went out dancing.

Her name was Kathy, and she was beautiful and we had a great time. So much so that I stayed in Denver for the entire weekend and took her and her four kids to some large park.

One thing led to another, and soon I was driving to Denver every weekend. I was romantically alive again for the first time since my divorce, and I loved the feeling. But I was concerned that she and her kids might not like living on a remote ranch, so I suggested they spend the summer with me.

I have always loved children, and I loved being kind of a dad to hers and I did come to love them. Her oldest son, Luke, was about 16 and I taught him many things and we got along fine. Rachel was next and we hit it off well. She used to love swimming with me at the rocks. Paul was next and perhaps was the one who had the most difficult time with me. I was a lot stricter than he was used to and at first he fought it tooth and nail. I do think that he finally came around, but only he could tell you that. Liz was the youngest and a real sweetheart. She was about 6 and still took her turn at doing dishes, even though she had to stand on a chair to get them done. Kathy was very supportive of my requiring all the kids to take on responsibility.

We went to Mass on a weekly basis. In the beginning she insisted we pray the rosary on the twenty-minute ride to church. To me that was too fast, kind of like racing through it. I got her to talk about our faith a time or two, but she was very traditional and wanted to say the Rosary. I am sad to say that those experiences kind of soured me on the Rosary. The Our Father is one of my favorite prayers, but if I say it too fast, it means little. When I say it with reverence, it makes all the difference in the world.

In the eyes of the church, Kathy was free to marry again because she had an annulment. She wanted me to get one. I told her that I was sure the church would not grant it because I was certain my marriage was sacramental. I did however apply for the annulment and was granted a hearing. I went before several priests and members of the church and answered all their questions. Did I believe my marriage was sacramental? Did I enter into it of my free will? Was I instructed properly? I answered yes to all of these questions and everything I told them indicated to me that I would not be granted an annulment.

When the annulment was granted, it actually hurt and bothered me deeply. It even shook my faith.

Things continued to go along fine until Kathy and I took a trip to Kansas.

I remember that we met her relatives at a Motel 6 because we joked about "we will leave the light on for ya."

On the night we met, we all went to a dance. There must have been eight or ten people in our group, and we were having a great time.

Halfway through the evening, with a few drinks under our belt, Kathy and I were out on the dance floor and had just finished a dance. As we started to walk back to our table a fast country western song came on that was a real toe stomper. I held her hand and said, "Let's dance." She said no, and I said, "Please, just this one." But she turned and walked away. Another young woman was right there and had observed what was going on. She came up to me and said, "I'll dance." By this time Kathy was already back to our table. Now in retrospect, I know I was wrong and even thoughtless to stay on the floor and dance, but that is what I did. It was a very fast dance and a lot of fun, and when it was over I just thanked the stranger and went back to our table.

Kathy was furious, and I had never seen her that way before. She lit into me, almost yelling in front of all her relatives. She went on like that for at least a minute and ended up saying, "Don't you ever, ever do anything like that to me again."

Right or wrong, nobody talks to me like that. I said nothing. I just got up and went back out on the dance floor and danced another fast dance with another stranger.

I do not have another memory of that evening, but I know I would have apologized later. But I also know I will not take someone getting in my face or yelling at me.

Kathy had many fine qualities, but she had a temper she was able to hold back for almost six months. Once the cork had been blown, it could not be put back in. Things were never the same after that night.

I was in love with a woman with a temper and our lives became one fight after another with awesome making up in between. The making up was really very special, and once we had done so all was forgotten.

A lot of people can live like that. Some shrinks even say it is good for two people to let off steam, and even for their children to see it and learn about conflict.

I was not raised like that. I never once, until I was over 30 years old, saw my mother and father fight and my first four sons never saw their mother or I have a fight. As far as Kathy goes, I eventually made my mind get control of my heart and knew that I could not live like that.

When I got to that point, I told Kathy I loved her but could not live like this; and then she told me she was pregnant.

Now what do I do? What do I owe this unborn child of mine? Do I owe him enough to live a life getting more difficult by the day? Perhaps.

We kept trying to make it work. During the pregnancy, I was building our new home and wanted to get it done so the baby could be born in it.

I didn't make it and Daniel was born in the trailer on January 28, 1991.

Things were still going pretty much the same between Kathy and I, and I was praying daily for guidance in what I should do.

I still wore my father's wedding ring. I remember putting my thumb on the ring and asking my father to help me decide what to do.

Right after that I walked into the new house and the phone rang. Kathy read me the riot act for eating a peanut butter sandwich so close to dinner. She really came unglued. I finally hung up on her and said, "Thanks, Dad, for your answer."

Within a month of Daniel's birth, we moved into the new house and I was still trying to make it work. Several months later Kathy got so angry at me, for who knows what, that she picked Daniel up and started to walk out the door. She said she was going to take Daniel back to Alaska and that I would never see him again.

I crawled like I have never crawled before or since and begged and pleaded with her not to go. She had won and actually brought me to my knees, so she turned around and stayed.

For me, it was over, but I could not lose my son. Kathy's uncle was, or recently was, the governor of Alaska and I believed her threat.

I went to an attorney, and I learned to hate our legal system. I was told if she got back to Alaska, I very well might never see my son again. To prevent that, I had to serve her papers here in South Dakota. Getting her served would take a week or more.

I believe this is why Kathy still hates me to this day. I deceived her for over a week, all the while knowing that papers were being drawn up to try to take her son from her.

I even had to go so far as to make sure her other four kids were away when I knew the sheriff was coming. It is still a horrible memory for me. It was not right, but our legal system gave me no other choice. Lose my son perhaps forever, or do what I did.

Our legal system sucks!

After she was served, I went to an attorney friend of mine. I asked him who was the best attorney in the state, and he told me Gary Coldbath. But he said it was more important to find out which judge would try our case and hire the attorney who had the best rapport with that judge. I talked to the right attorney for our judge, Ken D.

Then I went to the best attorney in the state and asked him if I should hire him or Ken and he said hire both of us. Ken refused to work with another attorney, so I had to make a choice. I asked Gary who to choose. He told me that on a scale of one to one hundred that he was a 100 and Ken was an 85, but because of the judge connection I should hire Ken. So I did.

More importantly I prayed and prayed and in my prayers I asked my Heavenly Father to be the judge and to do whatever was best for Daniel.

The court case went on for a long time. In the process, I lost my relationship with the rest of Kathy's children and I lost over 30 pounds.

The case went all the way to the Supreme Court of South Dakota, where I was awarded full legal and physical custody of my one-year-old son.

Kathy understandably never forgave me, but I want to end this on a positive note. When Daniel was a senior in high school and had just returned from visiting his mother in Alaska, Kathy called me. During the conversation she said I had done a good job raising Daniel. It was so shocking and so powerful that I lost it, and got all choked up.

Grandfather's quote

No matter how your heart feels, you must rely on your logic and reason when making decisions.

Daniel and me checking cows

36

Daniel

Prior to having Daniel, I lived on a horse. There were many days where I was in the saddle for six hours or more. I had even thought of selling all my motorized outfits and taking a horse and packhorse over the mountain once a month to buy groceries. Now that I had a one-year-old to take care of, I bought a Jeep and installed an elevated car seat so he could see what was going on.

The contrasts between raising my four sons in a traditional two-parent family and raising Daniel for several years by myself were many. In my traditional family, I was the bread earner, the disciplinarian and the authoritarian figure. I was the obvious head of our family, and the entire family looked to me for guidance and direction. I spent a lot of time with my four boys and taught them many things. I also had the luxury of being able to teach them to be tough and endure the hurt or pain. If they needed additional comfort, they could always go to Mom. Yes, I too could comfort my sons, but it was much easier to play the role of the traditional father. Because I wasn't with them continually, when I was with them, they valued my time more. They listened more intensely, and they wanted to be with me as much as possible. I also did not have to be the one changing diapers or cleaning up vomit or rocking a sick child to sleep. I did not have to wash their clothes and teach them how to brush their teeth and tie their shoes. I did not realize at the time how easy I had it.

With Daniel, all that changed, but I did not mind the poopy diapers or the laundry or the never-ending responsibility. I only had a lot of difficulty when Daniel got sick. It got to be almost more than I could handle when he was sick and I too was sick. Fortunately, shortly after Kathy left, I had a traditional family—Bob and Lorna Lauinger with their four children move into a second home on the ranch. Their youngest son, Tom, was the same age as Daniel. I paid Lorna to come and cook one meal a day for me and do a little house cleaning, and Bob occasionally helped me out on the ranch.

I tried to make sure I took care of their son more often than they took care of Daniel. But once when both Daniel and I were very sick, they insisted on moving their whole family into my house to take care of us both. No way was I ever able to repay such kindness and love.

But it helped a little that once Daniel and Tom got to be three or four years old, I took them with me way more often than they had Daniel. The two boys loved to come with me when I was doing ranch work, and I made sure they felt like they were helping out.

Bob and Lorna had a very deep faith, and Bob got me to join a men's church group called the Twelve Pillars. We met once a week at the Catholic church and just shared our thoughts about any and everything. I was very moved by our sharing, but I was way out of my spiritual league with that group. I even worried I did not belong there, or I was causing the group harm. Each of these good men had had some sort of religious experience, and one of them even said that he wanted to be in church, in God's presence all the time. He had several young children, and I had the audacity to suggest that at this time in his and his children's life, he needed to be at home with them. I never got asked to leave, but I was definitely the worldly one in the group.

For whatever reason, I seemed to draw or be drawn to people of faith. When a good friend from Cannon Falls bought property out here, he built prayer cabins on his 160 acres and allowed anyone to come stay in them free of charge. He built an octagon house with the top floor completely taken up with a chapel surrounded in glass. Daniel and I were there quite often.

Daniel and I attended Mass every Sunday, and he started religious education at the church. I was asked to become a teacher, but when I reminded the priest of my history, he agreed with me that it might not be acceptable to the other parents.

Daniel learned to ride a horse by the time he was four, and he had chores and responsibility from the time he could remember. I also taught him to read before he started school, and I only allowed him to watch a few hours of TV a week.

When the South Dakota Supreme Court made their final decision in Daniel's custody case, the only thing they changed was his mother's visitation rights. They allowed us to decide for ourselves.

Daniel learning to drive

If we were unable to agree, the standard court guidelines required every other holiday, one weekend a month and all of the summer, other than the first and last week. No way did I want him to be away for that long every summer. I proposed what I did, and Kathy accepted my proposal.

Right after the Court's decision, Kathy moved to Kansas. I don't remember exactly what we decided about visitation there.

When she moved back to Alaska, she got him every holiday and twice during the summer for two weeks each time.

On the ranch we could celebrate Thanksgiving, Christmas and Easter anytime. I thought I was doing the right thing by giving up the actual holidays. Later I realized that most of a child's memories are of extended family and holidays, so maybe I made a mistake.

In spite of my mistakes, Daniel grew into a fine young man. Daniel went on to college at the School of Mines in Rapid City and graduated *summa cum laude* with an electrical engineering degree. I required my boys to send themselves to college. But later in life my older sons told me they lived on ramen noodles all through college, so I paid for Daniel's

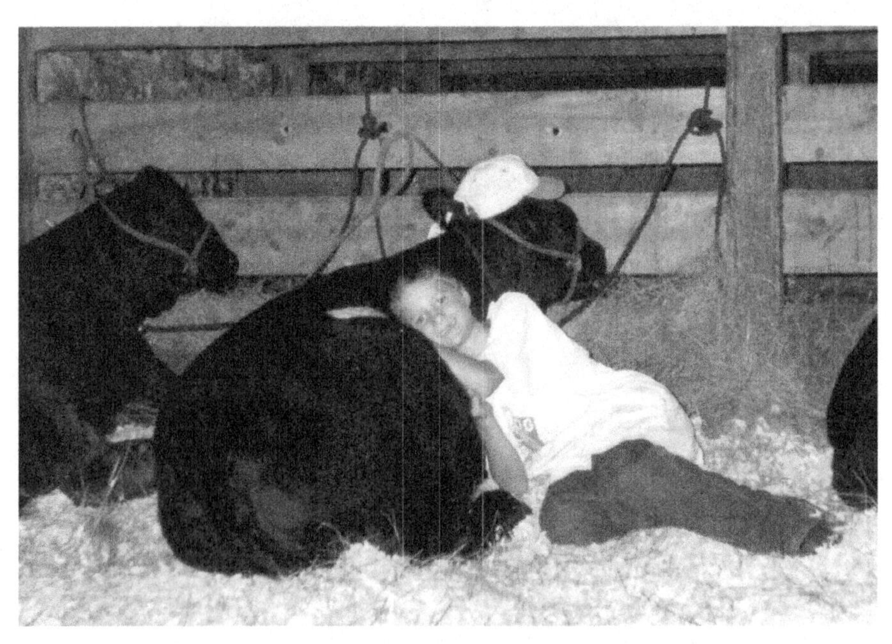

Daniel with his 4-H heifer

meal tickets. Daniel worked his tail off all summer and throughout the school year. With the help of several college scholarships, he paid the rest of his college expenses on his own and graduated in four years debt-free! He also bought his own home and rented rooms to five other students during his last two years of college.

Grandfather's Quote

Stories can teach without the child even realizing he or she is being taught. Tell them often and build an unbreakable bond.

Daniel, my mother and me in Germany at Mark's wedding

Jeanne helping out

37

Jeanne, a Gift for Daniel and Me

Here is how one of the great blessings in my life began.

I had my profile on some singles dating site and had taken it off a week or two earlier when I got a call from someone at the website. I was told that a young woman had contacted them and asked if she could get my contact information so that she could write to me. I said OK, and Jeanne sent me an email. Growing up, she spent many summers on her uncle's ranch in California and was interested in knowing more about life on a working cattle ranch. One thing led to another and soon we were talking on the phone. I was writing my children's stories; she was an illustrator, and she was possibly interested in illustrating my stories. We also sent tapes back and forth and on one of the tapes Daniel and I sang to her. When that didn't drive her away, we invited her to the ranch for a visit.

WOW! What an amazing human being, and as we were to find out, with so many talents. I was beginning to be taken in the first few times I had talked to her, and when I met her, the attraction kept growing. She and Daniel also had a real connection. Now I am not sure what she saw in this very different kind of guy, but she must have seen something. After several months and a few more visits, she came to spend the summer. The rest is history.

Taken on one of our rides to Midnight Mass

We hiked together, rode horses, both for pleasure and ranch work, and we went dancing a lot.

While Daniel was off at school, I can remember spending many hours riding together, either with a saddle or bareback; and often taking drives in the pickup all over the ranch and winding up on some romantic vista.

One Christmas Eve, while Daniel was off visiting his birth mother, we rode horses under a full moon over the mountain to Midnight Mass. The mountains were snow covered, and the snow on the trees sparkled in the moonlight. When we got to the edge of town, we took a shortcut through the VA parking lot and up drives this police car.

The officer rolled down his window, and smiling said, "I just have to ask?"

"We are going to Midnight Mass."

"Have a merry Christmas."

We rode the short distance from there through town to church. While answering many questions, we tied our horses up outside the church and went into Mass. Our trip is still talked about today.

On the way home I fell asleep in the saddle and was awakened by "Gary wake up!"

"It's OK, Loco (my horse's name) knows the way home," and I went back to sleep.

For the first time in my life, I had a woman who wanted to be with me as much as I wanted to be with her.

During the summers Jeanne, Daniel and I took many trips to Angostura, a large reservoir with miles of sandy beach. It was only about nine miles from the ranch and we always went during the week, so we usually had all of the beach to ourselves. Actually, many times we took several of Daniel's friends, which both of us thoroughly enjoyed.

Jeanne loved to cook, and she was more than fantastic at it. She was a great homemaker, loved the outdoors, the ranch, and the remoteness of it all. She also was a great dancer, loved horses and most importantly became very attached to Daniel and Daniel to her.

Jeanne put in a lot of effort for birthdays and holidays. For this party, Jeanne baked a football cake and made a "Pin The Football on the Running Back" game for Daniel and his guests.

Before Jeanne, I often said eating was a waste of time. If I could take three pills a day and forget about eating, I would do it in a heartbeat. Jeanne changed all that in a big way. For the first time in my life, I really looked forward to meals. Eating was a pleasure, and sometimes the meals were so good that I stomped my feet on the floor in excitement. Not only that, but she took great interest in my health and particularly in the foods that helped prevent prostate cancer. She spent hours and hours on the computer doing research, and with that newly acquired knowledge she went out of her way to make sure I was eating right. She also made sure we were eating only the best and usually organic food.

She made clothes for Daniel and me, and boy did she make Daniel's birthdays and Halloweens extra special. In fact, she made every occasion something to be remembered. For Daniel's high school graduation, what she did is still talked about today among other parents.

One of the most amazing things about her is that she is always thinking of others before herself. She seems to get some kind of satisfaction in doing things for others. And it did not matter if it was Daniel or me not feeling well, she was there waiting on us hand and foot. Going through my last major surgery without her being there for me would have been very difficult.

Yes, I have been blessed beyond all telling.

Grandfather's Quote

Don't ever give up. There is someone special for each and every one of us.

Daniel and me on one of our diving trips.

38

Scuba Diving

Daniel was twelve years old when we decided to become scuba divers. We bought all new gear except for tanks and signed up for a scuba diving class. I had fun studying alongside a twelve-year-old.

Sixty and twelve was not a bad combination, but I was a little embarrassed that he read the chapters quicker than I did. When we asked each other questions, he seemed to do better than I did. We took our initial hands-on lessons in a pool in Rapid City and did our open water dives in Cold Brook Reservoir. The cold water was bad enough, but the poor four to six foot visibility really sucked. When it was all said and done we both passed everything, but the old man actually saved a little face and scored higher on the written exam than did the twelve-year-old.

The year before we became scuba divers we had arranged an exchange with a family who owned a place on Eleuthera in the Bahamas. We got to stay at their place for a week and then they came out to the ranch for a week. We were on the island shortly after a hurricane, so the bottom of the ocean was really stirred up. The visibility was not as good as normal, but we still did a lot of snorkeling. I patched their roof while we were there. Daniel, his friend Laird, Jeanne and I played lots of cards and toured the entire island. We even found a sandy beach with huge breakers coming ashore.

Jordan, me, Duggan, Mark, Brent (back). Tristan and Paul (front)

Our first diving trip was really just a trip to Hawaii. We went to the big island and we once again let Daniel bring a friend along so there were four of us. Neither Jeanne nor Daniel's friend Casey were divers, so we did a lot of snorkeling. We went on two shallow open water dives. Casey stayed on the surface and snorkeled while we were diving nearby. Daniel did get to hold a baby octopus on one of the dives. We rented a villa on a lava rock beach so we could snorkel right in front of the place. We also hiked to a black sand beach and swam and goofed around so we had a good time, but it was certainly not much of a diving trip.

The following year we went with Luke and Jordan on a live-aboard catamaran in the British Virgin Islands. The water was the clearest I have ever dived in, before or since. You could see at least 100 feet. In fact, when we dove on the RMS Rhone, a sunken ship, we were in eighty to eighty-five feet of water and you could easily see to the surface. We even saw a large shark swimming near the ship. We swam in a place among rocks and caves, with lots of fish everywhere. I slept on deck at night and got up before the sun. I swam to shore, hiked along the beach for forty-five minutes, and then swam back to the boat. The bottom was very sandy, and I saw several sea turtles. Unfortunately, in the British Virgin Islands you are required to anchor on buoys and there were always several boats near our spot. When I was swimming back in the mornings, just as others were getting up, in all directions I could see toilet paper—and whatever else was being flushed down the toilet—coming from each boat. It was nice being able to sail and anchor in different spots each night though, even if you always had other boats around. Lots of cards, good food, and super clear water. All in all, a great trip.

One of the best diving trips we have taken was on Green Turtle Cay in the Bahamas. I rented a place called Tranquility. The entire family was there. Mark, Sandra and Sarah stayed with Daniel and I, along with Tim and Brent. Luke, Carolyn, Jordan, Paul and Tristan rented their own place close by, as did Matt, Kathleen, Duggan and Paige. I hired a cook for the evening meals and everyone ate and hung out at

Tranquility. Lots of cards and Scrabble, and the beach out front had rock pools that were very warm for Sara to sit and play in. A small island about 100 yards off the beach had a reef on both sides, so between the beach and island was a kind of cove. Every morning I would swim to the island, hike a little and swim back. The water between the beach and the island never got deeper than about twelve feet, and I saw fish and several sharks there. In fact two local boys, about twelve or so, caught a shark and brought it up on our beach so everyone got to be in a picture with a shark. The diving itself was just so-so, but having everyone there made it very special. We hired a fishing guide one day and went fishing. We got to eat fish on the beach and feed several stingrays that came around looking for a handout. Another nice thing about the island is almost everyone had golf carts, the preferred method of transportation, so there were few cars. We also rented our own boat for one day and went diving off of it. After the trip, Carolyn put together a super scrapbook with lots of nice pictures—it is one of my family treasures.

The best diving trip that I personally have taken was on Little Cayman Island. I had heard the diving there was spectacular, but there were hardly any sandy beaches on the island—and my family loved sandy beaches. So I got on Google Earth and found a sandy beach on the east end of the island, with one villa on the beach. I found out who owned the villa, a couple from Oregon. I got in touch with them and proposed a trade. They could come and stay on the ranch for a week or two in exchange for us being able to use their place on Little Cayman. I threw in a little cash and offered to fix some of their plumbing. The deal was made.

They had a large porch, so I asked if I could have a ping pong table shipped over. I would put it on their porch and then leave it there for them and their family. They agreed. On this trip, the divers—Luke, Paul, Daniel and I—were all ping pong and card players. We played lots of cards, lots of ping pong and the diving itself was on a wall that went straight down for over a thousand feet. Above the wall it was between thirty and fifty feet deep, with a nice sandy bottom with rock

Me, Paul and Daniel playing cards on Little Cayman.

Paul and me playing table tennis

outcroppings. There were several openings in those rock outcroppings where we could dive through a cave and come out on the wall. The villa on the beach was nothing short of spectacular. We could sit inside and look across the ping pong table through solid glass, ceiling-to-floor patio doors and see the ocean through the palm trees. The sandy beach was perfect, and at night you could see the Southern Cross in the evening sky.

The dive master was a card player too, so we had him come over for an evening or two and played lots of cards. He even taught us a new card game called Damage Control.

On the last night, we had a problem that perhaps is the reason we have never been able to go back. Before arriving, the owner told me to watch out for a feral cat and to make sure it didn't get in the house. He didn't like the cat, but his wife was fond of it. On that night, while making several trips to the car, the cat got in. In attempting to catch the cat, Daniel got bit by it. I was afraid of rabies, so I called a nurse on the island. She told me the only way to make sure the cat didn't have rabies was to kill it and test it. I called the owner and explained the situation; he gave me permission to kill the cat and have it tested. The cat was not infected so Daniel didn't have to get rabies shots. However, after that, the owners were very cool toward us. In fact, they never did come to the ranch and wouldn't even return my calls.

I believe it was the following year that we went back to Eleuthera. I found a church that would allow us to donate a ping pong table to them, so once again I had a table delivered to the Caribbean. We actually moved during this trip. The place we originally rented was not as it was represented, so I found another place. We moved mid-trip. The diving wasn't very good, but the second place had a nice beach so we enjoyed that. I can't remember for sure, but I think that it was Luke, Jordan, Paul, Daniel and I, the same as the year before.

As of this writing, my last diving trip was to Fiji, but that is a story unto itself. You can read about it later in the book.

Grandfather's Quote

Give of yourself with your children
and have companions for life.

Daniel, Mark, Matt, Dad, Tim and Luke on Green Turtle Cay

39

Fiji and the Great Lesson

This is not a story about a trip to Fiji or a diving trip—this is a story about the great lesson that I learned there.

For our annual diving trip in 2007, we chose Fiji. Four of us went—my 40-year-old son Tim, my 16-year-old son Daniel, my 16-year-old grandson Brent, and this 64-year-old father and grandfather.

On the third day there, we decided to drive to the far end of the island and hike in the rainforest to a remote, high, beautiful waterfall.

When we arrived, our guide told us it had been raining for several days and that the river was very high. He was not sure we could make it to the falls. We started anyway. The walk through the rainforest was the most memorable part of my entire experience in Fiji. When it began to rain lightly, the others seemed to hunker down. I took my shirt and hat off and loved the feeling of the water soaking my head, running down my face and all over my body. I wanted to feel what I thought the original native Fijians had felt while hiking through the rainforest in the rain. The scenery was spectacular, and I loved the rope bridge that we had to cross.

When we got close to the falls, the river was truly raging. There was no way that you could swim against that current, but a rope was attached along the shoreline. By hanging onto the rope, you could pull yourself upstream through the strong current. When we got closer

Daniel using the rope to get upstream

The waterfalls I dove off of in Fiji

to the waterfalls, the river was not dropping so dramatically and you could actually swim against the current. We all swam upstream between two steep cliffs and pulled ourselves up on the rocks, about 100 feet below the waterfalls.

Two large waterfalls crashed down into the river. One was about 20 feet high and the other, perhaps 40 feet high. The water at the base of the falls was extremely turbulent, causing a strong whirlpool. Our guide warned us not to get caught in the whirlpool, because it would pull you under the falls and suck you underwater. He said that it would spit you out again, but you may be underwater for more than a minute or two.

I was enjoying the roaring of the falls, the mist in the air, the company and just the joy of being alive. It was exhilarating.

The next thing I knew, the guide had disappeared. He had climbed up what seemed to be a sheer rock wall and was standing on top beside the first falls.

Now this is very important.

I did not want to prove anything. I was not being macho. I was not showing off to my sons and grandson—I was just caught up in the moment. I have never liked being a spectator. I don't want to watch racing cars—I want to race them. I don't want to be told or read what it is like to hand glide; I want to do it myself. Such has been my way my entire life.

I looked up at the guide and started to climb. Soon I was on top of the rock wall standing next to the first falls. The guide had climbed to the top of the second falls. He signed to me to jump into the river. I hollered at him, "Are you sure there are no rocks below? Are you sure it's deep enough? Are you sure it's okay?"

He signaled me to jump again.

I thought he was signaling me to dive.

I had dived from those heights before, and I had dived below waterfalls. I knew that if I dove in right at the outlet of the whirlpool, I would be spit downstream, and I would not be sucked back under the falls.

I stretched my arms above my head and dove into the water. The current was much stronger than I expected and/or my shoulder was much weaker than I had realized. When I hit the water, the current yanked my right arm right out of my shoulder socket.

My right arm was totally useless, and the turbulence whipped it around like a loose piece of string in the raging current. I fought for the surface with my legs and good arm. I thought I was below water for just a moment, but Tim tells me that it seemed like I was underwater for at least a minute. When I was finally able to take a breath, it was obvious that I was caught in the whirlpool and being sucked back under the waterfalls. I swam as best I could and got to the rock wall on the outside of the whirlpool. The current was sucking me towards the falls, and I kept trying to grab a handhold. Just before being sucked under the falls, I found a notch in the rocks and was able to hold on with my left arm against the current. Luckily, I had a foothold there too. I was able to stand in water that came between my knees and waist. I looked down in disbelief. My right arm was completely pulled out of my shoulder joint and bent abnormally 180 degrees backwards. Impossible! The arm was completely dead and useless. When I picked it up with my left hand, I could feel nothing. The fingers on my right hand were losing their color, and the pain in the shoulder was off the charts.

Soon the guide was at my side, but he did not know what to do. So he hollered to Tim and Tim swam through the whirlpool over to where we were.

I told Tim my shoulder was out of its socket and he had to pull it back in. He said he didn't know how. I told him if he didn't put it back in, I was afraid I would pass out from the pain.

He put one hand on my shoulder and grabbed my wrist with his other hand and gave a hard yank. I felt the arm and shoulder snap back into its socket. The color immediately started to return to my fingers, but the pain was still out of this world.

The guide could not swim out of the whirlpool against the current. He had to climb the rocks behind the waterfalls, get himself to the other side and jump into the river where it would push him downstream.

Once downstream, the guide cut the rope we had used coming up the river. When he got back to where Daniel and Brent were, he tied the rope on a pair of shoes and tried to throw it to us, but he could not get it across.

Finally, he tied the rope around his waist, swam across the stream and got within twenty or thirty feet of us. Tim helped me, and I was somehow able to get to the rope. The guide then had to climb back up behind the waterfalls and jump out once again.

I hung onto the rope with my left arm. The guide, Daniel, and Brent pulled me, as much under as above water, out of the whirlpool and across the raging river. Once out of the whirlpool, I let go of the rope and shot downstream in the current. Daniel followed.

The guide had to repeat the process to get Tim out of the whirlpool, but soon Tim, Brent and the guide were following Daniel and me downstream.

It took over two hours to hike back to the village because I stopped at several streams along the way and soaked my arm in the cold water. We rode another hour over a rough road to get back to our place, and another hour to get to a small hospital.

The x-rays showed that everything was back in place, and I was sent home. I did not take any pain medication because I was afraid that if the pain went away, I might roll on the shoulder in my sleep and dislocate it again. I was very fearful of permanently losing the use of my right arm and did not want to do anything that might hurt my chances of a full recovery.

Between arriving home and going to the hospital, Maria, the gal who was cleaning our home, told us that she would not be back for a few days because her brother was overdue at sea by more than a week. That perspective helped me make it through the next couple of nights.

The pain was as severe as any that I can ever remember, and I could not sleep at all. I kept giving my pain up as a prayer offering in hopes that Maria's brother would return safely.

Two or three days later Maria came back to our home to clean once again. Just as she walked up to the front door, she pointed excitedly out on the ocean and said, "That looks like my brother's fishing boat." I handed her my binoculars and sure enough, it was her brother. My prayers had been answered, and they had allowed me to make it through those first few nights and learn a life-changing lesson.

The next morning, Tim blew his stack at me. He said that he was not as good a swimmer as I was and that I had endangered his life. He called me many uncomplimentary names and said that I thought of no one but myself. I was hurt deeply, but the lesson was yet to come.

All my life, I have been a very proud person, and I have looked up to no one other than my father. I have often said that I would not walk across the street to shake the hand of the Pope or the President. If they wanted to meet me halfway, that was another matter, but I was not a hero worshiper and would not go all the way to them.

Pride can be a good thing, but when a person is proud and sure of himself, he has to be very careful not to be condescending.

Before this trip, I don't ever remember feeling as though someone was being condescending to me. I have been told by others that on occasion a couple of my sons had been disrespectful or condescending, but I never really felt or believed it.

This time was different. There was no doubt about it—Tim was angry, and for the next couple of days he treated me like a two-year-old child.

I was in extreme pain, weak and vulnerable, and I could not believe how one of my sons treated me in front of another son and grandson. He would do it ever so sarcastically, but very surgically. Finally, one time, I'd lashed back out at him in anger. To my surprise, Daniel jumped on me and said, "Cool it, Dad." That hurt even more.

In my pain, and during the sleepless nights, I had a lot of time to think about things. For the first time in my life, I realized that I had been condescending to others. Worse yet, I had only been condescending to women and usually the women that I loved and cared about. Most notably, and painfully and regrettably, I realized that at times I had been that way with Irene, Daniel's mother, and with Jeanne.

I had always been proud that I had never hit a woman and almost never lost my temper at them. I had not realized that being condescending could be as hurtful.

I had felt its pain, its lack of respect, its disdain and its seeming lack of love or even caring. It was much worse than being slugged in the mouth. I understood for the first time why it would be much easier to forgive someone who hit you then to forgive someone who treated you with disdain.

I made myself a promise. I promised myself that I would try, with every fiber of my being, to never again treat anyone in my life in a condescending manner.

Footnote

Being proud is a good thing, but being condescending to anyone is just not right. Being condescending to your wife or your parents is even worse.

It is an absolute fact, that wherever in this world the elderly are looked up to and treated with respect, that they live very long, happy lives.

Here in the United States, where each generation is so much more educated than the previous one, many tend to disregard and look down upon the elderly. How foolish they are.

Absolutely nothing can replace the wisdom gained through a lifetime of experiences.

Grandfather's quote

Wisdom comes with age, not with degrees.
Learn from those who have lived life the longest.

40

The Surgeon

The day after I got back from Fiji, I went to see the top orthopedic surgeon in Rapid City. When he reviewed the x-rays, he could not believe I had any movement in that shoulder even prior to that injury. He kept asking me, "Are you sure you could raise your arm above your head?" "Are you sure you could do ... this or that?" He must've asked me at least four times. He told me I had massive injuries inside the shoulder, but most of them looked like they were over twenty-five years old. He could see no rotator cuff whatsoever, and there were massive bone spurs. He thought I needed to have a complete shoulder replacement, but he ordered an MRI for the same day to see if there were any other options. He also told me to start moving the shoulder as much as I could, and to see a physical therapist. I was able to see my physical therapist before getting the MRI.

The first thing I did after getting home was to research what a shoulder replacement would entail and how active a life I could live if I had the surgery. It became obvious that I could not continue to lead the lifestyle that I was accustomed to with a shoulder replacement. The research said that a shoulder replacement was mainly to alleviate pain, and it should be done only as a last resort.

Although the orthopedic surgeon I saw in Rapid is noted for being very good at what he does, he's your typical doctor. He believes he knows best, and the patient knows little or nothing. He is the same one who told me if I removed all of the cartilage in my right knee, I could no longer hike mountains, ride horses or swim—in fifteen years I would no longer be able to walk.

After hearing that, I flew to Minneapolis and sought a second opinion on my knee. The sports medicine orthopedic surgeon recommended I have the cartilage removed. He agreed it was likely, with no medical advancements, that I would not be able to walk in fifteen years. But he also believed that in another fifteen years, medicine would have advanced far enough to do something for me. I elected to have the cartilage removed.

So for the second time in my life, I was going to seek a second opinion, but I wanted it to be from the best orthopedic surgeon in the nation.

The next day Tim came by the ranch during his move from Las Vegas back to St. Paul. He got on the Internet, did the research and found Dr. James Andrews, who many consider the best orthopedic surgeon in the nation.

The more research we did on Dr. Andrews, the more I was convinced he was not only the best orthopedic surgeon in the nation but perhaps in the world. The only problems were he was in Alabama, and all his former patients seemed to be super athletes or famous people. He had operated on Carson Palmer, Daunte Culpepper, Barry Bonds, Tommy John, Jack Nicklaus, Emmitt Smith and Bob Hope. I was afraid someone with his credentials was not about to take the time to treat a rancher from South Dakota, but you all know about my optimism.

I ordered a copy of the x-rays and the MRI taken in Rapid. I also gathered all the information that I could from my physical therapist. Then I called Dr. Andrews' office.

A nice young man named Scott answered the phone, and I told him a little about my situation. I also told him about my apprehension about whether or not Dr. Andrews would consider working on a rancher from South Dakota. He told me Dr. Andrews would consider seeing anyone, but in order to get to him I had to first contact an orthopedic surgeon under him. He suggested I send a copy of the x-rays, the MRI, the physical therapist's report, and a letter detailing the injury and what my expectations were to Dr. Andrews, in care of Dr. Hackel.

I gathered all the information I needed, and then I sat down and wrote a very long letter which I showed to my daughter-in-law, who is a doctor. She told me I needed to shorten it up to a single page.

I did worry this letter contained too much information to send to a man of his importance and that he would not take the time to read it. I went with my gut feeling and sent it anyway.

To my surprise, Dr. Hackel called me and said he would bring it to the attention of Dr. Andrews. But he too believed from the x-rays and MRI that a complete shoulder replacement was the way to go. We visited for quite a while. When I got through telling him the type of life I had lived and expected to live for at least the next 30 years, he agreed that if at all possible, I should not have a shoulder replacement. He added if anyone could do anything, it would be Dr. Andrews and he would get me an appointment with him the following week.

The week before the flight, during the flight and even the morning of my appointment, I continued to vigorously work my shoulder. I am sure that more than a few people wondered about this crazy cowboy doing shoulder exercises in the airport and squeezing a rubber ball during his flight. I even managed to swim laps for an hour the day before my flight and swim laps for another half hour the morning of my appointment. By my appointment time, although painful, I had a wide range of motion back in my shoulder.

When Dr. Andrews walked into the room, he stretched out his hand and said he wanted to shake the hand of his hero.

"Excuse me?"

"You don't realize what you have managed to accomplish. You are truly one in a million. With the massive injuries to your shoulder, there is no way that you should be able to move it at all."

He then asked me to show him my range of motion. I was sure glad that I had worked on it so diligently since the accident.

I showed him my range of motion and he just shook his head, "That is truly remarkable."

His intern, another orthopedic surgeon, came into the room and we were introduced.

Dr. Andrews told him I was a walking miracle. After showing him my complete range of motion, to my delight Dr. Andrews said he was willing to perform surgery and see if he could improve things a little. He then left the room.

His assistant told me in the two years he'd been with Dr. Andrews he had always gone first to prep a new patient. This was the first time he had ever seen Dr. Andrews go in the room first, because he was truly anxious to meet this anomaly from South Dakota.

When Dr. Andrews returned, we went over the new x-rays. I could see how the ball on the end of my arm had worn a groove in the bone in my shoulder. He also showed me how the round part of the top of my arm bone was about 20% bigger than it should be. My body had formed calcium deposits around the lower part of it, but they had been worn smooth, just like an addition to the arm bone. He thought my rotator cuff had been completely gone for many years. He could try to widen the space between the top of the arm bone and the groove carved in the shoulder bone. He could clean out any debris and smooth out a couple of jagged edges. He would repair any rotator cuff if any existed.

He had to leave the following afternoon for a two-week football camp, but if it worked for me, he would give up his lunch and operate before he left. He also said he would not be there when I came to, but would call me later.

Right after the operation, he personally called Jeanne, but she did not get to the phone in time, so he left his number. A couple of minutes later, Jeanne called that number. When a man said hello, Jeannie was stunned, because she had expected a secretary to answer. He said hello again. Jeannie said, "May I speak to Dr. Andrews?" He said, "This is Dr. Andrews, may I help you?"

He had given her his personal cell phone number, and then he talked to her for over 15 minutes, just like he had been a personal friend for years.

When he finally called me in the early evening, he told me there had been no rotator cuff to be salvaged. He believed my rotator cuff had completely dissolved years ago. He cleaned out some debris, widened some spaces, and smoothed out some jagged edges. The rest, he said, now was up to me.

When I asked him what I could expect to do, he replied, "Gary, whatever you believe you can do, you can do!"

When I got home, I worked faithfully an hour at a time, three hours a day on rehabilitating the shoulder. I was very sore but to my, and Dr. Andrew's surprise, there was no real pain. After a couple of months of constantly doing my shoulder exercises, I actually had more mobility than I had prior to my accident.

Dr. Andrews is truly a remarkable man. All the stories that I had heard about him being the best are true. Why he took a liking to this South Dakota cowboy, I do not know. Perhaps it was because he was born the same year that I was born and he, like me, thinks of himself as being 30 years younger than he actually is. Everyone says there is no stop to him, but his most admirable trait is that he does not think of himself as special. He truly believes each person is his own best doctor. It does not matter if you are some famous football player like Emmitt Smith or a cowboy from South Dakota. He treats you both the same and ultimately believes that your recovery, success, or failure is entirely up to you.

A side note worth mentioning is that the man who is the driver for the Alabama sports medicine clinic at St. Vincent's Hospital in Birmingham, Alabama, says that he has the best job in the world. For the last 20 years he has been picking up all of these famous people at the airport and driving them to the clinic. He gets to meet them all and spend time with them.

I asked him if all these famous people were down to earth or whether they were aloof. He told me that almost every one of them were just down-to-earth good people. Emmitt Smith, the most valuable player in the Super Bowl that year, had even invited the driver and his family to his home for a barbecue. In all those years he had only one really bad apple, some famous female tennis player.

He also told me that without question his favorite celebrity was Bob Hope. He said that Bob was the most down to earth and friendly person he had ever met. When Bob was there, he was between 90 and 95 years old and he was still as sharp as a tack.

When he drove Bob up to the clinic, two young nurses came and took him by the arms to walk him to the clinic door.

Bob asked these young nurses, "How far are we going?"

They said they were just going a little ways.

Bob replied, "Just my luck, every time I get a beautiful woman on my arm, I never can get her to go all the way."

Bob Hope and Dr. James Andrews, two very special people!

Grandfather's Quote

Always remember, your health and well-being is up to you.

41

Three Years in Court

A few years after purchasing my original ranch, an adjoining ranch came up for sale. I bought it knowing I would have to sell off some of what I had just purchased in order to pay for it. (You can read all about it in the appendix under "Buying and selling land South Dakota"). The new ranch bordered Highway 79, and the first piece I sold was to Steve H. He had a live-in girlfriend at the time and we all became friends. Shortly thereafter, I let them use a couple of my horses, and I picked up the minister while they rode my horses up the mountain. They were married on Battle Mountain, and I was one of the witnesses.

I had sold them 158 acres on a Contract for Deed. In the Contract I reserved an easement through their property, which allowed me to access another 160-acre parcel behind him. The contract also stated that the buyers understood their property would be treated as part of the rangeland of my ranch until they fenced it off at their sole expense. The contract was very clear, and I explained to them exactly what that meant so there would be no misunderstanding.

Early the following spring I called to tell them I was going to turn cattle out. This meant the cattle would be in their yard unless they fenced their property in. I volunteered to help them put in the fence, but Steve refused my help. He said he was going to resurvey his property before putting any fences in. I reminded him I had already had it surveyed and all the pins were still visible. He said he didn't want anyone to have six inches of his land and he didn't want to have six inches of his neighbor's land, so he was resurveying it just to make sure. A typical city person's mentality.

Two days before I turned cows out, I called him again. He still had not gotten the second survey done. With the cows in the pasture, he now had to open and close three gates to get in and out. That pissed him off. A couple of days later he called me and said a cow had attacked his wife right in their own yard and he would no longer close the gates.

After settling down, I called him back and asked him if he would keep the gates closed if I ran an electric fence around his yard. He agreed, but for whatever reason, he hated me from that day forward.

Several years later I was at a neighboring rancher's place with my son when Steve delivered some gravel there. He happened to have his son with him. Our sons were in school and sports together and knew each other well. Steve made his son stay in the truck, and he treated my son and I with disdain.

When I originally sold him the 158 acres, you only needed forty acres in order to qualify for agricultural status. This allowed your land to be taxed at a much lower rate. Then the law changed and required 160 acres for agricultural status.

Steve tried to buy two more acres from his neighbors, but only one could even consider selling because all the rest barely had enough land to maintain their own agricultural tax status. Gary Romey was the only neighbor who could sell him any land, but Romey had purchased his land from me. When I sold to anyone, I retained a first right of refusal. That meant none of them could sell to anyone else without giving me the first right to buy the same land at the same price. Gary Romey told Steve he would have to get my permission before he could sell to him. Steve told him he would not ask me for shit, no way!

Then one day at the courthouse I ran into Steve and he asked me if I would allow Romey to sell to him. I said to Steve, "I know you have a problem with me but if you promise to never show that problem to your boys or in front of my son, I will give Romey the OK to sell to you." He made the promise, so I extended my hand for a handshake. He would not shake it.

I should have told him to shove it right then and there but I didn't and boy, did that bite me in the butt later.

The 160 acres behind Steve's property was bought by Orin Draves, an old friend from Minnesota. Orin built a new home and used the easement through Steve's property for years. When his wife got very ill, he decided to sell his place and move to Florida, where most of his children were so they could help him take care of his wife. He tried to sell his entire 160 acres but settled for selling forty acres and his buildings to a Federal judge named Marcel G. When many more months had passed and he was unable to sell the other 120 acres, he gave me a call. He asked me if I would buy what he had left.

I told Orin I was very surprised the realtor had not been able to sell any of the 120 acres over all this time. I agreed to give him the $1,000 per acre he was asking but also told him I would immediately resell it in thirty-acre parcels for at least $1,500 per acre. Orin said he had no problem with that because he just needed to get it sold right away. Before making the deal, I went to Marcel, the Federal judge, and told him he should buy the 120 acres. If he didn't buy it, I was going to, and then I would sell it in thirty-acre parcels. He refused to buy it. But he asked me to put a covenant which would not allow anyone to put buildings just west of him. He wanted to keep his view of the mountains. I wanted to get along with the neighbors, so I agreed.

I made the deal with Orin and within two weeks I had a buyer for the thirty acres just west of Marcel. I told the new buyers to go introduce themselves to Marcel, and they did.

Then Marcel went ballistic. I don't think he believed I could sell the parcels because the realtors had not been able to do so. He called Orin and said he had changed his mind and wanted to buy the 120 acres. Orin told him it was too late. Marcel then called me and was not nice. He said he would not let anyone have access to their property. He then called my buyers and told them he was a Federal judge, and would not allow them access to the property they had just agreed to buy.

Decision time! Do I let this gorilla have his way or do I stand up and fight him? I called each of my sons for advice. One of them said if I fought him, it will be on his turf because he is a judge.

I should have let him have his way, but I called an attorney who assured me he could not deny access and so I let the fight begin.

Marcel examined all the abstracts and decided the best way to fight me was to have Steve H., who still hated me, be the one to deny access.

Once, before all this happened, I had gone to Steve's place and said I was sorry for whatever I had done to anger him and as neighbors I just wanted to get along. He told me he hated me and would always hate me and he told me to get the f* off his place.

Then I made another mistake. An attorney had just looked at one of the thirty-acre parcels. I knew he was not a very good courtroom attorney, but I called him anyway. He said it was an open-and-shut case and there is no way I could be denied access. He also said he would take the case and take his fees off the price of the land he wanted to buy. We made the deal.

Let the nightmare begin. The first time we went to court, Marcel—remember he is a federal judge—went into the judge's chambers for over twenty minutes before the hearing started. We got a change of venue and a judge change but the same thing happened again.

Even though I retained access through Steve's property, the access stated sixteen and a half feet on either side of the centerline of the then-existing road. Steve said he had moved a section of the road. When it was all said and done, I lost the middle of my access and my attorney no longer wanted the land. He wanted paid.

The thirty-three-foot access I did retain on each end should have allowed me to construct a new section of road connecting the two. However, like the nice guy I am, I had allowed Romey to sell two acres to Steve. Steve now owned property on both sides where I had to build my new road. If, while building the road, I spilled one drop of dirt on any of his property, he would sue me.

Even though Marcel was directly responsible for denying me access and Steve was still giving him access, Marcel now could say he had no legal access to his property. So he sued Orin Draves, the one who had sold to him. Orin then would have no choice but to sue me. Welcome to our wonderful legal system. Thank God there are still some good people in the world. Orin agreed not to sue me if I paid all his legal expenses in fighting Marcel in court.

I then approached Gary Romey, the adjoining neighbor who had sold Steve the two acres, and he gave me an easement through his property. I built an entirely new road, which gave legal access to Marcel and the rest of my property behind Steve's. Of course, that wasn't good enough for Marcel.

Once again we were in court against a federal judge, but this time I/Orin had a better attorney and this time we had a jury trial. It wouldn't be just a judge making the decision.

To my horror, this judge, in my opinion trying to help a fellow judge, said the jury had no right to know I had built another road giving Marcel access. That's when I learned the hard way, our legal system gives way too much power to our judges. Juries should be able to hear all the facts and then decide. To say a jury cannot know a person has been convicted of other crimes and the other person is a stand-up citizen is just not right. The jury should be able to see and hear all the evidence. If evidence is collected illegally, prosecute the person acquiring the illegal evidence.

Luckily my attorney was able to persuade or force the judge to allow the jury to see the new road.

In the closing arguments, which I was not allowed to hear, Marcel's attorney attacked Orin for being a liar and faking Alzheimer's. The jury was mostly women. According to Jeanne and Orin's wife, who were in the courtroom, when the attorney attacked Orin, they saw the women's expressions and knew, right then and there, Marcel had lost his case.

We went back to the ranch waiting for the verdict and Orin and I took a long walk. Coming back to the house, in the window, we could see the women jumping up and down with joy. We had won on all counts! With tears in our eyes, we fell to our knees and thanked the Lord.

I learned a person needs to stay out of court at all costs, especially fighting a judge, but between the new road and all the court costs I spent over $125,000 for the lesson.

And sad to say, within a few years Orin died from Alzheimer's.

I have never understood how others could hold hatred in their hearts, so a few years later I wrote another children's story entitled *The Gift of an Open Heart*. The story ended with these words:

> He walked the path of life in his own way, and his open, loving heart often saw things very differently than those about him.
>
> And when he approached the end of his journey, he himself became a wise grandfather, and in his wisdom he saw it was his gift that had brought him so many blessings.
>
> This rare and special gift.
>
> The gift of an open heart.

Grandfather's Quote

Don't let those who are hateful change who you are. Live your life with an open, loving heart and your journey through life will be a good one.

42

Writing a Book on Raising Children

I have done nothing in my life I have enjoyed more than raising my five sons. And despite the world they grew up in, what fine young men they all turned out to be!

In visiting with others who had raised children, I was always amazed when they said they would never want to go through that again, "especially the teenage years." When they asked me why I enjoyed my boys' teenage years so much, I told them it was partly because none of my boys ever told me no after the age of seven. I had no rebellious teenagers. I had fine young men who respected me and were my friend.

I wrestled for some time as to why other couples felt so differently than me. Why did they seem to have such a struggle, particularly with their teenagers? Perhaps they did not listen to their parents, grandparents or aunts and uncles when it came to raising their children. They were listening to Dr. Spock, modern society, and a bunch of learned child psychologists who supposedly knew best. They were told to never spank their children and to allow the child to express themselves. Don't tell them they have to come to dinner or pick up their toys—convince them to do it. And when they are teenagers, you need to understand they are going through a very rough time in their lives with many hormonal changes going on in their bodies. Parents had to be especially patient and understanding during a child's adolescent years.

Wow! In my experience, modern society has gotten it all wrong. If you can't control your child at three or four years old, how are you going to control them when they are teenagers? Maybe you can talk your four-year-old into picking up their toys. But you almost certainly will not talk your sixteen-year-old into coming home on time or wearing appropriate clothing to church—or going to church at all. If they respect your authority at age four, they will accept and respect it as teenagers. And in my view adolescence is a made-up word used as an excuse for bad behavior. One hundred and fifty years ago you were a young man or a young woman by the age of thirteen, and that is the way I feel it should be today.

So I wrote a book on raising children, hoping to inspire people to look again at some of the old ways. Parents' choices can make the teenage years part of a good journey to adulthood or cause those years to be full of conflict—treating them like a child for much longer than necessary.

Oh, that's right, our beloved government now considers your child a child until they are twenty-five years old. Barf!

Well, one of the tools I used in raising my boys was to teach them lessons, without them even realizing it, by telling them bedtime stories; so Jeanne suggested I write down and publish those stories. If I became a famous author, maybe people would want to hear what I had to say about raising children.

That is how I began writing down my children's stories. As of this writing, I have my book on raising children and seventeen children's stories written down and waiting to be edited.

Now, after watching my oldest son raise his three sons in more of a modern fashion, I realize there could be more than one right way to raise a child. As long as you shower them with love and are able to communicate with them, they should turn out just fine. His boys, like mine, turned out to be fine human beings who were no problem as teenagers or at any other time.

I still feel the so-called old-fashioned way is more likely to succeed, but perhaps I am mistaken. The Lord willing, I will get my children's stories and my book on raising children edited and get them published even if only for my family.

Grandfather's Quote

Don't look for education and degrees when seeking advice on raising children. Go to those who have done a good job of actually doing it.

To heighten your curiosity about my book on raising children, I will put the table of contents in here. Note what is written in (parentheses) are stories.

Walk a Little Plainer Daddy

by Gary W. Friendshuh

Table of Contents

m. Hidden Secret to Self-Esteem (Smiles A Lot)
n. Truth the Ultimate Friend (The Legend of Truth)
o. Choosing a Babysitter (Scary Things)
p. My Child Isn't Feeling Well. Should I make him mind? (Going Potty)

10. School (The Football Team)
11. Friends and Peers (Ode to My Father)
12. Raising My Child Alone (Holiday on Ice)
13. Raising My Child As A Stepparent Or With A Stepparent (The Birthday Party)
14. My Child the Person (The Rodeo)
15. The Opposite Sex (Girls in Colorado)
16. Difficult Subjects
    a. Sex (The Bull)
    b. Fighting and Kissing (Tim's Moccasins)
    c. Drugs and Booze (Jamie)
    d. Premarital Sex (The Double Date)
17. Adolescence, the Myth (A Legend)
18. My Teenager, My Friend (Mark and the Rocks)
19. Advice From The Heartland: Do's and Don'ts (Bath Time)
20. Letting Go (A Going Away Gift)

Epilogue

43

Writing Children's Stories

After writing my book on raising children, *Walk a Little Plainer Daddy*, and giving it to my sons to read, one of them came back with this comment.

"Dad, there may be a diamond within this lump of coal but who the hell cares what Gary Friendshuh has to say about raising children."

Within that lump of coal I had included several stories I told my boys at bedtime, and I wanted to have a few illustrations for each of these stories.

When Jeanne found me and I discovered she was an illustrator, we used that as an excuse to have her come and live with me and illustrate my stories.

After hearing my son's comments she told me, "Your stories are great and they teach children morals and values. Write your stories down and get them published. When you become famous for your stories, people will want to know what you have to say about raising children."

I ran that by my boys and they agreed.

My writing journey truly began.

I have never considered myself a writer—heck, I can't spell worth a darn—but I am a storyteller.

I bought a dictation system and told stories to my microphone.

As I got into writing, I actually used several of my real-life experiences as the basis for some of my stories. "The Difficult Path" and "The Gift of an Open Heart" are prime examples.

Then there was the story "Allowing Others to be Strong." My grandson, Brent, was here on the ranch for a week when he was six years old. He and Daniel, who was the same age, had a great time together for the first several days. Then things started going wrong. Brent was no longer having fun because whatever they did, Daniel did it better and worse yet, bragged about it.

I tried talking to Daniel, but it was like it was going in one ear and out the other. I decided to write a story about two young Native American boys who were faster and stronger than all the other boys. Yellow Hawk still knew what it was like to lose because when he competed with Little Bear, he always lost. Both of their fathers tried talking to their sons but, like Daniel, Little Bear did not listen. Because Yellow Hawk knew what it was like to lose, he listened and allowed the others to win once in a while. When they had all grown up, he was elected chief.

This story got through to Daniel and he started allowing Brent to do better and when Daniel won, he didn't brag but rather told Brent how well he did.

What I could not teach by words, I taught through a story.

A side note—several years later when Daniel was constantly beating Jeanne at a card game and gloating over it, she told him this was not fun for her. He didn't listen and did it again. This time she just looked at him and said, "OK, Little Bear."

Boy, did that get his attention. The next time he won, he complimented her on her good play.

Once again what words could not accomplish, a story did.

My heart was in the stories written for older children, but several people said I needed to start with stories for very young children.

Shortly thereafter, a friend came over with his four-year-old daughter and asked me to tell her a story. I wrote "Little One" and read it to her.

As I was writing these stories, I was amazed at how the words just seemed to flow out. Like I was supposed to be doing this.

I kept asking myself, "How is this possible? I can't write. Where is this coming from?"

I felt like I was being given an unbelievable gift, a gift I did not deserve. As I prayed about it, I made a promise. These stories did not belong to me, they were a gift and as a gift they shall be given. I promised I would not make a single penny on any of them.

In my pride, I even had the thought that someday I would be like Paul Newman and say, "If I knew how much money these stories were going to make, I would not have promised to give it all away."

I continued down the path, and the stories just kept coming and getting put on paper. Soon there were 17 of them.

Now what?

Jeanne never did get the stories illustrated, but she edited several of them, including "The Bear," which I consider one of my best. I read it to Daniel's third or fourth grade class and they loved it.

Jeanne was good, but she never seemed to have enough time to edit many more.

I started looking for an editor. I even found a Native American who taught college writing. He was also an editor and was very interested in my Native American stories.

He agreed to edit a couple for free to show me what he could do.

He edited "Little One" and "Little Beaver's Gift."

With all his talent and experience, he did not understand children's stories or my way of writing.

With "Little One" he told me I should not repeat myself.

Excuse me? Think "The Three Bears." Very young children love repetition.

He rewrote "Little Beaver's Gift" in his correct English/grammar style. Several people read both versions without knowing whose was whose, and they all liked mine better. So did I.

I tried at least two more editors and they too did not understand or would not allow my style of writing.

I tried a few more who would not even give me a sample edit. I paid $100 for one to read two of my stories and give me her opinion of them. But she would not edit even a few pages to show me what she could do. I did not want to deal with someone like that.

I gave up. I actually gave up for a few years.

During that time I contacted several self-published authors, some of the friendliest, helpful people I have ever talked to.

One from Arizona had 40,000 of her books bought by a school system, and she won several awards. Another, from Nebraska, printed 5,000 copies the first time out of the gate and sold them all within two years, mostly at craft fairs and the like. They both said go for it. Don't go to a publisher because you will be lucky to get thirty-five cents a book. If you do it on your own, you can donate five to ten dollars to charity for each book sold.

Then I started to look for an illustrator and found Maria Rask.

By this time, all of this was beginning to be a lot of work. Much more than I had reckoned with. Maria said she would illustrate my books for a reasonable rate plus a percentage of sales. More importantly, she agreed to keep the books at her place and market them. I pushed ahead.

Jeanne edited *Little One* and did a great job. I researched and found out the process, got my ISBN numbers, and found a printer at a reasonable price.

By the time I got my 2,000 copies back, Maria had gone through a nasty divorce and was out of the picture.

I got a website (grandfathersstories.com) and set up a tipi at Maverick Junction, and placed the books at the Mammoth Site, Wind Cave National Park, and local bookstores. I also contacted Crazy Horse Memorial but got no response.

Jeanne made a real nice sign to put outside the tipi at Maverick Junction, which invited people in. Inside the tipi she had a super sign and a *Little One* book on a rawhide cord. The sign invited them into the convenience store where Jeanne had created a nice display which held several books. All in all we sold about 300 books via the tipi and perhaps another fifty in other ways. I also gave away fifty books to the Shriners Hospital for Children in Minneapolis. I also bought boxes to mail books to twenty-one other Shriners Hospitals.

I didn't mind spending/donating the $7,000 to get the books done, but this was too much work!

Other than the website, I kind of gave up again, partly because the convenience store was shut down and we had no other place to put the tipi.

Jeanne and I talked about it and decided we needed to just send them off to several publishers.

More work trying to figure out how to do that.

I was dragging my feet.

My confidence was at a very low point.

Originally, I had envisioned a series of books. A Little One series, a Young One series and an adventure series. Now I am at the point where I just want to put the stories into one book, kind of like Grimm's fairy tales.

But writing has become part of my life and brought to the forefront my faith's journey. My different writing style is another instance of me taking my own path. So now that I have found a very good editor, for better or worse, I expect to continue writing. Hopefully my children's stories and my book on raising children will someday be in print.

Grandfather's Quote

Give the gift of a story and you will also be giving the gift of you.

44

Buying and Selling Land

The Beginning

Buying and selling land is really what has allowed me the freedom to pursue my dreams. It brought me financial independence, and like it or not, financial independence equals freedom.

In 1966, when I was twenty-three years old, I bought my first piece of land in Alaska. No one in the family that I knew of had bought and sold land to any degree, and no one was there to give me advice or guidance.

I was working on a plumbing job a few miles outside of Anchorage in a beautiful area of towering pine trees on the side of a mountain. In visiting with the homeowner, I asked him how he was able to find such a beautiful spot. I also asked him if he knew of any more land there that might be for sale. I don't know why I asked because I didn't have any extra money at the time. He told me a homesteader had just died, and the word was a grandson had inherited his property. I went to work. I don't know how I knew enough to go to the courthouse, but I did. I don't remember exactly what records I checked. I probably just asked around to see if anyone knew of a recent death and land transfer. When it was all said and done, I found the grandson and was able to get his phone number in Texas.

I made the call, introduced myself and asked him if he might be willing to sell his property. I don't remember if he had inherited only twenty acres or if he agreed to sell me just twenty acres for $700 an acre. He was willing to take $3,000 down and monthly payments for a few years. I had never heard of a contract for deed until that moment. I told him I would get back to him.

After I did a little more research on the value of the property, I felt confident I could immediately sell half of the property and pay for the whole thing. I called my father and asked him if I could borrow $3,000. I told him I thought I could pay him off in ninety days, but it might take up to a year. He agreed to lend me the money.

I bought the property and sold half of it within thirty days for the entire purchase price. I paid my father off and I paid the man in Texas off. Shortly after I moved from Alaska, I sold the balance of the property for $2,100 an acre. My real estate career had begun.

An interesting side note is that the property had no legal access to it. Perhaps this is why he sold it so cheaply. I do not know where I had the good sense to figure this all out ahead of time, but I did.

The only possible access was through a neighbor's property. Before I bought, I went to the neighbor who was an old-time homesteader and asked him if he would be willing to give me an easement. I needed to cross his property for about a quarter of a mile. He asked me what I wanted the easement for and I told him I wanted to build a road to access some property I was about to purchase. He told me a road would add to the value of his property, and he gave me the easement.

What a different world it is today. Today, anyone you ask for an easement would ask how much you were willing to pay for it. This man never asked for a thing. He just helped a neighbor out and helped himself a little in the process by getting a road put in on his property. He also profoundly affected the way I handled all my real-estate deals for the rest of my life. And being like this old-time homesteader and not making it all about the money, people liked and trusted me and the money just sort of happened.

Two years later in 1968, I began looking for my second piece of property because we had moved back to Minnesota and I could not stand living in a suburb. I found the forty acres that we eventually built our log home on. It had been on the market for more than two years because no one had the foresight that I did. The 40 acres had a four-acre slough on it, and the brush was so thick you could not walk through any of the timber. A year after I bought it, I put in a dam and created a four-acre lake, and I had cleared all the brush. Everyone asked me where I found such a beautiful piece of property. It was always there, but no one saw it or what it could be.

Buying it was no easy trick either. I could barely scrape together enough money for the down payment, and there was no way I could afford to make the monthly payments for any length of time. I did not let that deter me. After all, business life is just one big game of *Monopoly.*

I immediately offered thirteen acres of the forty acres for sale for one dollar down and monthly payments large enough to cover my monthly payments. I found a buyer and was on my way. The key here was that I knew the market and was not afraid to gamble.

The next few years were spent building first our basement home, and then our log home, and then a plumbing shop.

All during this time I was constantly reading want ads and keeping track of what real estate was selling for. I treated it like going to school and I really knew the market. In 1972 I found eighty acres for sale about four miles west of our home for a price just too good to be true. It was listed for $275 per acre, and I knew the value of land in that area was at least $500 per acre.

I called the realtor and asked him what was wrong with the property.

He said nothing was wrong with it. I asked him how long it had been for sale. He told me it had been over a year. I asked him again, "So tell me what is wrong with it." He insisted nothing.

I went and looked at the property and immediately knew why it had not sold. It was a rolling hillside with a small creek running through the middle, but on both sides of the creek were corn fields.

I bought the property and leased it out to a neighboring farmer with an arrangement requiring him to plant it to wheat or oats. Now I had a rolling green hillside with a creek running through the middle. I traded twenty acres of this eighty for the thirteen acres I had sold from my original forty acres. Within a year and a half I sold the balance of the eighty acres for more than double what I paid for it.

Since buying our forty acres and building our home, we had gotten to know the Rodamockers, an older couple who owned the 160 acres that joined our forty acres. I did several things for them and always told them to call me if they were ever going to sell their property.

In 1973, a For Sale sign went up on the Rodamocker property. I went over and talked to them. They told me they didn't believe such a young man could buy their farm, and that was why they had not told me they were selling it. I called the realtor who it turns out was related to the Rodamockers, and asked her what they wanted for the farm. They wanted $100,000 but they would sell it on a contract for deed with $25,000 down.

Time to play some more *Monopoly*.

I asked the realtor what her commission was, and she told me seven percent. I asked her if she would wait for her commission for one year. She told me she would wait for half of her commission for a year. I went to my banker and asked him how much money I could borrow on my signature. He told me $5,000.

Half of the commission was $3,500. I could come up with only about $500 of my own, so with the $5,000 of borrowed money the sellers would only be getting $2,000 down. The other problem was that at 7% interest, the payments on $95,000 would be over $1,100 per month. Interest alone would be close to $800 a month.

Prior to making an offer, I found a party who was willing to buy ten acres of the 160 acres for one dollar down and $800 a month for one year. Now I was covered for twelve months.

I told the sellers I would pay them the full $100,000. I would give them their $25,000 down payment, but would not make the down payment for twelve months. In the meantime, I would put $5,500 down, which put $2,000 into their pocket, and give them 7% interest. That would be $800 per month, on the $94,500 remaining balance. I assured them I would be able to perform and even if I couldn't, they would have all that money in their pocket and could sell the property to someone else. I did tell them I would need some release clauses but that no property would be released until after they received the $25,000 down payment. They accepted my offer.

Now all I had to do was sell the sixty acres from my previous land purchase or the Rodamocker farm buildings and ten acres for $25,000 cash. I also had to sell a couple more 10-acre parcels in order to be able to make the monthly payments after the first year. Finding buyers for the 10-acre parcels who were willing to give ten percent down was easy. Finding a buyer with $25,000 cash, or in the case of the sixty acres, a buyer with $48,000 cash, was quite another matter.

Selling property on a Contract for Deed with little down and payments over ten years was always easy. But I had never had to find a cash buyer before. Forty-five days prior to the $25,000 down payment being due, I still hadn't found a cash buyer. For the first and only time in my entire real estate career, I had trouble sleeping at night.

I do not know what I would have done had I not found a buyer. I believe I would have figured out some way to borrow the money, but I had been blessed my entire life, and once again the saint in my past came through. I sold the sixty acres for $48,000 cash, just in time. A little over $20,000 paid off what I owed on the eighty acres—remember I traded twenty acres off the eighty—and that left me the $25,000 I needed.

Within the following year, I sold ten acres and the farm buildings for $25,000. I also sold six ten-acre parcels, four wooded and two open, for over $1,000 an acre by Contract for Deed.

I now had the Rodamacker farm entirely paid for, on paper, and I was over the hump. The rest was all downhill from there.

I continued to read the want ads and kept my pulse on the real estate market.

A Man Who Changed My Life

Over the next year or two I looked for ranches and sold off a couple more 10-acre parcels of open ground from the original Rodamaker place. I took an extended trip through the Judith River basin of Montana and wound up in John Day, Oregon. What a spectacular valley up against the Strawberry Mountains! I spent a day in Dayville on a ranch with several thousand acres and even looked at a ranch north of John Day in the rancher's helicopter.

Irene found some problem with every ranch I found, and would not even go and look at any. Eventually I found a beautiful ranch near Klamath Falls, Oregon. I flew out to look at the ranch and fell in love with it. It bordered the national forests and had a 10,000-acre forest lease. A large fishing pond fed by springs flowed over 1000 gallons a minute and also irrigated over five hundred acres of land. I called Irene, and she agreed to fly out and take a look at it.

When I called her the temperature was in the 70s. Two days later when she arrived, a snow storm had set in and driven a skunk under the house. The weather was cold and miserable, and the house really smelled. Needless to say, Irene was not impressed.

We did not buy the ranch, but the trip and the man who was trying to sell me the ranch changed my life forever.

His name was Cliff Emmick and he was a real wheeler dealer. When I arrived in Klamath Falls, he had his spare Cadillac there waiting for me. The Cadillac had directions to a second riverfront home he owned where I stayed for the duration of my trip. We spent many hours visiting, and I learned he had been a millionaire a couple of times over. He made his money buying and selling property. He told me that while he lost it all once, they could not take away what he had learned. It only took him a short while to become a millionaire once again. Then he asked me how a man as young as I could afford to buy a ranch. I told him about my buying and selling property, and he said, "Let me tell you a story."

A man came over to the United States from the old country because he heard this was the land of opportunity. He had difficulty finding a job, and soon he went through his meager savings.

Finally, he decided to try his luck in a smaller town rather than in the large city. He went to several places seeking employment but still was unable to find a job. Soon he was very hungry and when the next place told him they did not have any work for him, he asked them if they could spare some food. They said they had none to spare, but told him a whorehouse on the edge of town was looking for help.

The man hurriedly walked to the whorehouse and knocked on the door. The madam answered the door, and he asked if she had any job openings. She yes, she was looking to hire an accountant.

The man said, "Great, I am very good with figures and I know I can do a very good job for you."

The madam asked, "You do have an education, don't you?"

The man replied that he did not have an education, but he was truly very good with figures and knew he could handle the job.

The madam replied that while she was very sorry, if he did not have an education, she could not hire him.

The man hung his head and asked if she might be able to spare him some food.

The madam said just a moment, and she went inside and came back with a crate of apples.

The man was so hungry that right after thanking her and waiting for her to go back inside, he sat down right there and started eating an apple. Soon a well-dressed man came to the whorehouse, looked down at the man, grabbed an apple and gave him a dollar. Then another man and another man, and soon the man had a handful of dollars. He bought another crate of apples, then another and another. Then he bought a truck to haul the apples, then an apple orchard, and another and another! In a few years he became the apple king of the world.

Then this great celebration was held where all the super rich and successful men of the world came and told their stories of how they became so successful. When it came time for the apple king of the world to tell his story, he told it just like I told it to you and the MC was astounded.

> The MC said, "There has to be more to it than that?"
>
> The apple king of the world said, "No, just buy and sell apples, buy and sell apples."
>
> MC: "Come on now. There has to be more?"
>
> Apple king: "No, just buy and sell apples."
>
> MC: "Wow! And to think that you did all of this without an education?"
>
> Apple King: "Yup, just buy and sell apples."
>
> MC: "Amazing, but can you imagine where you would be if you had gotten an education?"
>
> After a thoughtful pause the apple king of the world answered, "Yeah, I'd be an accountant in a whorehouse."

On the plane trip home, I thought to myself, if I had a plumber's license, which I had, I'd be a plumbing contractor, which I was.

To Irene's shock, within the next three months, I decided I was going to do nothing but buy and sell apples, and sold my plumbing business. Land! Buy and sell land.

Throughout the years I continued to read the want ads and kept my pulse on the real estate market. My first real estate purchase after selling the plumbing business was the Eide farm, which is close to where my oldest son Luke's present-day home.

My father had been watching my real estate transactions with interest and said he would like to get in on my next real estate purchase. So when I found the 115-acre Eide farm, I asked him to come along to look at it for the first time.

The farm had only been on the market for a couple of days when my father and I drove into the yard. I had already looked at aerial photos of the property, and when I drove into the yard, I knew I wanted it. The owner showed us the farmhouse and farm buildings, and I walked around the yard by the buildings. I told him I would pay him the entire $115,000 he was asking if he would give me release clauses. I explained how the release clauses would adequately protect his interest, and he agreed to give them. I asked him if he wanted to draw up the purchase agreement there or come back to my house, where I had blank purchase agreements available. He said he would follow me back to my place.

On the drive back, I asked my dad if he wanted in on the deal.

He sounded surprised. "You didn't even look at the entire property!"

"I didn't have to. I looked at the aerial photos and the soil maps, and I knew what was there."

"I never saw a person spend $115,000 so fast in my life."

"Dad, it's a great buy. If you want in, I'll give you whatever percent you feel comfortable with."

Dad just couldn't pull the trigger, and I bought the property myself.

The next day I got a call from one of Eide's neighbors and he offered me $10,000 more than I had paid. I respectfully declined his offer, but if I had not bought the property the night before, he certainly would have bought it the following day. (Rule number one: Know your market and pull the trigger as soon as you can.)

This property was so nice that I told Irene I wasn't going to have to go to work reselling this stuff. I never even had the property surveyed into 10-acre parcels. I just used a measuring tape and put in stakes of my own and told prospective buyers it was their obligation to survey their own property. I took several calls and talked to people on the phone and then gave them directions to the property. To my amazement, I sent over a half-dozen people out there, and not one of them bought any property. Finally, I told Irene that I would have to go to work.

Over the years it has always amazed me that people had to be sold. I certainly never had to be sold. I knew whether or not I wanted a property when I saw it, but the majority of people are not that way. When I took the next call, I set up an appointment to meet me at the property. When I showed them around, I pointed out the four-foot-diameter oak tree and how it must have been over a hundred years old. I also remarked on all the deer tracks along the creek and how private the property was. I told them how I fell in love with this property and that it was even a little difficult for me to let it go.

When they asked if I would hold it for them for a short while to give them time to think about it, I assured them it would almost certainly still be available and that they should not rush into anything. The more I tried to push them away and get them to take their time, the more they wanted the property. Before the evening was over, I had their $1000 earnest money and a signed purchase agreement. Within six months, I had sold the entire Eide farm and more than doubled my money.

All during this time I continued to look for ranches. Finally, I found one in Colorado that Irene agreed to give a try, but that's another story.

Obtaining a Brokers License and a Few More Deals

My buying and selling real estate was put on hold for about four years while we lived in Colorado, moved back to Minnesota, and operated an athletic club.

During those four years, I did buy and sell the 400 acres in Colorado and I did buy the 174 acres on the Cannon River, but not for speculation. I bought both of them to keep and live on.

Once I sold the athletic club, I knew I had to start buying and selling property again. Even while owning the athletic club, I read the want ads and kept somewhat abreast of real estate values. But once the athletic club was sold, I started looking in earnest.

Soon I found a resort for sale on Portage Lake in northern Minnesota. I went up and looked at the property and was astounded at how beautiful it was. With close to 1,000 feet of Sandy Lake Shore, it had six small but nice cabins and a large new barn. The only problem was it was a three-hour drive north of the Twin Cities and I did not have any money.

But I never let not having money deter me so why should this time be any different? They wanted $100,000 with $25,000 down.

I figured I could gamble $1,000 on this deal. I agreed to pay them their full price if they accepted $21,000 as a down payment, $1,000 paid immediately and $20,000 at closing ninety days later. Of course they also had to agree to some release clauses, but their interest was well protected.

They accepted my offer, so now all I had to do was to resell the property in ninety days.

In the game of *Monopoly*, it is important to consider where your piece is and where your opponent's pieces are when you mortgage all of your property and build hotels. Likewise, it is very important to buy real estate at the right time.

The ninety days I had to make my sales were the perfect months of May, June and July.

I made a lot of six-hour round trips. My father thought I was crazy for selling the cabins and lakeshore so cheaply, but I resold the entire resort in seven parcels within those ninety days. I got $2,900 down payment on each sale and the balance over ten years at 10% interest.

Yes, I could've gotten more money, but instead I gave my buyers a great deal and got the job done in time. I did not make a penny in cash but I made over $50,000 on paper coming in over ten years at 10% interest.

We also got all the equipment from the resort, which included six or seven boats and outboard motors. To Irene's great dismay, after I closed with my first few buyers, I gave each of them a boat and motor.

We were a little short of cash at that time, and Irene thought I should have sold those boats and motors. But the goodwill it created could not be measured. At least two or perhaps three of my subsequent sales were friends of the people who had originally bought from me and gotten boats and motors from me. They were so impressed they sent their friends to buy from me.

An interesting side note was that one of the buyers asked if they could tape me as I was telling them about the property. I smiled and said absolutely. They taped me for over an hour and they wound up buying the property.

Most of the properties I bought, if not all of them, were listed by realtors and realtors got anywhere from 6% to 10% of the sale. I knew these realtors cooperated with other realtors, which means if another realtor brings them a buyer they split their commission. I also knew that I knew more about real estate than any of them. I called the proper people in the state of Minnesota and asked if I could get a waiver and take my real estate brokers exam.

Apparently they had not given a waiver in over fifteen years, but I could come before the board and make my case. I spent well over an hour with the board. By the time I left, I had impressed them so much with my knowledge of real estate that they agreed to grant me a waiver. I was required to take some classes and pass the brokers exam. They did warn me that even after being a sales person for over two years, 60% of them failed the exam the first time they took it.

I took the classes, which were a breeze, and reinforced the fact that I knew more than most of the realtors out there. I passed my brokers exam the first time with over a 90% grade.

With a brokers license, whenever I bought a $100,000 farm listed by a realtor, I saved anywhere from $3,000 to $5,000 on the purchase.

My Portage Lake property was so easy that I concentrated on trying to find lakeshore properties.

The next farm I found was in Fergus Falls, Minnesota, on a small lake that was not very clear. But it had a nice three-bedroom home and over five thousand feet of lakeshore. I needed to test the market.

All kinds of lakeshore lots were for sale out there, but most of them had one hundred feet of frontage on pretty clear lakes. I started calling all the realtors in Fergus Falls, asking if they had any five to twenty-acre parcels for sale on a small lake. I told them the lake didn't have to be clear water, but it had to be fishable. None of them had any such property and all of them told me if they did, they could sell it in a heartbeat.

I took the plunge, saved half the commission, bought the farm and immediately resold the farm buildings. I divided the lakeshore property into large acreages. The nicest property I had for sale was nineteen acres on a point, and I gave that property to Luke to sell. Before the summer was over, I had sold all the other lakeshore acres, but Luke was unable to sell his nineteen acres.

At the end of the summer, I took the nineteen acres back and sold it within three weeks.

The next lakeshore property was on Net Lake, just south of Duluth, Minnesota. Net Lake was a brackish lake which means the water was kind of rust-colored. I was a little concerned about that, but five acre or larger parcels of lakeshore seemed to be in demand, so once again I went forward.

Here too I saved half the real estate commission. I divided the property into six-acre or larger parcels with each having about three hundred feet of lakeshore. Within a year, I was sold out.

Through all the years of buying and selling land, I kept notebooks with the names and numbers of all my prospective buyers and sellers in them. I had notes by each of my prospective buyers' names, telling me about them and what they wanted. Whenever I bought a new piece of property, I would start making phone calls to people who I thought might be interested. I don't know exactly how many pieces of property I sold this way, but it was a significant number.

While I was in the process of working on the Net Lake deal, a neighbor of mine in Cannon Falls asked if I would like to purchase his farm. I told him my money was currently all tied up but I would give him $1,000 earnest money contingent upon me getting financing. I explained that getting financing meant I would just be trying to resell his place, and if I didn't get financing, he could keep the money. He asked me if I had a real estate license, and he told me he would rather I just list the property for him.

I had never used my broker's license in this manner, but because he was a neighbor and friend, I decided to try it.

Right after I listed his farm, I started making phone calls to my notebook full of contacts. I also immediately ran a want ad in the paper and got a call from someone out of state who wanted to fly in and see the farm. I remember he had a voice that sounded like a four-year-old child, but I treated him seriously and with dignity and respect.

Now I had too many prospective buyers. I didn't want this man flying in from out of state only to get here and find the property already sold. I heard through the grapevine that another neighbor of mine, who was a pilot for Northwest, had been transferred to Seattle. I went over to see if he might be interested in selling his farm.

He told me he was definitely going to sell his place. But he didn't know what it was worth. He asked me to appraise his home and the forty acres. I appraised it for $180,000. He told me he wanted $220,000, and he wanted cash.

I got a ten-day listing for $220,000 cash.

Within those ten days I sold both farms.

Because I sold the farm so quickly, my first neighbor asked me if I would wait for half the commission for one year. I agreed, and he stiffed me. The Northwest pilot tried to back out on his deal because when it sold so fast, he thought he had sold it too cheap. I was able to hold the deal together, but the pilot hates me to this day because I put $12,000 in my pocket for what he thought was only a few days work. Hell, I only charged him a 5.5% commission, when any other realtor would have charged him 6% to 8%. A year and a half later, the person who bought his property was only able to resell it for $160,000. The pilot got way more for his property than he should have and instead of thanking me, he thinks I cheated him.

I vowed never to list another piece of property for anyone.

The above pilot story reminds me of something similar. Selling property is very easy. Buying it is difficult. Somewhere in between the Portage and Net Lake deals, I found 80 acres near Hazelwood just east of I-35W and just south of the Twin Cities. I signed a purchase agreement on the property and knew with absolute certainty that I was going to make at least $50,000 profit and do it in less than a year.

At the time we were good friends with Larry Blaylock and his wife Helen, and they too had been looking for property. When they saw the 80 acres in Hazelwood, they wanted to buy it from me. Because they were friends, or because I was a fool, I agreed to sell it to them.

I offered my position on the purchase agreement if they paid me $500. I explained that I was walking away from a $50,000 profit in order to help out my friends. Later I found out they didn't believe I'd walked away from a large profit. They were angry at me for making $500 while only owning the property for a day or two.

This gives you a fairly good idea about my experiences with buying and selling land. If you want to know a little more about the purchase of the ranch, and a lot more about buying and selling real estate, look in *A Path Less Taken: The True Life Adventures of Gary Friendshuh and His Faith Awakening*. Available on Amazon.

45

Ranch Stories

Throughout the years I have written stories about my life on the ranch. Here are a few of them.

Horse Wreck Canyon

The ranch is close to seven miles long and has seven pastures, so in order to communicate locations, every place of distinction gets a name. We have Girl Friend Hill where my number four son Mark took two girls horseback riding at the same time. On No Gate Flats, an old fence line was taken out, but the H posts on each side of some long-gone gate still stood. The Freeway is one of the roughest roads on the ranch. In Rattlesnake Canyon number two son, Tim, killed a rattlesnake with a stick. Broken Arm Gate is where I flipped a Razor while moving cattle and broke my arm. The bone was sticking out so they medevaced my off the mountain in a helicopter. And many other places of distinction.

Occasionally the name of a place gets changed. No Name Canyon, for instance, got changed to Elk Canyon after my brother saw four large bull elk in it while deer hunting. Jamie's Canyon got its original name because Jamie helped me build a trail up it. Based on the story I am about to tell you, it is now called Horse Wreck Canyon.

Several years ago a cowboy and I were going to ride up on the mountain and gather the eleven bulls that were in with the cow herd. I was still riding Loco, a half Arabian and half Morgan ranch horse that was athletic as hell. I ran him without shoes so he could really handle the rocks well. On one occasion, I even chased a bull over the rim of the Bowl and played the man from Snowy River (riding on an unbelievably steep slope). To the amazement of the cowboys with me, I got the bull back without breaking my or the horse's neck.

Whenever I went up the mountain on Loco, I would take the shortcut up Jamie's Canyon. On bull gathering day, I asked my friend Bill, a local cowboy, if he wanted to go that way. He said, "Why not?"

The trail up the Canyon is fairly easy, winding through timber and making a gradual climb until it gets to a rock wall. Here the horses have to go up a very steep, rocky incline. Loco had done it often with no problem, but Bill's horse had shoes on. At the steepest part, those shoes slipped on the rocks and the horse went down on its knees. It was so steep right there that, when the horse pushed himself back up with its front legs, it went right on over backwards. Bill was able to bail out, but the horse actually rolled over several times before it came to a halt at the bottom of the rocky incline. It just stood there shaking as Bill walked up to it and felt each of its legs for breaks.

I told Bill we could go back and gather bulls the next day, but he led the horse around a little and said, "She seems to be OK." But he added emphatically, "I am not going up this canyon." I rode back down the steep rocks, and we took the Freeway up the mountain. When we gathered the eleven bulls, one horned cow was still in heat and they didn't want to leave her so we brought her along.

Halfway down the Freeway, she headed off into the woods on a very steep slope. Because of what had already happened to his horse, Bill dismounted and went after her on foot. When he got too close, she turned on him and charged, putting one horn on each side of his waist and ripping his shirt in the process. He smacked the side of her head so hard he hurt his fist, but she backed off and headed back to the Freeway.

We got the bulls and the horned cow off the Freeway and down into the Bowl. Then we put them all in the corrals and cut out the cow. We pushed her up the Freeway and back onto the mountain.

Just another day on the ranch, but one in which a canyon got a new name. From then on Jamie's Canyon became Horse Wreck Canyon.

The Thanksgiving Eagle

On Thanksgiving Day, I had just enjoyed a super feast and I was ready for my daily walk.

I took my clothes off, put on my breechcloth and moccasins, and headed out the door. It was probably only thirty-nine degrees, but the sun was warm and the wind was calm.

I headed east to the creek which came out of Rattlesnake Canyon. By following the creek up behind the corrals, then crossing to the draw just west of the driveway and following that all the way to the barn, I could make the entire trip almost entirely unseen. A great route that I had taken often, and many times it allowed me to get very close to deer, turkeys or other wildlife.

Even though it was cold, especially for someone in a breechcloth, I did not feel uncomfortable. I could feel the branches on my legs and the direction of the breeze upon my skin. The movement of my muscles and the rays of the sun on my bare body more than kept me warm.

I often took these walks and used each one to thank the Lord for my life and my good health and the life and good health of my family. Each walk also allowed me to just visit, as might any son with his father. My attire or lack thereof seemed to allow me to become more at one with nature. To quote a poem by Lord Byron I once read:

From these our interviews, in which I steal
From all I may be, or have been before,
To mingle with the Universe, and feel
What I can ne'er express, yet cannot all conceal.

On this Thanksgiving afternoon, I had not seen any wildlife. So as I came up the draw towards the house, I decided to extend the walk up Rattlesnake Canyon. I had shot a turkey the day before and cleaned it there. I thought I might catch a coyote or bobcat dining on what was left.

I had cleaned the bird on the old road bed, beyond the cut off that went up the mountain. The cedar trees lined both sides of the trail on the old road. They formed a canopy over the trail just before it turns off towards the falls.

As I left the fork where the road began going up the mountain, I started walking as silently as I could. The grass was just moist enough that the passing of my feet made no sound. I could feel the breeze upon my legs as it made its way ever so slowly out of the canyon. I was intensely alert and aware of all that surrounded me. A slight bend in the trail just before the cedar trees afforded me cover. If anything was having dinner on what was left of the cleaned turkey, I would be able to get very close.

As I rounded the bend, I saw two eagles on the ground, not fifty feet from me. They saw me at the same time. Neither of them could take off and go straight up because of the overhanging trees. One took off and flew down the trail away from me. The other came right at me. His wingspan was at least five feet, and for an instant I thought he was purposely coming after me. I stepped to the side of the road as he flew towards me at knee height. I was looking down at a flying eagle, and for an instant, I thought I might touch his back. As the tip of his wing passed within four inches of my leg, he turned his head, beak, and talons in my direction. He was sending me a clear message, and I knew I was not to move. I watched him pass in awe.

It was over in but a moment, yet the experience and the memory will be with me for a lifetime.

The Lion

One day when I was checking cattle I came across four bucks, one of which was a 4x3 and still in velvet. He had a spread of at least 28" and good height to boot.

They were in Little Spring Canyon in Rim Rock Pasture, about a quarter mile above the spring and water tank. The big boy stepped behind a deadfall, and stood motionless for over five minutes just staring at me. When he finally moved out into the open, he was only fifty yards away. He stopped and looked at me again for another five minutes.

What I wouldn't have given for a camera. Little did I know how much I really would need one.

I have lived my life as an outdoorsman. Between here and Colorado, I have lived in mountain lion country for over twenty-four years. Yet I had only seen a lion twice. Once one crossed my driveway, and another watched Daniel and I as we walked back from hunting elk.

That was about to change.

As I slowly drove farther down Little Spring Canyon, a large lion crossed the trail less than thirty yards in front of me. The cat was over five feet long and his tail was at least that long.

I shut off the Ranger and went after him on foot. The level land on the other side of the trail ended once I got twenty feet off of it. A sheer rock cliff dropped at least thirty feet and there was no lion in sight.

I walked back towards the Ranger for at least thirty yards and the canyon began to curve around away from me. I was looking at the head of a portion of the canyon that had at least a thirty-foot drop on all sides for as far as I could see.

At the head of the canyon a large overhang, just off the bottom, proved a perfect place for a lion's den or for a man to get out of the elements. I didn't see a way down there other than to approach the overhang from below.

I retraced my steps and noticed a large pine tree fallen against the wall, the solution to the puzzle. The lion had climbed down the tree.

I continued down the canyon, along the wall looking for a place to climb down and there the cat was, less than forty yards below me. It was frozen in mid-step, staring at me.

Both of our views were unobstructed, so we just froze and stared at each other.

WHERE THE H*** WAS MY CAMERA!!!

After several minutes, the cat moved his front leg ever so slowly and set its foot even more gently upon the ground. The paw was so large it seemed like a snowshoe and its tail and all its paws were very fluffy or furry.

The lion took a few more steps, all in slow motion and all very deliberately, slowly disappearing into the underbrush.

I came home full of life and thankful for the way I have been privileged to live it.

Not all the amenities, luxuries, comforts, safeguards, and financial gains of civilized man could make me live in the city or suburb. I thank God every day for my life and the way I have been able to choose to live it.

Only next time I hope I'll have a camera.

Mean Cows

I have been culling my cow herd for disposition for many years, so my herd is fairly safe. But I will tell you about a few cows I had to get rid of.

In my starter herd in South Dakota, I had a cow with the number 13 for an ear tag and she had some Brahma in her. She was gentle enough during most of the year but at calving time she was real mean. She let you know in no uncertain terms you were not to get close to her newborn calf. To tag her calf for the first time, I picked a time when she wasn't looking and was a few feet away eating hay. I grabbed the calf and threw it on the back of my flat bed truck. When old 13 heard her calf beller, she came running and got both of her front feet up on the flatbed trying to get at me. From then on I just never tagged her calf until I could get them in the corrals to do it.

Then there was the time when I had a red cow charge me after I tagged her calf. She lifted me off the ground with her head and I hung on as she carried me over twenty feet across the pasture. When she let me go, I managed to land on my feet and got out of her way.

I knew I had to be careful with 13, Red and a couple of other cows. But a cow that gave me no warning caused me to take my first-ever ride in an ambulance. Lucky for me a girlfriend was along that fateful morning because I am almost always out there by myself. Evelyn was watching from the pickup when I went to tag this cow's calf. I kept the calf between the cow and me, but the calf struggled so much I got down on my knees to insert the tag. When I snapped the tag in, the calf bellowed and the cow knocked me over with her head and proceeded to dance on my chest. Most cows will knock you over and run away, but this one wanted to stomp me and she weighed over 1,300 pounds. When she finally left, I was light-headed and my ribs hurt like hell. I got in the truck and drove down to the renters' place, got out of the truck and passed out. I came to almost immediately but was in no shape to drive, so Evelyn drove me to the ER where they did an EKG. The results scared them enough that they loaded me into an ambulance and rushed me sixty miles to Rapid City Regional Hospital.

Rapid City was better equipped to handle heart problems. That's when I found out your heart is in a sack. If it is hit with a sledgehammer, or jumped on by a 1,300 pound cow, it almost certainly will swell up. If it swells too much, the sack will prevent it from beating. They kept me under close observation and x-rayed my ribs. I had a couple cracked and two broken. They wanted to keep me overnight, but by early evening the swelling of my heart was down. The heart doctor said if I could climb the stairs he would reluctantly allow me to go home. Evelyn drove me back to the ranch.

Those ribs took many months to heal, and on doctor's orders I had to make myself cough often during the process. Man, was that painful.

After that I really started culling in earnest, and I figured I had all the mean cows out of the herd. Then a cowboy friend of mine asked me if I would run ten of his cows on shares. (I run his cows on my place and I get a percentage of the calf crop for doing so.) I said I would without asking about disposition because they already had month-old calves at their sides.

About a month later, I had a sick calf on the mountain and I roped him off of my horse Loco, who was not trained to hold a dally. Holding a dally is when you rope the calf, then you wrap the rope around the saddle horn, and your horse pulls back to keep the rope tight. So when the calf hit the ground, I jumped off of Loco and quickly worked my way down the rope. The calf, of course, was back on his feet in no time and I had all I could do to get to him. It took every ounce of strength to throw him off his feet. When he hit the ground, I jumped on top of him. As I was trying to tie his feet together, a cow knocks me off him with her head. The cow moved on and the calf, free of my weight, jumped up and ran off with the rope around his neck.

And that damn cow wasn't even the calf's mother! It was the Brahma-looking cow of Bill's. Needless to say, I told Bill in no uncertain terms she wasn't welcome at my ranch ever again.

As I have matured, or as some might say, gotten older, I no longer leave my feet when tagging a calf no matter how hard it struggles. I now have Wade Allison doing a lot of work for and with me. Wade started out as a hired hand and has become a good friend. He does the work that might be considered dangerous for an old guy, and we now only tag calves when both of us are there.

I have never lost a calf to a coyote and no wonder! Even these even-tempered cows come a-running if a coyote even passes through the calving pasture. Many a time I have heard the entire herd bellering and looked out over the calving pasture to see seventy-five cows all charging to the same spot.

I just love this way of life and I love my cows. Mean or not, I hope to have cows until the good Lord takes me home.

You might think after all these years I would have gotten smarter (as well as older), but perhaps it's just the life of a rancher.

Broken and cracked ribs on my left side gave me my first ambulance ride. But at age seventy, I was sorting two-year-old heifers in a muddy sorting alley when I lost my footing and fell to the ground. The fall spooked the heifers and one of them tried jumping over me but didn't make it. Her thousand pounds of weight came down on my chest. I was on my side or I wouldn't be telling you this story. This time, I broke five ribs on my right side.

Six months after I had my first knee operation and had a pacemaker put in, I was branding my calves. A couple of inexperienced hands there were told to wrestle a calf only with an experienced wrestler. On the last calf, those two figured they could try wrestling together and the calf started to get away from them. One guy had a hind foot and the other guy had the calf by the tail. Without even thinking, I stepped in front of the calf to slow him down so they could throw him to the ground. Just as I got in front of the calf, they both lost their grip, the calf dropped its head and it came up between my legs. For a few seconds I was riding the calf backwards. When I finally hit the ground, I had pulled a groin muscle and pulled the lead wire out of my pacemaker.

Too soon old and too late smart.

To Touch a Rabbit

On a Saturday after Thanksgiving, a neighbor stopped over to borrow the jeep, and I was telling him about a book I had been reading by Tom Brown Jr. I told him about the Thanksgiving eagle and how Tom Brown claimed to be able to sneak up on a deer and touch it.

His eyes showed his doubt, but he had Native American blood in him, and he liked the idea of moccasins and breechcloth for silent walking.

After he left, I fed Jeanne's horses and set off on my morning walk. A steady breeze blew out of the north, but I wore nothing but a breechcloth and moccasins so I could better practice walking Indian-style. That is to walk with the heel directly in front of your toes. The toes are turned slightly in or straight ahead, arms and hands close at your side or in front of you. Point your toe down with each step and the outside of the ball of your foot hits first. Roll on to the balls of your feet, when you feel nothing beneath.

As I walked, I was conscious of the sound my foot made in the snow, like a tap-tap. It sounded nothing like a man. Many times while hunting, I had heard other men approaching, and the sound was very distinct, a *cruuuuunch.* Nothing like the tap-tap of an approaching deer. I stepped white man style for a few steps and sure enough, you or any animal could sure tell the difference. When a man walks Indian style, you sound like a deer or other animal, not like a man. I stopped to examine my own tracks. When I walked normally, even with my toes pointed straight ahead, you could see the heel hit first. The heel mark was deep and the entire track was outlined. Often times a scuff mark showed in the snow behind the heel. Walking in the Indian way, the tracks hardly showed the heel print at all, and the outside of the ball of the foot left the deepest print.

About ten minutes beyond where I had examined my tracks, I caught a movement out of the corner of my eye and froze. There, not six feet from me, was a rabbit. He was now dead still and looking right at me. I never moved a muscle, but in Tom Brown's book, he claimed that he and any animal staring at each other never blinked. The rabbit and I were eye to eye, and both he and I blinked several times.

Taken on a family canoe trip years before, but nothing has changed except my age.

The wind was in my face and I was aware of the fact my breech cloth was moving in the wind. The rabbit didn't care or didn't notice—he just stared. The sun was warm on my bare skin, and the wind had a warm feel to it, so I decided to let Mr. Rabbit have the next move. I tried to empty my mind, but my thoughts kept coming back. In the course of a rabbit's lifetime ten minutes are of greater significance than the same ten minutes should be to a human. I figured I could outlast him. We both just waited.

I then noticed where he had come from. There was a bare spot on the ground beneath a log, facing the midday sun, only three feet from where I stood. I could see where he had slept in the sun and where he had relieved himself and even where he had nibbled.

As if nothing was out of the ordinary, the rabbit dropped one of his ears and nibbled at the snow. Then, like a sudden flash of memory hit him, he froze once again and looked right at me. This time he only stared for a minute or two. Then once again, as if nothing were out of the ordinary, he nibbled some snow, dropped one ear and moved a little bit away.

I decided to see if I could touch him. When he was facing directly away from me, I tried lifting my foot out of the snow, but it made a sound and he froze. Within thirty or forty seconds he was back about his business. Twice more he heard me and twice more he and I froze, but now my left foot was out of the snow and my right was on bare ground. The next step he never heard. I slowly moved each time he faced away. Soon I was about three feet from him and about 18 inches from where he had been bedded.

Suddenly he turned and hopped back onto the bare ground beneath the log, only eighteen inches from my feet. I now could see his fur moving in the wind and his little body move ever so slightly with the beating of his heart. He lowered his head a little, dropped his right ear and relaxed his left. I could not see whether his eyes were open or closed, but I could see the tops of his eyebrows and I watched them relax.

I started moving my right arm away from my body so slowly I could barely see it move. After three or four minutes, my hand was directly above his head, but I would need to bend over to touch him. Moving as slowly as I could, I needed to bend down and to the side. My fingertips were only about four inches from the top of his still-up right ear. I thought about reaching down quickly to touch him. But I decided to see if I could do it gently. Besides, if he moved now, I could quickly tag him as he left. As I bent my legs and knees a little more, the old bones made a cracking sound. In an instant the rabbit was gone. My reactions never even had a chance, let alone my brain trying to tell me to move. If I am ever to touch a deer, I had better figure out a way to keep my bones quiet.

I learned a lot that day. I relearned lessons I had once known but had forgotten. I learned a rabbit couldn't see me less than two feet away as long as I didn't move. I relearned a man can outwait an animal if he wants to. And I do believe that I will one day be able to touch a deer. If my old bones will be silent, that is.

Deer Hunting on the Ranch

Before I moved to this ranch, I never missed the opportunity to go deer hunting. Once I was living here it was like I was in the deer hunting woods or mountains every day. Yes, I love the camp comradery and seeing others get excited and enjoy their hunting experience, but for me it had never been about killing a deer. It was about being out there alone in God's country.

Once I was on the ranch, I was alone in God's country every day and no longer felt the need to be hunting unless I needed the meat. When I did hunt, most of it was with family. In the beginning, most of the time our crew consisted of all five of my sons, my brother Brent, my cousin Big Mark and sometimes Dick Roxberg. In the early years Bob Lauinger lived on the ranch and would often join us. We stayed in the mobile home where Daniel was born and had great success.

When the grandkids got older and were able to join us, we moved to a wall tent on top of the mountain and began hunting with bows. One year I rented three tipis, one of which was the actual tipi used in

Me and Daniel (1992). In back, trailer where Daniel was born.

Tipis used for one of the deer hunting seasons

Matt, Daniel, Brent, Luke, Duggan, me and Jordan

Wall tent used for hunting before cabin was built

Ranch Cabin

the movie "Dances with Wolves" in the scene where Stands with a Fist met Dunbar. Then when the cabin got completed, we moved in there.

None of the years with the grandkids were very successful because the mountain lions had more than cut the deer herd in half. In fact, before the lions moved in, every September I did a ninety-minute tour of the ranch and my average deer count was 125 deer. A couple of years after a trapper caught a lion on the ranch and the Game Fish and Park tagged her, she was spotted with three adult cubs. A few years later, I made the same deer count and only counted 43 deer. All but three were in the open grassland. When I was counting over a hundred deer, at least 85% were in the timber. I attended a meeting with the GFP and several other ranchers from the Black Hills where everyone told the same story. In our view, the lions had cut the deer and elk numbers by more than half and caused the deer to stay out of the timber.

I will share one story from hunting on the ranch. We were hunting during the rifle season and staying in the trailer. We had a rule in camp that you could only shoot a 4x4 or bigger buck. One morning I came across a mule deer buck, whose mount is currently on the wall in the cabin. For those of you who haven't seen it, it only missed the record book by an eighth of an inch. It is a beauty.

I was walking very quietly down the road that leads to the cabin today and runs along the north slope through the heavy timber. As I got close to the clearing, I saw this trophy buck and a doe feeding. The wind was right and I made no sound as I actually got very close and watched the deer lay down. I knew my brother Brent was over the ridge to the south, so I just watched the deer until they got up. If they headed any direction but south, I would shoot the buck. But when they got up, they went south over the ridge where I knew my brother would be. He shot the deer and we dragged it back to camp.

When I told my boys I was in bow range of this buck they said, "Bull shit—There is no way you would let that big boy go." I said, "You assholes, next year I will hunt with a bow and bring back the first 4x4." And the next year I did just that!

My Cows Need Me

(Another day on the ranch)

This morning I began my day a little late when my grandson Brent woke me up at 6:00 a.m. with his usual morning phone call. I had gotten up in the middle of the night to do some things I couldn't get off my mind, so I was still in bed at that late hour.

After our talk I threw another log on the fire, did my hour of exercises, ate my usual breakfast, and sad to say, spent over an hour on the phone with several people.

I spent about fifteen minutes on my robo pong and then got dressed and brought in more firewood.

It was beautiful out despite the seven degree temperature. I shoveled some snow and worked on my tractor and did a little in the shop/barn. Then I loaded an 1,800 lb bale on my Haybuster and drove down to the East pasture and fed my cows. My tractor pulls the Haybuster which grinds up the bale and spreads it out on the ground in a windrow. Once the hay was spread out, I got off the tractor and walked down the line of cows eating the hay. It was so beautiful I could hardly stand it. As I walked along the cows, I thanked the Lord out loud for blessing me with this way of life. It also settles the cows down to hear my voice and makes them more familiar with it.

In more than thirty-two years on this ranch, I have never had to feed so much hay. The snow has never been this deep—at least eighteen inches on the level with a hard crust over the first four to six inches. No way could the cows get through it to the grass. The banks are heaped up over thirty inches high along the driveway and the deer are constantly at the alfalfa bale I left out for them.

We have moved our main meal to the middle of the day so I came back home to a super salmon dinner.

After a 40-minute break, I hooked up the stock trailer and picked up Wade, my hired hand, on my way by. We went to Romey's and picked up six heifers and their first calves. We put one heifer and six calves in the front of the trailer and closed the division gate. The other five heifers, hearing their calves, jumped in the rear of the trailer and off we went.

I have never had to plow out my corrals, but this year I did. I plowed a large double-wide circle inside the corrals and a path to the calving barn which was full of straw. This left a big pile of snow in the middle of the corrals. I also had to plow a path so we could back the trailer up to the corrals and unload. A bale feeder and salt and mineral sat in the section of the corrals by the calving barn that was plowed out.

The calves ranged in age from three to seven days old and because of all the snow they had been confined to a very small area at Romey's. When Wade went to unhook the trailer, I stood and watched the calves run in circles, kicking up their legs with the joy of just being alive. One was so full of it he found himself caught for a moment with his front legs up on three feet of snow. Their mothers watched with concern but the calves paid them no interest. They just continued to let off steam.

As I stood there watching with feelings I cannot even begin to express, I looked up on the hill at this beautiful home I built with my own hands and marveled at the surroundings. How blessed both Jeanne and I were to be able to live this kind of life.

How I wish one of my sons could share in all of this, but alas, if we all liked blondes, the redheads would be in trouble.

To each his own.

I was going to hit a few ping pong balls and then come back and check on the calves. But the last time I looked, they were all on the straw in the barn and their mothers were eating hay. All was good.

On one of the phone calls I took that morning, I was invited to Rapid City to play table tennis with the best player in the state, but I turned down the invitation.

Actually, I quoted a t-shirt Jeanne gave me for Valentine's Day.

SORRY
I CAN'T
MY COWS
NEED ME

Me on Loco

46

A Year on the Ranch

For those of you who have never experienced life on a ranch or have little idea of what it might entail, I will share with you what a typical year on the ranch is like.

January first, of what could be any given year, arrives without fanfare because holidays are just like any other day on a ranch. Most January mornings are around fifteen to twenty degrees, and often there is a light cover of snow on the ground. It usually melts off before the sun goes down. The days are short so I am up before the sun rises and I do my forty-five minutes of exercises, and make and eat my breakfast.

While eating, I gaze out across the bowl, often seeing several turkeys rummaging through the grass and a few deer grazing on the distant hillside. The bowl is a large circular valley about a mile across with 600-foot mountains surrounding it. A small creek runs through the center with large cottonwood trees lining its banks. A couple of draws coming off the surrounding mountains have a few cedar trees and some buck-brush in them. The balance of the bottom of the bowl is all grassland with no pine trees in it. The pine trees start halfway up the mountain and get thicker the higher up you go. Those surrounding mountains only have one gap, through which a two-mile-long canyon enters the bowl.

My home sits part way up the mountain on the north side of the bowl, offering an unobstructed view of the entire area with no buildings or lights of any kind in sight. I can look down this beautifully timbered canyon and see the prairie several miles away.

After I finish my breakfast, I spend an hour or so on my computer checking the weather, reading emails and posting on the Friendshuh family forum. Having noted the day before that the salt and mineral was getting low, I drive my outfit (a rancher's description of his pickup) to the barn and load some on the back. Once in the East Pasture, I unload the salt and mineral into a tub, then drive slowly through the cows.

On occasion I drive about five miles into the little town of Buffalo Gap and go to the Ranch and Feed store. I usually pick up a few items, including some more salt and mineral and several bags of cake. Cake is what we call the cubes you buy in bulk or in 50-lb bags, which contains 13% or 20% protein. It is fed to the cows if the grass or what they are eating needs additional protein. The cake is stored in the barn as is the extra salt and mineral.

After lunch I load an 1,800-lb round bale of hay onto my DewEze, which is a flatbed on one of my trucks. It has hydraulic arms that can lift, haul and unload the bales.

When I go back to the East Pasture, all I have to do is honk my horn and the cows will come on the run to get their hay. I lift the bale off the flat bed and hold it just off the ground to take the nylon netting off. Once the netting is off, I lower the bale to the ground and drive slowly across the flat and the entire bale rolls out on the grass. The cows line up nicely along the rolled-out hay and start eating. If the weather is nice enough, I walk along the line of eating cows to get an accurate count and look over their body condition. If it is extremely cold, I can make my count from the outfit.

FEBRUARY / LATE WINTER / HEIFER CALVING

All of January and half of February are all about the same day-to-day process unless we get a lot of snow or a severe winter storm. Lots of snow requires spending time on the tractor plowing the three-mile-long driveway. A severe winter storm may necessitate feeding the cows in a protected area and feeding them more than normal. Usually mid-February is when most ranchers begin their most difficult task. That's when the heifers start calving. Heifers are young females. Cows are females who have had two calves.

Now a few ranchers let nature take its course, but their losses are usually greater than the ranchers who check their heifers every four hours around the clock. First-calf heifers sometimes have difficulty calving. Then the rancher gets out the calf puller—something like a jack seated on the heifer's rump—and wraps chains around the calf's hooves, which are sticking out of the vagina. He then jacks the calf out of the heifer.

Along with calving heifers, the most difficult things a rancher has to do are handling bulls, putting up hay and feeding cows in extreme cold. For the last several years, I have gotten out of all four.

I used to do everything except put up hay. I ran my cows on grass year round and only bought a few bales of hay in case of a real bad storm. Then one day a neighbor came to me and said he had more hay than he knew what to do with and he was short of grass. He proposed a deal where I would run a large number of his cows for five months on my ranch in exchange for him running my smaller number of my cows on his ranch for one hundred days. Plus, he would calf my heifers, and furnish the bulls and hay for my cows. He would take complete care of my cows for one hundred days and I would take complete care of his cows for five months.

Because that deal was made, I have one hundred days a year when I don't even have to be on the ranch.

SPRING AND CALVING

If my cows have been wintering at the neighbor's, around the fifteenth of February I bring them home and put them in the East Pasture. About two weeks later, we move them to the bowl where they will have their calves.

Then I start bringing my heifer pairs back from the neighbor's and put them in the East Pasture. I check the heifers every day and feed them cake. They also have hay in a feeder in front of them at all times. When they come to the sound of the horn to get their cake, I spread it out on the ground. While they are eating the cake, I slowly walk as close to them as I can, all the while talking to them. This is called taming the heifers and their calves. I get them used to me and the sound of my voice so they become gentle cows.

Now that my cows are in the calving pasture (the bowl) and the heifer pairs are in the East Pasture, I get up every morning and am out the door as soon as it is light enough to see. In past years I did the rounds by horseback, but now I do them in a side-by-side Ranger with a cab. The driver side door is off the outfit, but a really good heater still keeps the cab fairly warm. If no new calves have been born, I can usually do the rounds in about forty-five minutes.

If a newborn calf is on the ground, the mother will almost always give that fact away by intently watching every move I make. If a cow does not have a calf, she will lie there or eat grass and pay no attention to me at all. If the temperature is above fifteen or twenty degrees and it is not snowing or raining, a cow will almost always have her calf without any problems. If it gets down to fifteen or twenty degrees below zero, the condition of the newborn calf will depend a lot on its mother.

If the mother licks the calf off real good and butts it with her head to get it up and moving and the calf sucks, the calf will be fine. It is imperative the calf gets up and sucks as soon as possible, but in no case later than three or four hours after it is born. When the cow first has her calf, the milk in her bag is full of colostrum, which has all kinds of antibodies and other protection to help the calf survive.

The most difficult condition, even for a very good mother, is when it is raining and freezing at the same time or when it is snowing a very wet snow. If the calf does not get dried off or does not suck right away, it will die. I have seen some mother cows, usually older, bang their calf around so much you would think she was trying to kill it. She is in fact just stimulating it to get up and suck. In a lot of cases,a really wet, cold calf will just lay there and die if I don't come along first. That is why I feed the cows late in the day, which usually encourages them to have their calves during the daytime or early morning hours rather than at night.

While I am doing the rounds, if I find a newborn calf I believe has sucked, I will catch the calf, put its head between my legs and insert a tag in its ear. The tag will have the number of the calf's mother on it. If it is a bull calf, the tag gets put in the right ear, and if it is a heifer calf, the tag gets put in the left ear.

If I come across a calf that appears to be in trouble or looks like it has not sucked, I will stick my finger in its mouth. If the mouth is cold, I pick the calf up and get him into the cab of the Ranger with the heater blowing a lot of hot air. I always keep a few towels in the cab

Calf in the kitchen

Daniel and me in the kitchen taking care of two calves

to rub down the calf to help stimulate him. In a few cases the calf will respond, his mouth will warm up and I can put him back out with his mother and watch him suck.

In most cases I will have to drive him back to the calving shed with his mother following close behind. I put them in a stall filled with straw and watch them. If the calf does not suck within ten minutes or so, I put his mother in a head gate, tie one of her back feet up, and put the calf on the cow's bag. If the calf still doesn't suck, I force the calf's mouth over one of the cow's teats and squeeze the mouth of the calf so it tastes the milk.

If I am unable to get the calf to suck on its own, I have to milk the cow into a bottle and try to get the calf to take the bottle. If I can't get the calf to take the bottle, I have to put the milk in a bag. The bag has a long tube with a small ball on the end to protect the calf. I put the tube down the calf's throat into its stomach and let gravity fill his belly with milk. Once the calf has that first belly full of milk, he will usually start sucking on his own.

If I find the calf in the pasture and it is close to death, and its mouth is very cold, I will bring him into my kitchen where we have a tub with straw in the bottom. The calf is put into the tub until he is warm and oftentimes tries to get up. Any calf brought into the house will almost always require having the first milk put in him by the tubing method.

When I used to start calving in the middle of February, I probably averaged one calf a year in the house. When I moved my starting calving date back to the first of March, I probably only had a calf in the house every other year. Now that I start calving on the fifteenth of March, I haven't had to bring a calf in the house even once.

We only leave our bulls with the cows for about fifty-five to sixty days, so our calving season only lasts for about sixty-five to seventy days. Most years we have over seventy percent of the calves on the ground in the first three weeks.

All through the calving season I do my rounds at first light and sometimes again around noon. In mid-afternoon I feed the cows with my hay buster. The hay buster is pulled by my tractor and grinds up

Tractor pulling hay buster

Ready to roll out a big round bale

the big round bale I put in it. As I drive along, the hay buster lays the ground-up hay in a nice line. Once it is empty, I get off the tractor and walk along the feeding cows looking at their condition and getting a count. If I am short, I sometimes do the rounds once again.

I do enjoy feeding the cows during the calving season, and it isn't long before the cows start bringing their calves to the feeding area. Then not only do I get to look the cows over, but I am constantly checking the condition of the calves as well. If the weather is particularly warm, I will sometimes lie on the ground and the braver calves will often come and nibble on my pants or sniff my head. On the other hand, if a storm comes in, I have to feed the herd down along a cedar draw where they all have more protection. They can even get under the cedar trees for more protection yet.

LATE SPRING, EARLY SUMMER AND BRANDING

About the time the calving season ends, I go up the mountain and make sure the well supplying six 10,000-gallon water tanks is working. I then need to open all the valves and check the floats in each tank.

About two weeks after the calving season ends (now around the first of June), we have our annual branding. We still do it the old-fashioned way. We separate the cows from the calves and vaccinate the cows.

Then a rider ropes the calf by the hind feet and drags it out of the roping pen. Two wrestlers flip the calf on its correct side, take the rope off and hold the calf down. Then three other cowboys do their job. One castrates the calf, another gives the calf its shots and the third cowboy brands the calf.

You usually have two ropers, three wrestling pairs, one cowboy doing all the castrating, another giving the shots, and another the branding. A young cowboy or two keeps the calves from escaping the roping pen.

Our herd is fairly small, so it only takes our crew about four hours for the entire process. Afterwards everyone returns to the house for the annual branding feed. Most ranchers help out several other ranchers with their brandings and the ranchers help them in return so no one has to hire a crew of any size.

One of many brandings. Daniel, Will, Gary Romey on horse, and Wade

I am branding and Daniel is the bare-armed wrestler (2016).

SUMMER

Before the cows are put out to pasture, all the exterior fence lines of the pasture must be checked and repaired if needed. We have over sixteen miles of exterior fence line and almost as much fence separating the seven different pastures.

A few days after branding, the herd is moved to one of the summer pastures. The occasional cow that has lost her calf is hauled in a stock trailer to the sales barn. No rancher can afford to keep a cow without a calf over the summer.

Once the cows with their calves are in their summer pasture, I check the herd at least every third day. I am constantly checking fences, checking the salt and mineral and keeping it in front of the cows at all times. Most importantly, I make sure the cows always have water. Some pastures have springs, but some are dependent on a well to keep a tank full. The cows can never be without water.

I put the bulls in on June 5. For the sixty days the bulls are with the cows, I check them on a daily basis or at least every other day. I am constantly on the lookout for a crippled bull or one with a broken dong. The bulls will often fight and cripple one another or hit another bull when his penis is inside a cow, sometimes causing it to break. If a bull's dong is broken, it will hang down at an awkward angle and he will not be able to piss. He will die in a few days if he is not attended to.

The pastures also have to be monitored constantly. I do not allow cows to graze grass that is regrowing. If it is raining heavily, it only takes about 11 days for regrowth to begin. If it is dry, the cows can stay in the same pasture for up to a month. Either way, nature dictates how often we move the cows to the next pasture in the rotation.

We used to move the herd from pasture to pasture by horseback and still use horses to help in the process, but the side-by-side Rangers now do the bulk of the work.

The 6,000-plus-acre ranch is close to seven miles long and we lease 3,000 more adjoining acres. When I did everything by horseback, it was very romantic and fun. But by the time I saddled a horse and rode him for up to six or seven miles to check the herd, at least a half a day

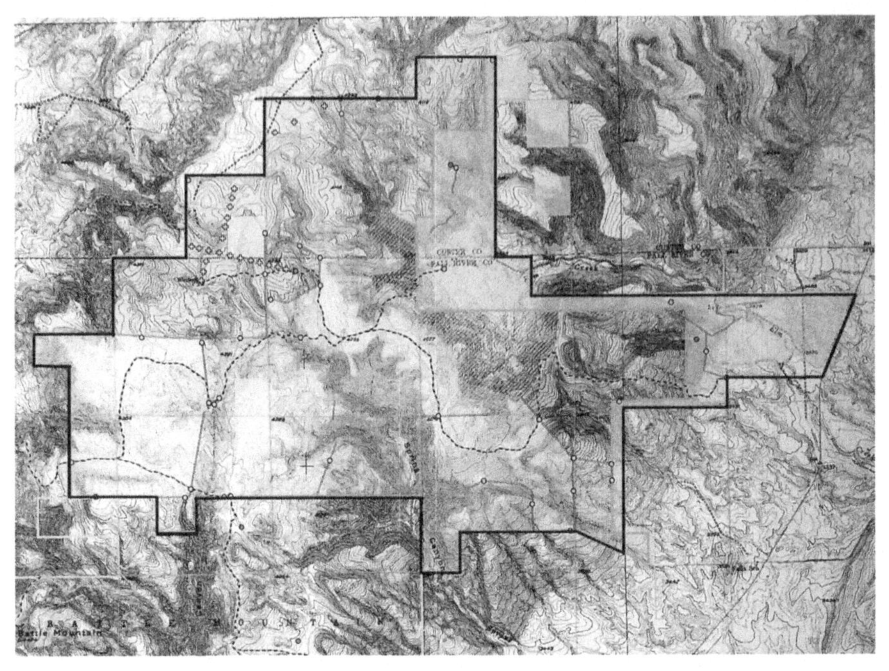

7 Arrows Ranch

was shot. On a side-by-side Ranger I can do the same job in less than an hour. I can haul salt and minerals without having to take along a pack horse to get the same job done.

I am constantly checking water, tank floats, fencing, salt and mineral tubs and looking over the cow herd for possible problems. If I get a sick cow or a calf with pink eye, or a runny nose or a serious cough, I carry a dart gun. I load a dart with the proper medications and then shoot it into the sick animal, which almost always solves the problem.

On rare occasions I have to push a cow or calf into a holding pen and either doctor it more extensively or load it on the stock trailer to take it to the vet. In the past, doing everything by horseback, I often doctored cows like a lot of ranchers still do today. The horse is trained to run alongside the calf as you rope him. Then you jump off your horse, work your way down the rope and throw the calf on the ground. You tie three of the calf's legs together so he can't move. Then you get the necessary medication out of your saddlebags and doctor the calf.

If I keep the cows on fresh pasture with lots of water, vaccinate them properly, and keep them away from outside herds, I can go an entire grazing season without having to treat a single animal.

Flies can become a problem, so we usually push the cattle into a fence corner about once every six weeks and spray them for flies.

We try to keep the weeds under control by spraying them at the appropriate times of the year. I have a weed sprayer on one of my Rangers, and my hired hand does the spraying.

SUMMER FIRES

We also use the weed sprayer to fight fires should we get a lightning strike that causes a fire. Lightning strikes probably cause one or two fires a year, so we are constantly on the lookout. We have an older jeep that we use exclusively as a fire fighting outfit. It has a 100-gallon water tank, high pressure nozzle and lots of hose.

The worst fire we ever had on the ranch happened two years after I bought the place. It burned over 4,000 acres of land and took out over four miles of my fence line. My 16-year-old son Mark and I, along with eight other ranchers and their fire units, fought that fire for nearly fifty-two hours straight. Mark and I managed to squeeze in four hours of sleep during those fifty-two hours.

A year or two later I was on the Buffalo Gap volunteer fire department and fighting what they called the Custer fire. We thought we had it controlled on the west side of Highway 16 when it jumped the highway and started a fire on a hilltop on the east side. There were several units right there, but they were trying to figure out what to do. I grabbed one of the ranchers who had his own unit and asked him to follow me. I later found out it was Gary Romey. I headed off through the timber and brush finding a path I felt his pickup with a fire unit on the back could follow. We got off the highway quite a distance and found ourselves at the bottom of the steep hill that the fire was burning on top of. I grabbed the end of the fire hose, and Gary fed it off the roll. I headed up the hill. After the first hundred feet, Gary ran part way up to help with the heavy hose. When we got almost the entire 200 feet of hose out, we had reached the fire. We put it out. Gary, who I got to know later, knows no fear. He still has his own fire unit and is almost always the first on any fire within a ten-mile radius.

Over the thirty-plus years I have been on the ranch, there has been a fire on the place at least once every two or three years. One night I saw lightning strike the side of the mountain across the bowl and watched the grass burst into flames. I called the local volunteer fire department, then jumped into my Jeep. I couldn't find the fire. I reached Jeanne with my walkie talkie, and she could see my headlights and the fire. She got me close enough to see it, but I had to pull out all my hose to be able to reach it. I started putting water on it until the fire crew got there about thirty minutes later.

Another time while doing something in the Mountain Pasture, I saw lightning strike the grass across the canyon in North Pasture. I had no cell phone. So because the fire was above my house and in the grass, not timber, I got there as quick as I could. I started trying to contain it with nothing more than the McLeod, a firefighting tool, I had with me. I knew someone would soon see the smoke and help would be on the way. We contained those fires, like most other fires, within one acre or less.

In five fires, I have seen lightning strike and the flames begin. I saw two from my home. I saw another one when I was showing the original homesteader's family the root cellar their ancestors built, actually on my birthday. Two others I saw while out on the ranch.

The key is getting to them early before they have time to build up heat, get into the tree tops and start spreading in the wind. There have been many times, after a lightning storm, that I have gotten into the Ranger and got on a high spot and just looked for smoke. Of course, all the other ranchers are doing the same thing, so we often catch a fire early.

Some of the most dangerous ones are what we call sleepers. Lightning strikes a tree and it smolders for two or three days. Then with the right heat and wind conditions, it just bursts into flames.

FALL AND SELLING THE CALVES

Back to the cows. About a month before shipping (the day when we sell our calves), we gather the herd and separate the calves from the cows. We treat the cows for flies and vaccinate the calves again. This second round of vaccinating the calves is called preconditioning, and it helps protect the calves when they are in the feedlot.

A month or so later, at the end of the summer, we gather the herd once again. We separate the calves from the cows and ship the calves to market. We then pregnancy test the cows and haul any open (cows not pregnant) or crippled cows to market. All the bred healthy cows are vaccinated and kept on the ranch.

Shipping the calves and pregnancy testing the cows is done the same way as branding and preconditioning the calves—with the help of neighboring ranchers in exchange for our helping them. But occasionally we just have to hire enough cowboys to help out with whatever is going on.

After the cows have had four days to dry up and forget about their calves, we turn them back out on pasture. We usually ship the calves around the end of October. Sometime in November, we take the cows off the winter pasture and move them onto some corn stocks.

WINTER AND COMPLETING THE CIRCLE

The best thing for any ranch is its owner's footsteps.

No matter what time of the year it is, we are constantly checking all the machinery and outfits to keep them in top condition. And we always seem to be replacing some corral timbers or adding or replacing some fencing.

You are your own man on your own schedule, but you are constantly monitoring every part of the ranch.

The weather dictates how the herd is handled for the balance of the winter. Usually we feed cake or hay, depending on the amount of open grass available. In the case of a severe winter, we feed them a lot of hay. With a severe storm, occasionally straw is put down to give them a dry place to lay.

When Christmas rolls around, like all families, we enjoy the holiday, but the cows must be tended to on a daily basis, Christmas or not.

Soon we are back where we started, starting another year. The circle of life just continues on. I thank the Lord every day for being able to be part of that circle and to have been blessed enough to live this kind of life.

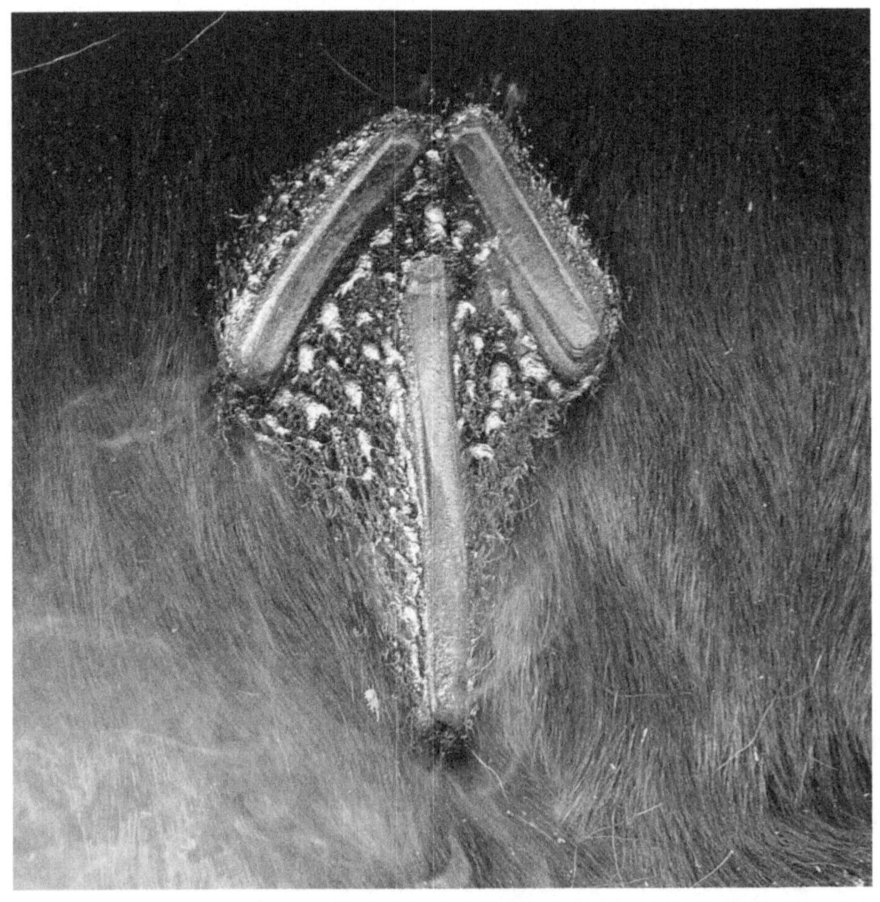

My brand on the right rib, immediately after being put on

AN ADDITION

Just before this book went to print, I had a memorable ranch experience I thought I should share.

Tough Days

As of this writing I have lived on this ranch for a little over thirty-three years, and I have never had a rougher 36 hours than I just went through.

Three days before the rough 36 hours we found the oldest cow on the place dead and bloated. She was laying with her back slightly downhill up against a tree. We thought she had died with the calf in her. Two days later a calf shows up in the same area. It climbed a steep bank and tried to follow the Ranger and then us on foot. We determined that the old cow had had her calf and the calf must have sucked at least once before she laid down and died. Otherwise there is no way that calf could have lived for two more days without being fed.

We picked up the calf and got it to the house. We put him in a tub in the kitchen. He took a bottle like he was starving to death and I am sorry to say we let him have too much. That caused problems later.

The evening before the start of my 36 hours it started raining. It rained all night, and before morning it turned to ice and then snow.

My day started at 5:00 AM because I had to tend to the calf in the kitchen. It now had a bellyache because I had given it too much milk.

After taking care of the calf, I got outside as soon as there was enough light to see. Everything was a solid sheet of ice covered with snow. And it was still snowing.

We started our rounds. The first newborn calf we found had slid down a steep bank and was sideways in the creek. She was still trying but couldn't get up. When we got to the calf its mother was really on the fight. Wade managed to pick the calf up as I stood in the creek and beat the cow with my sorting stick as hard as I could. I had to keep her from knocking me over and getting at Wade. We got the calf into the kitchen with the other calf still there in the only tub we had. I used that tub as one wall, the end of the kitchen cabinets as another wall, the (thankfully) tiled outside wall of the house as the third wall, and a garbage can to finish enclosing a space.

After dumping straw on the kitchen floor inside of our homemade enclosure and putting the new calf inside, out the door I flew.

The next calf we found in trouble was a two-day-old calf. It was covered in a solid sheet of ice, and the inside of its mouth was cold. This calf was in real trouble. We put it on the floor of the pickup with the heater blowing on it, and managed to get its mother into the calving barn. But during the hour it took to get the mother in the barn, the calf had died.

The third calf we found also slid down a steep bank and was laying in a puddle of water and tangled in a barb wire fence. We got her out and she was able to follow her mother away. Late that evening the mother brought the calf to the hay, and it was doing fine.

During the day we had to put hay out three times for the cows and once for the heifers in the East pasture. They have to have lots of feed to keep them warm and they couldn't get at the grass because of the solid sheet of ice and snow.

When we hayed the heifers, one heifer and two calves were missing. One of the missing calves was only two days old. We were able to find the missing heifer and she had the two calves with her, so we decided to leave them for now.

Big mistake!

Later in the day the heifer was in the hay yard without the two calves. The mother of one of the two calves was out looking for her calf. We managed to hook them up and made our second mistake. We pushed the pair back to the hay yard and left the two-day old calf. I was sure its mother knew where it was and would come back for it.

She never did. Stupid heifers.

During all of this I had to run to the vet for the calves in the kitchen but that gave Wade time for a quick breakfast around noon.

After giving shots and electrolytes to the calves in the kitchen, we went to find the missing two-day-old calf in the East pasture. It took some doing to find it again; it had moved from where we and its mother had left it. We picked it up and drove it to the hay yard. It mothered up (meaning the cow and calf found each other and the calf sucked) and is now doing fine.

During this time, we had to get the mother of the calf that fell in the creek into the calving barn. After shifting her around with the other cow in there, we got her in the head gate. Once in the head gate we tied up one of her back legs and milked her. Milking a range cow is nothing like milking a tame milk cow but we got it done.

We took the milk to the kitchen but her calf was too far gone to take a bottle. We put the milk in a tuber and tubed the calf. That is where the milk is put in a sack attached to a hose which is attached to a plastic tube. The tube has to be pushed down the calf's throat, making sure not to get it into its lungs. It has a small ball on the end of the tube that we lubricate with a little butter and once it is in the calf's stomach, we hold the bag up high and allow the milk to flow in.

Then we went back to the barn and put the mother of the two-day-old calf that had died in the head gate. Once in the head gate we tied up her back foot and milked her. I wanted the milk for the other calf in the kitchen.

I finally got to eat my breakfast and have my first glass of water for the day at 3:30 PM.

Then I was out the door again until it was too dark to see.

During the entire day the snow never stopped and until I was able to eat my breakfast I was walking on frozen feet, wet from being in the creek. My hands were none too warm either.

The next morning it was three degrees but thankfully it was not snowing. Maybe we will get lucky today.

No such luck.

Three calves were born during the bitter cold of the night. Two were doing fine but the other one had to be taken to the calf warmer in the barn. In getting the calf away from her mother, Wade was almost crushed by the cow. She even hit the Ranger but I was finally able to beat her off with my sorting stick.

Several hours later we took the calf out of the calf warmer and put it back with its mother. By this time the calf had lost its instinct to suck and the mother, because of having her calf taken away once, was really on the fight.

Back to the calving barn. We milked out the two cows in the calving barn again but the one who had lost her calf broke the head gate. Still, we got enough milk to be able to feed both calves in the kitchen and both were now able to take it from a bottle.

Back to the calf that had been in the calf warmer. It still had not sucked so we had no choice but to put the cow and calf in the calving barn.

While driving them to the barn the cow got herself tangled in a barb wire fence. We had to cut the wire to get her out. In order to have room for this cow in the calving barn we had to let the mother whose calf had died into the corrals.

Wade had since spliced the broken head gate. When we got this mother in the head gate we brought in the calf. With the mother's back leg tied and held by me, Wade was able to put the cow's tit in the calf's mouth and got him to suck.

I finally got in for breakfast at 12:30 PM.

We kept the pair in the barn overnight. After seeing the calf suck the next morning we let them out.

I had originally posted this on our family forum and a couple of my boys responded, "Dad, you love it."

I responded, "No way." I really don't like days like this but I am willing to put up with an occasional bad day and a couple of horrible days every four of five years to be able to have the more than one hundred days a year that I truly love.

That's the life of a rancher.

Actually, no—

That is life.

47

Summing Up Ranch Life with a Story

I couldn't ask for a better way of life. Outdoors all the time, experiencing the circle of life and feeling close to my Creator.

Often times I will stop the Ranger, get off, lie in the grass, and fall asleep under the Lord's magnificent sky.

I'll share something I wrote one Easter Saturday that will give you a sense of this way of life and how I perceive it.

Hardly a single day goes by without me thanking the Lord for all my blessings, but this day, the day before Easter, was special.

There was a chill in the air when I went out to do my normal rounds this morning, and I was thankful for my coveralls, jacket, stocking cap, and gloves. The sun was trying to fight its way through the clouds and the winds were calm. The cool morning air filled my lungs, and the majesty around me warmed my heart.

There were no lights, no buildings, no automobiles, no other people, and no sounds to intrude on the wonder about me. A few wild turkeys scampered off on my approach, and a mule deer stood motionless as I rode by. A hawk soared above the trees as I headed to the cedar draw, and the cows grazed peacefully on the distant hillside.

As I rounded a bend, I noticed a cow was off by herself about to give birth. In her confusion, after each labor pain she would look around for her calf and call out to it. As I drew nearer, another calf approached the calling cow and tried to suckle her. Both cow and calf paid me little heed until I was within twenty feet of them, but when I stopped, they slowly ambled off. I kept my distance as they walked about a hundred yards away, and she once again had a labor pain. The calf had now given up, but the cow kept turning in circles looking for the calf that had not yet come.

She was one of only two cows yet to calf and I soon found the other, so I headed back to the buildings.

When I got back to the house, I set up my spotting scope on the cow so I could check her every so often. It wasn't very long before I

could actually see two of the calf's feet protruding from her. I now could be fairly certain the birth would be no problem.

I tended to a few household chores, and soon a newborn calf was on the ground. I smiled as I watched him on wobbly legs trying to find the right spot on mama. She kept wanting to lick him, and in trying to do so, kept pivoting away from him. But at last nature's instincts took over. Mama stood, baby latched on, and his tail went a hundred miles an hour.

A few hours later I spread the round hay bale across the flats and walked among the cows and calves. When I headed back towards the pickup, one calf was licking the truck door and another was using his head to batter the six-inch round core of the bale left on the ground.

I went back to the house, got the Ranger and slowly drove up to the new cow/calf pair. She was a very gentle mother and just lay next to her calf, allowing me to walk up within two feet of her before she stood. When I lifted the calf's leg to see I had a new heifer, mama just mooed softly. I inserted the tag in the calf's left ear and slowly walked away. As I looked back over my shoulder, I saw the youngster latch on to mama once again. All was good with the world.

In driving back towards the rest of the herd, I looked at our home at the base of the mountain and I was overwhelmed with emotion. Everything around me was so beautiful. It was so perfect and I could not believe how blessed I was.

I stopped the Ranger, stepped off and got on my knees. The emotion was so powerful I did not know what to say. I prayed the "Our Father."

Upon its completion, I slowly got to my feet and looked all about me and said part of the prayer I say almost every day of my life.

> "Thank You Lord for this day and thank You for my life and my good health and the life and good health of my family. And thank You for Your Son, Jesus, and for my sons Luke, Tim, Matt, Mark, and Daniel. And thank you for Jeanne and her daughter Kim, and all those who share this life with me."

Then I went on to say something like "I have been so blessed I can hardly believe it. There is no way I deserve all these blessings. Whatever relative earned these blessings for me, I thank you. I thank you.

"It is said somewhere in Scripture that when a man is truly good, his children shall be blessed for seven generations.

"I truly am not deserving. I am a sinner, I am too proud, and I am very difficult to live with. Yet I am blessed beyond all measure. Someone else's goodness has brought this upon me and I am truly grateful."

When I got back to the warmth of my home, I felt the need to try to put into words the powerful experience I had just been a part of. I found pen and paper and tried to write down something that seemed beyond words. Several days later, when I shared the words on the family forum, one of my sons responded.

A quote from my oldest son, Luke

Dad, you have been given yet
another gift, the gift of gratitude.

48

My Awakening

A year or two after my Easter experience, I went to Mass one Sunday when we had a visiting priest, Father Jack La Rocca. The deacon gave a sermon about spreading the gospel, but Father Jack said just enough during the Mass to draw me in.

There was something about him and there were several things he said during Mass that were all summed up in what he said after Mass. After Father gave the final blessing, the deacon said, "Go forth and spread the gospel." Father Jack said, "Go forth and spread the gospel by letting the light of Christ shine through you."

When Mass was over, I leaned forward in my seat with my arms on the pew in front of me and my head bowed. I prayed for a while as the congregation was leaving the church. When I finished, I realized I was late and hurriedly went to my outfit and started driving away. I got about three blocks from the church and something just made me turn around. I went back to the church hall where they were serving coffee and rolls and saw Father Jack sitting there. I went up to him and introduced myself and asked if we might be able to get together sometime. We exchanged contact information.

Several days later I gave him a call. When, he asked what our meeting was supposed to be about. I told him it was spiritual, so we set up the meeting at a church in Rapid City.

We were in a small room and I was sitting directly across from him with my head bowed. He waited patiently as I searched for the right words.

Then I began, “Father, I just had this feeling during Mass you were someone I needed to talk to. After you gave the final blessing, Deacon Craig said to go forth and spread the gospel. You said, ‘Go forth and let the light of Christ shine through you,’ and I knew I had to talk to you.

“Many years ago while at deer hunting camp, I went to Mass at a small church and the priest gave a sermon that really meant a lot to me. He talked about how the church no longer sent missionaries out to tell the uncivilized they were living in sin. They now go out and help those in need and eventually ask them what their understanding of God is. If they ask in return what the missionaries’ understanding of God is, they then tell them about Christ. They don’t preach the gospel—they live the gospel and the light of Christ shines through them and draws others to Christ.

“That is basically what you said after Mass and it really grabbed me. So much so that even though I had driven away from church heading to a meeting I was already late for, I had to turn around.

“I don’t understand these feelings, the feelings I had during Mass or the feeling that made me turn around. They were just there.”

Father leaned forward and said, “Feelings are the windows to your soul.”

He just let what he said sink in and sat there looking at me.

I continued and painted him a picture of my life. I told him I had 12 years of Catholic education, but my mother taught me to think for myself. When I was young, that presented some real problems. Other kids didn’t have to decide what was right or wrong, they just believed without question. Whatever the church said was wrong, they accepted as wrong. If the nuns told them they couldn’t attend if a Catholic was getting married outside the church, they didn’t think about it—they just didn’t go.

I, on the other hand, had to make a choice when my mother’s sister chose to get married in a Lutheran Church. The nuns told me the church had forbidden me to go. I was still in grade school at the time, but I just had the feeling the nuns were wrong, so I went.

When at age sixteen I was about to go on a hundred-mile canoe trip into the wilderness for thirty days, I went to a Catholic priest and asked for permission to miss Mass on four Sundays. When he told me I couldn't go, I just knew he was wrong and I went anyway.

I had always believed life begins at conception and I saw nothing wrong with a form of birth control that prevents conception; my wife and I used it for a short time before eventually having four sons.

My twelve years of Catholic education included four years in high school being taught by Christian brothers. They constantly brought home the point of how serious a sin masturbation was, and at the time I believed it. But when I taught my sons, I did not give them that hang-up. Instead, I taught them that they had to be in control of their body. They should not eat all the sweets their body craves, or stay in bed just because they were tired and didn't want to get up, or hit someone just because they were angry at them. They had to be in control of their bodily desires. Although one of the greatest desires of the body is sex, they certainly should not sleep with a girl before marriage or give into their body's desires every time they felt the urge. They had to make sure they were in control of their body at all times, which would take a lifetime of practice.

I went on to tell Father Jack that I tried to pray every day, but I prayed like Tevye from *Fiddler on the Roof.* I just talked to my Father in heaven like I would talk to my father on earth.

Father Jack said he loved that movie, and he too liked to pray in that manner.

I then told him I believe we all have been given special gifts and that my gifts were many, but sometimes our greatest gifts were our greatest crosses. I had been given the gift of communication but I tended to talk too much. My father was a quiet German who said little, and I always felt he was somewhat ashamed of me for all my talking. Once while riding with him for two hours, on the way to his brother's farm, he said nothing the entire trip except to answer me when I asked what he was thinking. He just glanced at me like I was nuts and said, "Nothing."

Dad also didn't like showing affection in public, not even holding hands. When I returned from Alaska, he offered to shake my hand. I took his hand in mine, pulled him in and gave him a hug. Later in life he learned to give and accept hugs.

I also told Father Jack that I have been given the gifts of an enormous love of life, of forgiveness and of gratitude. In fact I try to thank the Lord every day for my life, but I also have tried to pray every day for the gift of faith.

I was once given a small gift of faith when my father died. The day after he died I went to Mass and for the first time in many years my mind was completely empty. There were no words in my mind, no thoughts at all. I just knew it was right to be there.

But I confessed to Father Jack that I have always been too proud. For years I had taken pride in the fact I had almost never asked God for anything other than a greater gift of faith.

Not until my wife of twenty-four years walked away did I actually beg for something. I was on my knees crying and begging Him, "Please don't let this happen." Later, I realized this was one prayer God could not answer. He would never take away anyone's free will. But all of that is another story.

I told Father Jack that over all these years every time my mind got into the act, religion always lost. I often challenged it, asking how could God in the Old Testament be so cruel? How could anyone put a story on paper twenty-five years after they lived or were told the story? How could a loving father condemn one of his children to hell for all eternity? How could the church say I have to do this or that or—

Father Jack leaned forward and spread his arms wide apart as he interrupted in a very loud voice, "FORGET THE STRUCTURE! FORGET THE STRUCTURE!

"It is your open, loving heart that God wants and He doesn't give a darn about the structure. The Church put the structure there, not Jesus. Some take comfort in structure. And children, as they are learning, need structure. But too often it gets in the way. Don't let it get in the way of your soul.

"Feelings are the window to your soul. Let them out. Let them guide you. Forget the structure and let your soul guide you. Let all the love within you out and allow the light of Christ to shine through you!"

"Gary, you are full of faith; don't let the structure hold it back."

I cannot explain what happened to me at that moment, but the feeling was incredible. All the burdens of church structure were gone, my doubts were gone. I felt full of grace and I was at peace.

My life was changed forever.

We met a week or so later, and he shared with me some of his life experiences. I learned he was raised in an orphanage and had always wanted to be a priest. Back then, they didn't need priests and they wouldn't accept him because he was an orphan. He spent two tours in Vietnam and afterwards he spent several years among the Hmong people in the remote jungles and mountains of Vietnam, Laos, Thailand and southern China. Finally at age forty-three he was ordained as a Catholic priest.

But what had the greatest impact on me was the fact that he had worked with Mother Teresa, a canonized saint, and he told me this saint actually struggled with her faith. My struggles no longer seemed so troublesome.

Several days after our second meeting, I received a card from Father Jack that is difficult for me to share. It sounds too prideful for sharing; but later Father and I talked about it. He thought what he wrote should be shared and so did my oldest son, Luke, who I did share it with. Luke also had an insight that made the sharing easier. He said to me, "Dad, what was written to you could have been written to almost anyone."

So take my name out and replace it with yours, and he could have been speaking to you.

Here is part of what this man, Father Jack La Rocca, who has spent his life serving others and radiates the light of Christ, wrote in the card he sent me.

My dear brother in Christ:

I am indeed very humbled being with you. You are a source, a divinely inspired source of God's creation.

Be ever mindful, reflective and praise God for you, His special son called Gary, His true disciple.

You, dear Gary, are blessed as I am. Together we will rock and roll joy unto the wonderful creations of humanity who have forgotten to love.

Always remember that you have been and continue to be a true disciple of the Lord.

WOW! How could anyone ever hear something like that and not have it change them forever?

A few days after I had received the card, Father Jack came to the ranch. He anointed me with oil, and in his capacity as a Catholic priest, he administered the sacrament of matrimony. With Jeanne and I holding hands, in the presence of a friend, we exchanged our marital vows and Father Jack pronounced us man and wife in the eyes of the church. Then he laid his hands upon each of us and blessed our marriage.

49

Epilogue

At 77 years old, I now have to pay a price to live the life I want to live. I eat right, including almost no sugar or dessert, and I exercise every morning for close to an hour. If you count the following as working out, I lift weights, swim laps, hike the mountains, and play table tennis for over twenty hours a week. That doesn't even count the time I spend working the ranch.

Over the last three of four years I have had run-ins with cows two or three times, breaking and cracking ribs and pulling my groin in the process. Not because of the injuries themselves because I healed nicely, but rather because I am not as quick on my feet as I used to be, I finally have accepted the fact I am no longer the man I used to be.

My wife still worries and tells me all the time I work too hard, and my boys have asked me, "Dad, when the hell are you going to sell your cows and take up golf?" My response still is, "My cows are my golf game and I hope to have cows until the good Lord takes me home."

I just hope and pray that my time comes when I am alone on the mountain somewhere and my remains are never found.

If I am to be remembered at all, let it be through these stories, and by a plain stone marked with a cross with the following words below the cross:

Gary W Friendshuh
Born July 2, 1943

And some say he is out there still

Made in United States
North Haven, CT
20 May 2023